TO THE RE

Dianetics (from Greek *dia* "through," and *nous* "soul") delineates fundamental principles of the mind and spirit. Through the application of these discoveries, it became apparent that Dianetics dealt with a beingness that defied time – the human spirit – originally denominated the "I" and subsequently the "thetan." From there, Mr. Hubbard continued his research, eventually mapping the path to full spiritual freedom for the individual.

Dianetics is a forerunner and substudy of Scientology which, as practiced by the Church, addresses only the "thetan" (spirit), which is senior to the body, and its relationship to and effects on the body.

This book is presented in its original form and is part of L. Ron Hubbard's religious literature and works and is not a statement of claims made by the author, publisher or any Church of Scientology. It is a record of Mr. Hubbard's observations and research into life and the nature of man.

Neither Dianetics nor Scientology is offered as, nor professes to be physical healing, nor is any claim made to that effect. The Church does not accept individuals who desire treatment of physical or mental illness but, instead, requires a competent medical examination for physical conditions, by qualified specialists, before addressing their spiritual cause.

The Hubbard® Electrometer, or E-Meter, is a religious artifact used in the Church. The E-Meter, by itself, does nothing and is only used by ministers and ministers-in-training, qualified in its use, to help parishioners locate the source of spiritual travail.

The attainment of the benefits and goals of Dianetics and Scientology requires each individual's dedicated participation, as only through one's own efforts can they be achieved.

We hope reading this book is the first step of a personal voyage of discovery into this new and vital world religion.

THIS BOOK BELONGS TO

_____

DIANETICS 55!

DIANETICS 55!

THE COMPLETE MANUAL OF HUMAN COMMUNICATION

L. RON HUBBARD

Bridge
Publications, Inc.

A
HUBBARD®
PUBLICATION

BRIDGE PUBLICATIONS, INC.
4751 Fountain Avenue
Los Angeles, California 90029

ISBN 978-1-4031-4422-5

Printed in the United States of America

IMPORTANT NOTE

In reading this book, be very certain you never go past a word you do not fully understand. The only reason a person gives up a study or becomes confused or unable to learn is because he or she has gone past a word that was not understood.

The confusion or inability to grasp or learn comes AFTER a word the person did not have defined and understood. It may not only be the new and unusual words you have to look up. Some commonly used words can often be misdefined and so cause confusion.

This datum about not going past an undefined word is the most important fact in the whole subject of study. Every subject you have taken up and abandoned had its words which you failed to get defined.

Therefore, in studying this book be very, very certain you never go past a word you do not fully understand. If the material becomes confusing or you can't seem to grasp it, there will be a word just earlier that you have not understood. Don't go any further, but go back to BEFORE you got into trouble, find the misunderstood word and get it defined.

GLOSSARY

To aid reader comprehension, L. Ron Hubbard directed the editors to provide a glossary. This is included in the Appendix, *Editor's Glossary of Words, Terms and Phrases*. Words sometimes have several meanings. The *Editor's Glossary* only contains the definitions of words as they are used in this text. Other definitions can be found in standard language or Dianetics and Scientology dictionaries.

If you find any other words you do not know, look them up in a good dictionary.

DIANETICS 55!

CONTENTS

P R E F A C E

PREFACE

ECRET! Secrets, secrets, SECRETS! Ah, the endless quest, the far, far search, the codes, the vias, the symbols, the complications, the compilations, the mathematicity and abstractacity of secrets, secrets, SECRETS.

And truth. TRUTH! From Keats to Johnny Jones, we all have traffic with the truth, truth, Truth! The professors have a truth, the religionists have a truth, the stars and almost anything but government have a truth, truth, truth.

KNOWLEDGE! Endeared as a precious torch, abhorred as a neurotic's nightmare, it is all knowledge, knowledge, Knowledge! You get diplomas for it and buy books full of it. You perish for the lack of it or triumph in the absence of it. But whatever it might be, knowledge is precious, dangerous, valueless and horrible and craved.

And what is KNOWLEDGE? And what is the SECRET? And what is TRUTH?

Pontius Pilate asked the question when he washed his hands. Alexander executed messengers when the truth was unpalatable. The Chaldean priest corralled a bit of truth and ruled Chaldea into yesterday and Babylon into dust motes. And rulers and men, scholars and generals have condemned with it, dedicated their lives to it, fought for it and denied it and…have never defined it.

What is TRUTH? What is KNOWLEDGE? What is the SECRET? Are they inventions from a shaman's dream? Are they connected with science? Do they belong to philosophy? What are they? Whence do they come? Do they exist? Are they owned? Have they ever been written or spoken or guessed? And would one go mad if he knew them?

Dianetics moved into the world on May 9, 1950, with the publication of a book, *Dianetics: The Modern Science of Mental Health*. It moved with violence although its message was peace. A half a million Americans read it. Many, many of these acted upon it and are still acting upon it. And every year it sells still more copies–more copies than the average "bestseller."

Dianetics was an adventure into the dark realms of the Secret to accumulate Knowledge and to establish the Truth. Until Dianetics, these commodities have been owned by philosophy of either the esoteric or the monotony schools, or had been used by the charlatan–with or without surplice–to lure and ensnare.

Dianetics moved into a Dark Age of Reason where only a physical universe fact was given credence. When Dianetics was born, every freethinker Man had known had long since been burned or poisoned or dustbinned into the curriculums of "universities." It was an age where renown awaited only the manufacturer–not the inventor–of the new can opener, where sanity was adjusted with electrodes and philosophy was made with UNIVACs. Knowledge and the Secret being the total assets of vested interest, Dianetics was hit with violence from many quarters.

PREFACE

Medicine, entirely cognizant that it could not cure nor even alleviate the majority of Man's ills – yet like a prima donna who can but croak, yet resists the incoming next act – bluntly and viciously condemned, in leading weekly magazines, any further glance toward knowledge and truth. The government, fighting a war at the time, entirely cognizant that its pilot supply was old and slow, yet could not communicate on any subject which might remedy the matter. The Better Business Bureaus of the US, an organization solidly behind anything "good and solid," upheld the objection of capital to this new idea. The Communist Party, being solidly against any alteration of the mind (since that would undoubtedly alter devotion) went to considerable lengths to assist the stand of capital. To anyone who wanted a monopoly on knowledge and truth, Dianetics was an enemy. To them it was a degraded, wicked, fraudulent hoax – or so they said.

However, there happens to be a principle that anything which is thoroughly understood ceases. Their opinion of Dianetics could not have been correct because Dianetics is still here.

During the ensuing four years of commotion, much happened. The only orderly and progressive thing which happened was that Dianetics went on encroaching into the territory of the SECRET along the roadway of KNOWLEDGE to discover nearer TRUTH.

The primary assault of Dianetics was upon reverence and forms. The first book was written as a javelin directed into the doubtlessly sacrosanct vitals of philosophical departments and literature. It was carefully careless with its commas in the belief that commas, contrary to the prevailing mode, have little power to disturb an ultimate truth. The first book was written to be read and understood and it was written to upset and override and warn off those who would give it the fate of being "reverable." And the first book was written to be used by anyone who could understand it and the way it was written.

This, of course, could not include the extant mental charlatan (spelled "psychiatrist"), nor the professional dabbler in abilities (the "psychologist"). As one had learned these two could not be trained (and if they could have been, wouldn't have been interested in the proposed goals), it was necessary that a new breed of feline come into being–the *auditor*–and the auditor did.

Now this adventure, along the road of knowledge toward truth, was very shiny new in 1950. It is not quite so new, but much shinier in 1954. Certain promises were made in 1950. And these promises have now been kept.

Man *can* be *cleared*. He can be cleared (brought to the condition described in Chapter Two of the First Book) by a well-studied and competent auditor in a relatively short length of time.

This book contains the processes by which clearing can be accomplished. This does not mean that auditors do not have to be trained–for we have found that they do. It does mean that an auditor who has been trained and processed can now take these newer processes–and run them as directed–and can achieve the result of *Clear*.

Thus, in *Dianetics 55!* we have, actually, the Second Book of Dianetics. Everyone has assigned the title "First Book" to *Dianetics: The Modern Science of Mental Health*. But nobody has ever referred to *Science of Survival,* published in 1951, as the "Second Book." They haven't because it obviously wasn't. *Science of Survival* was a "First Book" in its own right. It was the first book of and under "Plan C" in the last chapter of the *real* First Book. *Science of Survival* adventured into causation, not into the resolution of problems outlined in the First Book.

Thus there has never been a Second Book of Dianetics. Such a book would have to take the exact problems of the First Book and, in the terms and references of the First Book, resolve those problems.

Well, as one looks over fiction novels and technical volumes in general, he finds that a four-year—almost five—lag between an author's first and second volume would discover his public to have waned. But when we take up a subject of the status of Dianetics and when we realize that it is condensing into a few years some thousands of years of doing, we see that a lag of four or five years between volumes isn't so very bad.

What happened in those four or five years? Many things. Somehow, for one thing, research and development was financed and the basic organization, after many limpings, survived. A lot of petty things happened which in another decade will be bone dust. For none of these things, none of the tales of terror, the attacks, the financing, the business advances, were permitted to interrupt the only thing that *can* mean any difference—the product of years of steady gain on the road of knowledge toward the goal of ultimate truth.

Knowledge, Truth, Secrets—they are the guts and anatomy of life. They must not then be owned. They must not then be hidden or bent. They must be permitted to stand out in the bold sunlight for all to see. For only when they are to be seen are they safe things to have, to hold, to know.

This is the Second Book of Dianetics. It *could* mean a new Earth. It could mean a new Freedom. But whatever it means, it cannot mean *nothing* in the sense Man uses that word. For you cannot unveil the SECRET and have it ever be quite so secret ever again.

L. RON HUBBARD
PHOENIX, 1954

C H A P T E R

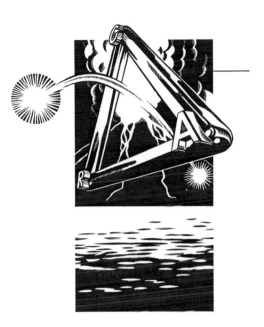

DIANETICS

DIANETICS

W HY SHOULD ANYONE want to know anything about the Human Mind? And for that matter, why should anyone believe that knowledge of the human mind is either unobtainable or undesirable? Why should men, ostensibly seeking answers to the mind, stray so far from it as to examine rats and entirely avoid looking at human beings? And why should anyone, pretending to treat the mind, stray so far afield as electric shock?

The answers are relatively simple. Anyone who knows the structure, function and dynamics of the human mind is very difficult to control. The only way a mind can be controlled is by enforcing upon it *ignorance* of itself. As far as study in treatment is concerned, a mind which has been made ignorant of itself would have to have restored to it *awareness* of its fundamentals before it could be considered to be recovered. When one restores full awareness to a mind, one is no longer able to victimize it. And a profession or a society would have to move out of "slave orientation" into action by "freedom and consent," were it to be effective.

Just as you do not want people to control you, so you should want knowledge of yourself and others. Just as you fight away from knowingness concerning self, so you will be controlled.

A simple and conclusive Science of Mind is a vital necessity in any society which desires to become free and remain free. The only elements in a society which would combat or contest or dispute an effort to attain such a science would be those interests which desired, by ignorance, to maintain their control of a slavery. Each and every impulse of freedom is an impulse toward sanity, toward health, toward happiness. Every impulse toward slavery is an impulse in the direction of misery, disease and death. One can say alike of the arthritic and the neurotic that the basic cause of disturbance–physical or mental–germinated in efforts to reduce the freedom of the individual, the group or Mankind.

Dianetics is an effort toward the attainment by Man of a level of freedom where decency and happiness can prevail and where knowledge of the mind itself would prevent the unscrupulous use of the mechanisms of slavery. Dianetics can be contested, it can be vilified, its founder and practitioners can be publicly pilloried. But Dianetics cannot be ignored. It could neither be drowned in praise nor burned in some purge to its total eradication. For it is a wonderfully observable fact that the one impulse in Man which cannot be erased is his impulse toward freedom, his impulse toward sanity, toward higher levels of attainment in all of his endeavors. This is Man's one saving grace. And because Dianetics is such an impulse and because its basic purposes from the moment of its conception have been dedicated unswervably to the attainment of even greater freedom, it cannot perish–a fact which will become doubtlessly more annoying to the slave masters as the years roll on.

There is much argument upon which we could adventure concerning whether Dianetics is an art or a science, whether it is a humanity or a hoax. But all this would avail us very little, for we would only be quibbling with words. Dianetics is what it is. And the totality of it can best be summed by the description, "An understanding of Man." We do not care whether or not it is a science. We do not care whether or not it is more properly cataloged under "adventure" or "mystery." We do care whether or not it is promulgated and known, for everywhere it walks slavery ceases. That mind which understands itself is the mind of a free man. It is no longer prone to obsessive behavior, unthinking compliances, covert innuendoes. It is at home in an environment, not a stranger. It is the solver of problems and the maker of games. A mind that is enslaved is weak. A mind that is free is powerful. And all the power there is, is defined by and contained in *freedom*.

Why should you know something about your mind? A question of a similar magnitude would be, "Why should you live?"

A science fiction writer once conceived a world composed entirely of machines–composed to a point where the machines were repaired by other machines, which in turn were repaired by yet other machines, and so the circle went round and the machines survived. He wrote this story from the fondest belief of nuclear physicists that there is only a machine, that Man derived from some spontaneous combustion of mud, that the soul does not exist, that freedom is impossible, that all behavior is stimulus-response, that causative thought cannot exist. What a world this would be. And yet this world, this pattern is the goal of the slave makers. If every man could be depressed from his freedom to a point where he believed himself but a cog in an enormous machine, then all things would be enslaved.

But who would there be to enjoy them? Who would there be to profit?

Not the slave maker, for he is the first to succumb. He succumbs to his own mechanisms. He receives the full jolt of his own endeavors to entrap.

What would be the purpose of this world of machines?

There can be no purpose worth contemplating which does not include *happiness* and *experience*. When a man is no longer able to envision happiness as a part of his future, that man is dead. He has become nothing but an animated robot, without understanding, without humanity, perfectly willing then to compose missiles of such detonative quality that an entire civilization can perish and that the happiness of all could be destroyed in the experience of radiation – an experience which might be considered digestible by an atomic pile, but not by a human being.

Thus as we depart from the concepts of freedom, we depart into a darkness where the will, the fear and the brutality of one or a few, no matter how well educated, may yet obliterate everything for which we have worked, everything for which we have hoped. This is what happens when the machine runs wild and when Man, become a machine, runs wild. Man can only become a machine when he is no longer capable of understanding his own beingness and has lost his contact with it. Thus it is of enormous importance that we understand something about the mind, that we understand we *are* minds, that we are *not* machines. And it is of enormous importance that Man attain at once to some higher level of freedom – where the machine reaction of destruction may be controlled and where Man himself can enjoy some of the happiness to which he is entitled.

Dianetics: The Modern Science of Mental Health was written into a world where atomic fission was yet in its early stages. *Dianetics 55!* is being written in a world where bombs exist of such fury that a continent could be laid waste. The recent declaration of the Secretary of War of the United States of America that such weapons exist and are capable of being used – and his assumption that men exist with such insufficiency of humanity that they would use such weapons – tells us that it is time someone, somewhere, took a hand in this game.

CHAPTER ONE
DIANETICS

The intimacy of his promises cannot be escaped. You would think anyone a madman who assayed to destroy every book in every library in the United States and Russia. You would think a man quite insane if he insisted upon the destruction of all of your personal possessions. You would know he was mad when he insisted that the only course for the future was the destruction of your body and any future race to remember it. Only a raving, drooling madman could contemplate the ending of all goals everywhere on Earth. And only an apathetic fool would stand by motionless before the inevitable destruction of his most intimate dreams, his fondest hopes, his possessions–even on down to the identification cards and money in his wallet. Such destruction permits no inheritance. It means an end of everything for which we have all hoped, for which we and our ancestors have strived. And it is my belief that an individual who can contemplate this with equanimity and without an impulse to act is so lost to the race and lost to himself, to his family and to his friends, that he must personally believe there is no hope for anything, anywhere, at any time. Such depravity is difficult to envision.

We know, definitely, that the wrong thing to do is nothing. Whenever any situation may develop, we always have that answer–*it is wrong to do nothing*. The only time anyone has ever gotten into serious trouble was when he decided he could do nothing about something. This was the entering threshold toward death. When one *knew* at last that he was powerless in the face of all fates or of any one particular fate, he was to that degree a slave of those fates. Thus the wrong thing to do in this world, at this time, is nothing. No matter what fantastic or incredible plan we adventure upon, no matter how we put it forward, it would still be better than the abandonment of all plans and all action. It may be that we have better plans than "fantastic plans." It may be that we, possessed of a knowledge of the mind and of Man, can yet restrain this dreadful crime of oblivion from occurring.

Dianetics, then, is a weapon. It is a timely weapon. It is the only weapon of defense in existence which can confront, with equanimity, nuclear fission. Dianetics can fail only if it is not used, only if those who know about it do not use it to its fullest extent.

Were you to take the technologies of Dianetics this day and seeking out anyone even remotely connected with the responsibility for waging atomic war, apply these techniques to them, you would soon have the man into a sufficiently high strata of humanity that he would recognize some of his responsibility to the human race. Your task would be made hard, for all those who are connected with the waging of war with atomic fission are restrained by law from receiving any psychotherapy. If this seems incredible to you, you should realize that anyone in a "top-secret" or "confidential" classification in a government is not supposed to impart any information of his calling. And it is the fear of governments that some of this information might be imparted to someone practicing in the field of mental healing. Thus if anyone connected with nuclear fission is discovered to be undergoing processing of any kind, he would be immediately relieved of his post and his top-secret classification would be cancelled.

But this is not a hopeless picture. Supposing one processed them all? And had all their top-secret classifications cancelled? Who would be left? Or supposing one pointed out this idiocy with sufficient conviction to those in charge of, but who are not responsible for, the destinies of Man? And made it mandatory that the sanity of anyone connected with the creation or use of atomic fission be required to have a sanity passport? Only the insane will destroy. Remember that. Only the insane would bring about the end of Earth. One of these men – fumbling forward, uncomprehending, a mere machine – given processing, begins to realize that he is not without responsibility for the safety of humanity. Only when he is a slave could he be forced to use such weapons against Mankind.

There is no argument on Earth of sufficient emergency or violence to require war, much less war by atomic fission, with the consequence of a destruction of at least one continent and within a few years the destruction of the planet Earth. Who would believe that anyone could wipe a continent clean of life without at once so polluting the atmosphere of Earth as to endanger or eradicate all further life forms on this planet? What argument could there be amongst men which could occasion such a fate for Earth? There is no such argument amongst men. Such an argument could arise amongst machines which consciencelessly, by pushed buttons, reach conclusions for which they have no responsibility.

There are many ways in which a higher state of security could be attained for Earth. None of these ways include violence or revolution. All of them include a greater freedom for Mankind. Dianetics is the key technology necessary for the control of atomic fission. Remember that. And remember also that Dianetics is a precision science, that it works only when it is used as a precision science. For if you are to accomplish anything with it, whether the rescue of a relative (from the pain of continued psychosomatic illness), of a group, a nation or a world, it works exactly along the lines it is designed. It does not work with innovations. It is a precision science. It has a precision mission. It contains more answers than Man has ever had before. And it contains enough answers to make Man free–*if it is used!*

CHAPTER

THE
FUNDAMENTALS
OF LIFE

THE FUNDAMENTALS OF LIFE

MUCH MORE BROADLY COVERED in Scientology, the fundamentals of life yet differ in no way for Man.

The basic subdivision in life is between:

ABILITY and MECHANICS.

This could also be described (but less accurately) as a subdivision of:

QUALITY and QUANTITY.

Where mechanics have ability, the ability is only apparent and has been endowed into the mechanics by life. It is all right to suppose that an electronic brain is capable of thought, as long as one realizes that life itself must necessarily be present in order to give cause and quality, or direction, to such a brain. An electronic brain will sit all day and do nothing unless life starts the machine running. It will give millions of answers. But none of these, no matter how sharp, have any meaning until they are viewed by life. The machine is never anything more than a servomechanism to life. Indeed, a machine cannot even exist in the absence of life.

By mechanics we mean "any and all of the objects, motions or spaces which exist." Foremost of these and foremost in any mechanical scheme is *space*. Next is *energy*. Next is condensed or solidified energy, called *matter*. And finally, always present in any mechanical arrangement or mechanic, that relative change of position of particles or objects known as *time*. Thus we have space, energy, matter and time. Whether we are considering a body (running on any energy), an automobile or a mountain, we are still dealing with what we call here "mechanics." Mechanics are always quantitative. There is always just so much distance, or so much mass, or so many hours. The quality of space, energy, matter and time has value only when viewed, used or monitored by life and, indeed, cannot exist in the absence of life. Correct or not, this is workable and is our primary assumption. We have a word for mechanics (compounded from Matter, Energy, Space and Time) which is *MEST*. By MEST we mean "any or all arrangements of energy of whatever kind, whether in fluid or object form, in space or spaces." We do not conceive life to have an energy and therefore any energy, even if directly produced by life, can be found to be embraced under the quantitative term MEST.

Life, itself, has quality and ability. The products of quality and ability are mechanics. Ability is demonstrated by the handling of matter, energy, space and time. Quality means, simply, "valued or having a value." No values (that is to say, opinions) exist in the absence of life. In the matter of such a thing as an automatic switch, we might consider that the switch is capable of making a decision—whether to be "off" or "on." However, we must remember that the original decision that "a switch was to be made" and that "off and on could be accomplished" and, indeed, the design of the switch itself depended entirely upon life quality.

In the field of mechanics, we do not discover *creativeness*. We discover varying condition, varying arrangement, deterioration and destruction of one or another form. But we do not discover any alteration in quantity. Indeed, the entire science of physics is predicated upon the assumption of "conservation of energy" (which is to say, that energy itself cannot be created and destroyed, but can only alter its forms). To this we might add "conservation of space," "conservation of matter" and "conservation of time." None of these things are capable, in themselves, of altering. They are not capable of more than change of position or alteration of form. The physicist is very fond of demonstrating that the breaking of a vase does no more than alter the relative position of the particles and the form. And that the burning of a piece of coal does not change the basic particles of matter, since if you were to collect all the smoke, all the ash and the particles which radiated from the burning and weighed them, you would have the same weight as before the coal was burned. In other words, the quantity of matter does not change and, as above, it does not create to itself or add to itself in any way.

Life (it has been adequately established) can, however, *create*. It can create particles and it can add to mass. The demonstration of this on a man is an easily accomplished thing and is quite conclusive. A process known as the "Remedy of Havingness" is capable of altering the weight of a man, upwards of twenty to thirty-five pounds, even though there is no change whatsoever in the diet or living habits of that person. In other words, the life which is in the body of the man (and which *is* actually the man) can, by a certain process, increase the amount of mass of this man. Another process known as "Perfect Duplication" can reverse this and again, without change of diet or the living habits of a man, decrease the amount of mass of a man without the complications of heat or waste products being present. Thus, forthrightly and directly, in the same frame of reference as that used by the physicist, it is easily demonstrated that life does create mass and can cause mass to disappear.

"*Thus, forthrightly and directly, in the same frame of reference as that used by the physicist, it is easily demonstrated that life does create mass and can cause mass to disappear.*"

CHAPTER TWO
THE FUNDAMENTALS OF LIFE

As long ago as fifty years, as represented by an article in the *Encyclopaedia Britannica*, it was fairly well understood that the study of physics should have begun with an examination of the mind. This article, under the heading of "Time and Space," states that "as space and time are mental phenomena, their proper delineation and study begins in the field of the mind." Nineteenth-century "mental sciences" were insufficiently schooled in science to comprehend this. And the physicist, unaware in general of such a fact, did not consider that his proper province was the mind. Thus a misunderstanding existed in the humanities and in the sciences, where one was depending upon the other. And the result came about that neither knew his proper field of endeavor. By undertaking a study of the mind from the orientation of physics and with the application of all the principles known in chemistry, physics and mathematics (items in which the nineteenth-century psychologist was entirely unfamiliar and which the twentieth-century psychologist utterly disdains), it was only then possible to produce some comprehension of this thing we call "life" in this place we call the "physical universe."

Thus that thing which considers, that thing which has opinions, that thing which creates, that thing which monitors, that thing which has goals and desires and which can experience, is *life*. What we call space, time, energy, matter, forms of any kind, are the byproducts of and are monitored by life. Energy, whether in the form of a mental image, a body, a tree or a rock, are alike the byproducts of life. There is no faintest difference, save only density and wavelength, between the space you behold around you with your *physical* eyes and the spaces and forms you see when you close them and behold a *mental* image. These things, alike, are energies and obey the various laws of energy.

Here, then, we have a unit, or a quality, capable of bringing into being quantities such as spaces, energy, masses and time, capable of changing and controlling these masses and energies, capable of adding to them or subtracting from them.

There was a considerable dissertation in *Dianetics: The Modern Science of Mental Health* concerning the "awareness of awareness unit." When this subject was first under investigation, it was established that all was not a machine. Somewhere, in tracing back the various lines, it was necessary to strike a cause-point–either simply to assume that there was a cause-point or to actually discover one. Two names were used in connection with this causative agent. One of them was "analytical mind" and the other, much more properly, the "awareness of awareness unit." The awareness of awareness unit was (as its name implies) aware of being aware, or aware of being alive. When one was looking at or discussing the analytical mind, one was aware of something else–that the awareness of awareness unit became connected in some fashion with computers, or "analyzers," in order to handle and control the remainder of the physical beingness. The term analytical mind then meant "the awareness of awareness unit *plus* some evaluative circuit, or circuits, or machinery to make the handling of the body possible."

The other item discussed broadly in *Dianetics: The Modern Science of Mental Health* was the "reactive mind." This mind was a stimulus-response mind which depended upon exterior direction for its action and reaction. The reactive mind was conceived to be a collection of records in picture form, so arranged as to make a complete pattern of experience, capable by its pattern alone of evaluating the conduct and behavior of the individual. The pictures contained in the reactive mind are now called "facsimiles." For they are no more and no less than pictures (like photographs) taken of the universe around the individual and retained by him. A specialized kind of facsimile was the "engram." This differed from other mental pictures because it contained, as part of its content, *unconsciousness* and *physical pain*. The definition of an engram is "a picture of a moment of pain and unconsciousness." The reactive mind was conceived to have more of these engrams than the analyzer. But the analyzer was seen to have some of these too, except they were a lighter form and were a "lock" on the engram in the reactive memory bank. Indeed, when one considered the reactive mind, he was actually considering what is, in the electronic brain, a "memory bank." Instead of cards or a card-file system, the reactive mind contained pictures. These pictures were filed. And, were drawn out of the files by the environment, which contained "restimulators." The presence of these pictures could alter form and could alter behavior. The eradication of one of these engrams, by the early erasure techniques of Dianetics, was found to alter the stimulus-response behavior of the individual.

Here, we were confronting three kinds of minds. One was the causative agent–the awareness of awareness unit–which did not appear to have any byproducts, but which was impinged upon another mind–called the analytical mind–which on a machine basis analyzed situations rationally and was sane and rational. And a third kind of mind–the reactive mind–even further remote from the awareness of awareness unit, which acted without the consent of the causative agent and did not in any way consult it. Now, on a very careful review of this, we see that the analytical mind and the reactive mind, alike, are byproduct mechanical minds. Alike, they depend upon energy, spaces, storage and other quantitative things. The awareness of awareness unit, however, is itself *decision*, is itself *knowingness*. It delivers into the analytical mind and its systems various "knowingnesses" to be handled on a mechanical basis. And, unwittingly delivers into the hands of the reactive mind, which is totally a mechanical thing, the right to alter and correct the analytical mind. Apparently, then, we have here a causative agent and two machines. We might as well, then, take the obvious conclusion that there is the awareness of awareness unit and that this in some fashion handles machinery. And, that the analytical mind, the reactive mind and even the body and the environment are mechanical.

One item here is qualitative and decisional – the awareness of awareness unit. All other items are subordinate to it and depend for their conclusions either upon it or upon the environment. Here, again, we have quality versus quantity.

A further demonstration of this awareness of awareness unit in action is quite convincing. A machine (a meter) which is built in every tradition of physics and electronics, and which is composed of nothing more or less than the usual meters and gauges and electrodes, can detect the production of energy by the analytical mind. This machine (one of which is at the headquarters of Hubbard Professional College) demonstrates conclusively that the awareness of awareness unit can predict and cause an energy reaction to occur at will. It goes further and demonstrates that the awareness of awareness unit can bring about, without further contact, an energy flow in a body at a distance. This is a very startling demonstration and is one of the more significant electrical discoveries of recent times. The conditions of the experiment are sufficiently rigorous to dispel any doubt, in the mind of a physicist, concerning the authenticity of the current.

If there were no energy being created by the awareness of awareness unit, then one would be at a loss to account for mental energy pictures. For these things, being made at a tremendously rapid rate, have considerable mass in them – mass which is measurable on a thing as common and as everyday as the bathroom scales.

As soon as it was discovered how facsimiles (these mental energy pictures) came into being, it was also discovered that they were actual energy and not "an idea of energy" as they have been supposed to be in the past. The facsimile and the engram come into action by *resistance*. The awareness of awareness unit resists a scene in the physical universe, either resisting its approach or departure, and thus by this resistance makes a "print." This print is made in a moving fashion (like a motion picture) and is complete in every detail. Later on the individual can call back this print (and take a look at it) and will find it to have in it the exact forces which were in the original version in the physical universe. The awareness of awareness unit does this so easily that it has been completely unaware of what it was doing. Now, when the awareness of awareness unit makes a print (trying to restrain something from going away or trying to restrain it from approaching) and considers that the survival of its body is being violated or threatened, it files this print in such a way that it will not have to look at it again. But this does not mean that an approximation of the print by the physical environment cannot reactivate the print independently. In other words, when the awareness of awareness unit puts away and does not want to look again at such a facsimile, the facsimile itself begins to have a power over the awareness of awareness unit. The collected files of these non-survival experiences come together and are the reactive mind. The awareness of awareness unit could be conscious of these, but chooses not to be. Thus the environment can restimulate this reactive mind and can cause changes of behavior and bodily form, such as overweight, psychosomatic ills, or even fixed expressions or gestures.

The essence of time is *change*. Where there is no change, there is no time. Thus something which is unchanging is enduring. If a thing has no change in it, it will then "float" in all time (since it does not assign itself to any "changingness," being a thing of no change). Thus we discover that silences and no-motions "float" in time. And we discover that every place on the time track where the awareness of awareness unit has taken a picture of silence (has resented or restrained silence), it then has an energy mass which will "float," or stay with it, whatever time it assigns to itself. And we get the composition of the physical universe. The physical universe is composed of "floating," or *forever,* energy. If this did not work out in processing and if it were not a usable principle, it would not be included in this text.

In view of the fact that these facsimiles (particularly those of silence) can "stay with" the individual, then we get the entire mechanism we call "restimulation"–where the environment reactivates a facsimile which then acts back against the body or awareness of awareness unit of the person. This is a very simple system of stimulus-response. We discover, then, that engrams, or facsimiles in general, have a tendency to "hang up" on all of their silent or motionless spots. Thus a facsimile may contain considerable action and yet be stuck at one point of no-motion. Here we have a no-motion, on either side of which there is motion. The no-motion point hangs up and is not contacted by the awareness of awareness unit, since the awareness of awareness unit is looking, in general, for motion. Thus we get a phenomenon known as "stuck on the time track"–where an individual can believe himself to be at some distant point in the "past." The facsimile or engram in which he is "caught" has almost as much reality to him, as a condition of existence, as his present time environment. When he becomes entirely psychotic, the facsimile or engram has far more reality to him than his present time environment. Thus we have aberration, psychosomatic illness.

In early Dianetics, the way this condition was alleviated was by addressing the pictures themselves and persuading the awareness of awareness unit to erase them by recounting them and re-experiencing them. Because this took a long time and because auditors had a tendency to abandon half-erased incidents, the technologies, while workable, were not conclusive. Thus, more research and investigation had to be entered upon in order to establish the best way to handle this situation.

"… a facsimile may contain considerable action
and yet be stuck at one point of no-motion."

C H A P T E R

THE
AWARENESS
OF

THREE

AWARENESS
UNIT

THE AWARENESS OF AWARENESS UNIT

IN EXAMINING the individuality and identity of the individual, one discovers that the individual *is* himself and not his byproducts. The individual is not his analytical mind, he is not his reactive mind, he is not his body any more than he is his house or his car. He might consider himself to be associated with his analytical mind, his reactive mind, his house, his body, his car, but he is not these things. He is himself.

THE INDIVIDUAL, THE PERSONALITY, *IS* THE AWARENESS OF AWARENESS UNIT AND THE AWARENESS OF AWARENESS UNIT *IS* THE PERSON.

As this awareness of awareness unit confuses itself further and further with the pictures it has made of its surroundings, it conceives itself more and more to be an object until, at last, when it has gone entirely down Tone Scale, it has arrived at the point where its fondest belief is that it *is* an object.

Just as you would not say that John Jones was his car, so must you also say (when you perceive this clearly) that John Jones is not his analytical mind or his reactive mind, his body or his clothes. John Jones is an awareness of awareness unit. And all there is of him that is capable of knowing and being aware is John Jones—an awareness of awareness unit.

When we have arrived at a state where John Jones himself *knows* that he is an awareness of awareness unit and is not his analytical mind, his reactive mind, his body, his clothes, his house, his car, his wife or his grandparents, we have what is called in Dianetics a *Clear*. A Clear is simply an awareness of awareness unit which knows it is an awareness of awareness unit, can create energy at will and can handle and control, erase or re-create an analytical mind or a reactive mind.

The difference of approach is this: Instead of erasing all the things with which the awareness of awareness unit is in conflict, we make the awareness of awareness unit capable of besting and controlling all those things with which he thought he had to be in conflict. In other words, we raise the determinism of an individual up to a point where he is capable of controlling his mental pictures and the various byproducts of life. When he is capable, so far as his ability is concerned, of controlling and determining the action of these things, he is no longer aberrated. He can recall anything he wants to recall without the aid and assistance of energy masses. He can be what he wants to be. He has had restored to himself a considerable freedom.

About the only difficulty we have in accomplishing this state of Clear, with all the power and ability appended thereto, is the fact that individuals come to believe that they have to *have* certain things in order to go on surviving. Actually, an awareness of awareness unit cannot do anything else but survive. He is unkillable. Yet his byproducts are destroyable. And confusing himself with his byproducts, he begins to believe that he has to have or do certain things in order to survive. His anxiety becomes so great on this that he will even believe that he has to have problems in order to survive. An awareness of awareness unit is very unhappy unless it has some mass or space of some kind and has various problems to solve.

For a very long time, in Dianetics, we looked far for the "One-shot Clear." Such a thing has come into existence and is workable on over 50 percent of the current populace of Mankind. The One-shot Clear depends, of course, on getting the awareness of awareness unit at a distance from and in control of its various byproducts so that it no longer confuses itself *with* its byproducts. The astonishing speed with which 50 percent of the human race can be cleared is believable only when you put it into action. The magic words are:

"Be three feet back of your head."

This is the One-shot Clear. If the existence of a One-shot Clear (or the process) is indigestible to people, it is because they have so long contemplated objects and have their attention so thoroughly fixed upon objects that they can no longer view space. And the idea of viewing space, the idea of being without objects, is so antipathetic to them that they feel they must condemn any effort which might take from them the proximity of some of their fondest possessions.

It is so strongly antipathetic to Man to look at space that one of the basic processes of Dianetics—causing him to look at *spots in space*—will cause a rather low-toned individual to become quite violently ill at his stomach. The nausea resulting, simply from contemplating empty space, is discoverable only in those who have a great deal of trouble with possessions and who are unable to have things. From having to have things, they have gotten to a point of where they do not believe they can have anything any more. Thus, being asked to contemplate an emptiness of any kind is enough to cause a violent physical reaction.

Hence, this whole subject of Clear and "exteriorization" (as it is technically termed) is very antipathetic to the remaining 50 percent of the human race, who cannot be hit instantly with this one-shot button.

Fifty percent of the people you walk up to, if you do not preselect your "preclears" (a person on the road to being Clear), will immediately exteriorize (be a distance from their body) and behold themselves as capable of handling a great many things they before considered impossible to control, the moment you say, *"Be three feet back of your head."* The remaining 50 percent will look at you with varying puzzlement. These "know" they are a body, these "know" they are an object and these "know" (most of them) that they would get sick at their stomachs if they contemplated being all by themselves in space. They would believe it would be impossible to control a body while being three feet behind it. Thus, one gets into an immediate argument with such people and they wish to go into the various "deeper significances."

If these people were lost to us with current Dianetic processes, we would still have gained many percentiles over any past effort to do something for the race or about the mind. In the past, even when we look as short a time ago as 1949, we discover that Man in general did not possess the ability to get a recovery percentage in patients higher than 22 percent. Oddly enough, whether it was a witch doctor at work, a psychoanalyst, a psychiatrist, a psychologist, a medical doctor or any other practitioner, simple assurance and a pat on the back yet brought about 22 percent cure. This fact, not looked at very carefully by practitioners, caused people to believe that the only thing that was wrong with the mind was that "people thought something was wrong with the mind" and all anybody needed was "a cheery word" and it would all be all right. Twenty-two percent of any population will recover if anything is done for them. The remaining 78 percent are not quite so lucky.

When we can raise the percentage, even to 30 percent, we are doing more than has ever been done before. When any practice gets less than 22 percent recovery, then that practice is actually, definitely, harming people. For if all the practitioner did was be at home in his office and give cheery reassurance to his patients, he would get this 22 percent. He would have to be very active and depressive in order to decrease this amount of "cures." Now when we suddenly vault to the figure of 50 percent, we know we are closing with the answer. Thus, we could relax at this very point, confident that we have done more in the field of healing than has ever before been done.

However, it is not good enough within our framework. In the first place, if we wish to treat people involved with the government, people involved with ruling, people involved with the material sciences (such as physicists and chemists), we are dealing with almost entirely the remaining "resistive" 50 percent. This does not mean that a person simply by exteriorizing is weaker. It means that a person with continuous contact with the physical universe, and continuous harassment and concern over the state of objects or energy, is apt to get what we call "interiorized."

A recent series of cases, undertaken to demonstrate how far we had to go and what we had to do in order to bring results in this remaining 50 percent, has now concluded successfully. With modern techniques very, very closely followed, auditors trained by the Central Organization have been successfully clearing cases which were resistive and did not improve on all earlier processes as of 1951, '52, '53 and the bulk of '54. The certainty of clearing the first 50 percent simply with the "magic words" has been followed now with a certainty of handling the remaining 50 percent. This presents a rather different scene and attitude than 1950, where an auditor had to be "intuitive" and had to work endlessly (it seemed) to produce gains on cases–much less clearing.

My own percentages in clearing people do not count. And I learned early (with some puzzlement) that what I did with a preclear and the results I obtained with a preclear were not the results which would be obtained by another auditor. It was this fact alone which caused research and investigation to be continued at such lengths and for processes to be codified so closely. For first we had to know the processes. And then we had to know how to train auditors. And finally we are obtaining these clearing results.

Any Clear, earlier obtained, was known to be Clear simply by the fact that he could recall at will, by pictures, or could perform certain other feats. Actually, a person was only Clear to *stay* Clear when he was not immediately involved with either his analytical or his reactive mind. And those Clears which remained stable had been put unwittingly into a much more advanced state than had been supposed even by the auditor. It was an investigation of these Clears which led forward into the techniques we have now. It was found that many of them were simply "wide-open cases" which had become rather able to read their own facsimiles. Several had simply increased their abilities to a point so senior to other people's ability that everyone agreed they should be called "Clear." And then there was the *actual* Clear. The actual Clear, on close questioning, even though he himself had not always noticed it, conceived himself now to be some distance from the body. Those Clears which remained stable and continued to perform and function despite the convulsions of life were these who had been stably exteriorized. This may be a datum which is very hard for some Dianeticists to assimilate. But again, the difficulty would stem only from the fact that these would be unwilling to look at space or would be afraid of being disenfranchised (such people are very frightened of losing their bodies).

But this is a fact with which we cannot argue: That so far as psychosomatic ill is concerned, it is best resolved by exteriorization. One has the individual step back from his body, look at it and patch it up. And that is about all there is to psychosomatic illness. There is, of course, an electronic structure of the body, which one can direct a person's attention to. But I have seen the shape of a face change in moments, I have seen psychosomatic illnesses disappear in seconds and, as long as there was any physical structure left to work with at all, I have seen the problem of psychosomatic illness pushed so far in the background as a "problem" that we no longer think in these terms and, indeed, do not consider Dianetics well used when it is only addressed to psychosomatic illness and aberration.

Our emphasis today is upon *ability*. We have found that the more we increase the ability of a person, the better the byproducts around him become. Simply by increasing an individual's ability to walk or talk, we can change his physical beingness and his mental outlook.

By this theory, it would be enough to have somebody learn how to make pottery, or drive a car, or sing, or speak in public, to increase his mental and physical health. And, indeed, on investigation we discover that these things are therapeutic. But we discover that they are limited in their therapy because the talents which an individual learns in this fashion are talents involved entirely with the handling and orientation of the body. And he is not being entirely influenced merely by his body. He is being influenced, as well, by the computing machinery which he calls his analytical mind and by the more insidious and less obvious machinery called his reactive mind. Furthermore, by these increases in ability, he is not brought up to a point of where he can control or handle his entire environment. Such an ability can be developed only *by* and *in* the awareness of awareness unit itself. When it is learning to do something via the body, it is not learning to do something directly. It is learning to do something with help–the help of arms and legs, face, voice, eyes–and thus "hobby therapy" is limited, even though it is quite positive.

Looking a little further along this line, one discovers that the awareness of awareness unit has peculiar abilities. First and foremost of its abilities is to "be where it likes to be" and "look." It does not need eyes. It does not need a vehicle in which to travel. All it needs to do is to "postulate" its existence in a certain location and then look from that point of existence. In order to do this, it has to be willing to be *cause,* it has to be willing to be an *effect.* But if it can do this, it can go much further. It can create and change space. Furthermore, it can erase at a glance facsimiles and engrams.

Now, when we get into such capabilities, people are liable to believe that we have entered the field of mysticism or spiritualism. But an inspection of these fields demonstrates the people in them not to be very able. Mysticism and other such practices are reverse practices. Rather than controlling the reactive bank, the analytical mind, the body, the environment, they seek very markedly to withdraw from the necessity to control. This is downward ability. (And while I might be accused of maligning these fields, I can only look at the people I have known in these fields and at the fact that I, myself, studied in these fields in the East and know their limitations.)

People are apt to confuse exteriorization with "astral walking." As you sit there reading this book, you are definitely and positively aware of sitting there and of this book. There is no question about whether or not you are looking at a book. You don't believe yourself to be projected. And you don't have to guess where you are. And you don't think you have to create some sort of image in order to look at anything. You are simply sitting there reading a book. This is exteriorization. If you were cleared and (with your body at home) you were in a library, you could read in the library just as well–with the limitation that you might not have a good grasp on pages. You would certainly know you were in the library. There would be no question about this. There would be no question about the text on the periodicals on the table, be no question about the quality and personality of the librarian and other people sitting there.

"Looking a little further along this line,
one discovers that the awareness of awareness unit
has peculiar abilities. First and foremost of its abilities
is to 'be where it likes to be' and 'look.'"

Being Clear does not enter into it "guesswork." You would not be concerned with telepathy, with reading people's minds and with other such bric-a-brac. You would simply know what you wanted to know. Further, you wouldn't have to use a "system" for finding out what you know. You would simply *know* it.

If Man cannot face what he is, then Man cannot be free. For an awareness of awareness unit, surrounded entirely by energy masses and believing that it itself is completely these masses, is in a difficult and desperate state. It believes, for instance, that in order to go from one address to another, it has to take the energy mass along with it. This is not true. One might carry a body around in order to speed up one's conversation, in order to have a problem, in order to get some attention and interest from people. But one would not carry a body around because one "had to have a body."

The general attitude of a person who is cleared is the most interesting thing to observe. Only a cleared person has a very definite tolerance for the behavior of others. People, before they are cleared, are in a varying degree of distrust of other people. They are hiding, or protecting, or owning things to such a degree that they do not dare separate themselves from them.

There is a certain fear of an exteriorized person. There is a belief that he might do them wrong. Actually, one is done wrong by the weaklings of this world, not the strong men. One does not have to enslave and control by force those whose conduct he does not fear. When you find an individual who is bent entirely upon a course of the arduous control of the motions of others, you are looking at an individual who is afraid. By their fear you shall know them.

Another slight difficulty in the state of exteriorization is that one has a tendency to let things be more or less as they are. Up to a certain point, one is content to let the game run and take part in it and have fun with it. The point, of course, is the destruction of the playing field. Life, to a Clear, is no more and no less than a game.

And the only thing which he would consider somewhat unpardonable in behavior would be the wiping out of such a playing field. But if he were even higher, in such a state, he could theoretically make his own playing field. However, if he did this, he would find difficulty getting into communication with other live beings unless, of course, he made them–which is a rather unsatisfactory state of affairs, since one never quite forgets that he did so.

Moral conduct is "conduct by a code of arbitrary laws." Ethical conduct is "conduct out of one's own sense of justice and honesty." When you enforce a moral code upon people, you depart considerably from anything like ethics. People obey a moral code because they are afraid. People are ethical only when they are strong. One could say that the criminals of Earth are those upon whom moral codes have been too forcefully enforced. (As an example of this, take the cliché object–the minister's son.) Ethical conduct does not mean promiscuous, abandoned or lawless conduct. It means conduct undertaken and followed because one has a sense of ethics, a sense of justice and a sense of tolerance. This is self-determined morality.

A Clear has this to a very marked degree. By actual check of many such cases, their moral behavior is intensely superior to that of people who pride themselves on "being good." The point arises because "law and order" depends, for its existence, upon its necessity in the field of morals. And it looks with a sort of horror on somebody who would be good without "recourse to" or "threat from" the forces of law and order. Such a person would be rather hard to have around–he would cut down the number on the police force quite markedly.

The state of Clear, then, is obtainable and is desirable. And, now that we can accomplish it with greater positiveness than in 1950, is found to be superior to that described in the second chapter of *Dianetics: The Modern Science of Mental Health.*

The way one goes about being Clear or creating a Clear is simple. But it requires a certain code of conduct (called the "Auditor's Code") and requires, we have discovered, a considerable amount of training. Clearing another person is a highly specialized ability. This ability must be raised in individuals before they can easily and successfully undertake such a project. Witnessing this is the fact that while many of the processes involved in clearing have been available for a very, very long time, very few people have successfully used them. The discovery of why this was, was quite as important as the state of Clear itself. The remedy of this disability lies in training and processing. The activity of creating a Clear is known as "processing" and is undertaken by one individual on behalf of another individual. "Self-clearing" has not been found possible where the individual was badly mired in his own case.

Enormously subordinate to the goal of Clear–but enormously senior to Man's various healing activities in the mind, spirit and body–the very processes which lead up to Clear remedy, whether one wants them to or not, a great many of the ills of the individual. One can take one of these modern processes and run it all by itself and accomplish more with Dianetics than Man had previously accomplished in the field of healing. When one has the answers, of course, applying those answers to minor psychosomatic difficulties, or aberrations, or spiritual unrest is elementary. But again, we have discovered that there is no real substitute for training, either at the hands of an already trained and skilled auditor or, best, from the Central Organization.

The awareness of awareness unit was not readily discoverable in the field of physics because physics is entirely concerned with mechanics. Physics starts with the assumption of the conservation of energy, the existence of space and goes on into further complexity from there. The awareness of awareness unit is one step earlier than all this and its existence was unsuspected by a misdefinition in the field of physics. That was the definition of a "static."

CHAPTER THREE
THE AWARENESS OF AWARENESS UNIT

A static, in physics, is called "something which is in an equilibrium of forces." This "object at rest in an equilibrium of forces" is an interesting semantic puzzle.

If we put a glass upon the table and then say that it is a static, we are telling a very bad lie. It is not in an equilibrium of forces. That glass happens to be traveling at 1,000 miles an hour just by reason of the fact that Earth is turning. It has seven other directions and speeds by reason of being part of the planet Earth, the solar system and this galaxy. It cannot, then, be considered "at rest." Thus no object can be considered at rest unless one considers something "relatively at rest" (the glass is at rest in relationship to the table), but this is not the physical definition.

The definition of a static disclosed something else of interest. There was a missing definition in the field of mathematics and that was the definition of "zero." The mathematician for ages has been using, in all of his formulas, a wild variable without suspecting it was there. He did not really encounter it until he got into the higher fields of nuclear physics. At this time he encountered it so forcefully and knew it so little that he had to alter most of his mathematical conceptions in order to work with nuclear physics at all. This wild variable was no less than zero. Zero, put down as a "goose egg" in a mathematical formula, would introduce many interesting variables.

In the first place, an absolute zero has never been obtained in this universe. It has only been approached (that is, in terms of temperature; that is, in terms of non-existence). We can say there is "a zero of apples," but that is still a qualified zero. We can say there "were no apples," but that is further qualified as being in the *past* and is a past zero. We can say there "will be no apples" and, again, we will have a zero qualified as being in the *future.* Zero was "an *absence* of a thing" and this immediately violated the definition of a zero as being "*no* thing."

The absoluteness of "no thing" had to be examined while we were examining the field of the mind and actually led to some very astonishing discoveries with regard to life itself and immediately pinpointed the existence of the awareness of awareness unit.

The proper and correct definition of zero would be "something which had no mass, which had no wavelength, which had no location in space, which had no position or relationship in time." This would be a zero. One could state it more shortly, if a little less correctly, as "something without mass, meaning or mobility."

It would be almost impossible to detach a dyed-in-the-wool physicist from the concept that "everything was a somethingness" and that there was actually a "nothingness." However, there is a nothingness which has quality. It has potential. It has ability. It has the ability to perceive, the ability to create, the ability to understand and the ability to appear and disappear, to its own satisfaction, in various positions in space. Furthermore, this thing could (we have demonstrated conclusively) manufacture or cause to vanish space, energy and masses and could, quite additionally, reposition time.

These new concepts are actually advances in the field of physics and mathematics and, from the viewpoint of the physicist and the mathematician, would only incidentally apply to the mind.

From this data, we get the basic definition of a static, which is "an actuality of no mass, no wavelength, no position in space or relation in time, but with the quality of creating or destroying mass or energy, of locating itself or creating space, and in re-relating time."

And thus we have the definition of an awareness of awareness unit. It *is* the definition of a static. It does not have quantity, it has quality. It does not have mechanics, it can produce mechanics. And it does have ability.

"From this data, we get the basic definition of a static,
which is 'an actuality of no mass, no wavelength,
no position in space or relation in time, but with
the quality of creating or destroying mass or energy,
of locating itself or creating space, and in re-relating time.'"

The foremost ability of the awareness of awareness unit is to have an idea and to continue that idea and to perceive the idea and its continuance in the form of mass, energy, objects and time. In the field of Scientology, the fact that this awareness of awareness unit can also control or even make physical bodies is almost incidental. That is only a specialized branch of the game. In Dianetics this is a very important function, for one in Dianetics is working with Man.

A static could also be called an "orientation-point." It would be from that point that it made and directed space, energy and objects. It would be from that point that it assigned meanings. And thus we have an essential difference between the awareness of awareness unit and its byproducts. These byproducts we can categorize as "symbols." When we say "mechanics," we actually mean, to some degree, symbols. A symbol is "something that has mass, meaning and mobility ('three Ms')." That is the technical definition of a symbol. An orientation-point is "something that controls symbols." The difference in ability of an awareness of awareness unit is how much it is an orientation-point in relationship to how much it believes itself to be a symbol, or to have mass, meaning and mobility. Reduction from the state of awareness is into the condition of the symbol (mass, meaning and mobility).

To get a clearer idea of this, you see the word "a" on this page. That has *mass,* even if very slight mass. It has *meaning,* since it converts an idea when glanced at. And it certainly has *mobility,* since you can move the book around. Now you, looking at the book, have the role of an orientation-point to the degree that you do not conceive yourself to have a fixed identity, a fixed position, a fixed mass. If you, looking at this book, have no real mass, if your name is not a tremendously fixed idea with you, and if you know you can move your body around without having to move with it–then you would very clearly and decisively be an orientation-point. But if you think you have mass and are mass, and if you think you are your name, and if you think you have to move around only by moving the body around–then, of course, somebody else, something else, can be your orientation-point. It may be your mother. It may be your hometown. Or if you are a mystic, it might even be some spirit. You would think of yourself as a symbol. Similarly, a symbol does not remember anything more than it symbolizes. And thus your memory, to a large degree, might be the memory of past allies (people who took care of you and to whom you were attached affectionately). And if you were in a lecture, you would probably take notes rather than remember what was being said. An orientation-point has the power of memory *without* record. A symbol has the power of memory only to the degree that it *is* a record.

Thus we see that it is desirable that an individual does not *identify* himself with masses, but that he retain his ability to *handle* masses and objects and energy, to remember at will without the need of "records" (such as those in the reactive bank) or "facsimile machines" (such as those in the analytical mind bank).

In any good, thorough investigation, one investigates to see what he will discover and to find better ways to do things. In any reliable investigation report, one tells what he discovered and reports its character and nature. In this science we are doing just that. When we talk of the awareness of awareness unit, we are not talking to be "pleasing," to "win friends" or "influence professors." We are simply telling you what has been discovered after twenty-five years of research and investigation in the field of the mind, having taken off from the platform of physics and mathematics rather than philosophy. The awareness of awareness unit is a fact. It is a demonstrable fact and the best way to demonstrate it is to use the processes which accomplish it and then discover that the individual is more well, has a better memory, is better oriented, is more capable, is more ethical, is happier, has a better command of time, can communicate better, is more willing to have friends, is less antisocial than the average person and has a greater zest for living and getting things done. All these things can be accomplished by test.

In 1950, we often had occasion to demonstrate the existence of the engram. It seemed to be highly in question amongst those people who were "extremely specialized" (it said on their diplomas) in the field of the mind. To be accomplished in the field of the mind and yet not know anything about engrams or facsimiles would be an idiotic state indeed. Because the mind *is* composed of facsimiles and engrams, if one wishes to examine items or energy products.

Well, then as now, we are only interested in results. What can we *do* with this technology?

If we can demonstrate with this technology that we can better the lives, tolerances, abilities of those around us, then certainly we will have done something. We have no place for philosophical arguments concerning this material. It is simply workable material. You do not argue with the directions on how to open a vacuum-packed can. If you don't follow them, you don't get the can open. Or not following them and still being insistent upon it, you smash the can and ruin the contents. One would not go into a philosophic dissertation about the directions of opening a can. Obviously, they are written by somebody who knows how to open cans and any hours spent on getting this person to demonstrate that he "really could" open cans would be wasted time. The thing to do is simply to read the directions, follow them very closely and see whether or not the can is opened. Although this seems to be a rather common sort of an example to apply to that noble creature, Man, it is nevertheless the bluntest statement that could be made about the status of Dianetics and Scientology and their uses and purposes.

Dianetics has as its goal the repairing and patching up of this thing called (by the uninitiated) "A Civilization," taking its destiny out of the hands of madmen who think that the entire organism is simply a machine and putting it in the hands of the same people–only this time with the ingredient of *sanity* added.

There isn't even any point in trying to categorize Dianetics or say that it "compares" to psychology or mathematics or engineering or any other activity, because it is obviously senior to all these activities and doesn't have to take any of these activities into account to work. All Dianetics needs to work is a trained auditor, preclear and a little time in which to accomplish its processes. If these ingredients (the auditor, the preclear and a little time) were not available, then there would be no purpose in having any Dianetics at all since there wouldn't be any human race.

The spirit in which these conclusions are advanced is intensely practical. And now that some nitwits (who probably don't get along with their wives and hate dogs, but who have worked themselves into the position of being able to) can knock a couple of atoms together, either by orders or by actual skill, and so tear up a very nice playing field – the presence of Dianetics in this world is not simply a practicality, *but an urgency.*

CHAPTER

ACCENT ON ABILITY

ACCENT ON ABILITY

ALMOST ANYONE REALIZES that he can be better than he is, that he can do things better than he has been doing them. It is an entirely different thing to ask someone to realize that he is ill, aberrated or stupid.

Why is it that a man can understand that he can be more capable and very often cannot understand that he is incapable? It would seem to follow that if a man realized he could be more capable, then he would realize at once that he was to some degree less capable than he could be.

For various reasons, however, this does not follow. One is confronted, many times too often, by his insistence upon brilliance of a very stupid man. It could be said with some truth that the person who asserts he "needs to know no more to be fully as bright as his fellows," would upon examination be discovered to be quite deficient in capability and understanding.

Earth has had many examples of this. The fascist is probably best described as "a very stupid man who insists upon a status quo which is intolerable for all others, yet who believes himself to be brighter than all others." But even the fascist of the most modern sort – the "fission fascist" – would be the first to admit that both he and others could do a better job of being fascistic.

The basic reason for this is a simple one, almost idiotically simple. One can understand "understanding" and can see that understanding can increase. Stupidity, ignorance, illness, aberration, incapability are only a fall away from "understanding" and are, themselves, "*less* understanding" and so are less understandable. One does not understand that he might get worse and so does not have any great communication with people who tell him that he will get worse. The dying man believes right up to the moment of the last breath, no matter what he is saying to his doctor or family, that he is going to get better. He has no understanding of that state of non-understandingness called "death." One can understand the understandable. One cannot understand the incomprehensible because the definition of "incomprehensibility" is "non-understandability." As I said, this is an almost idiotically simple situation.

Life in its highest state is understanding. Life in its lower states is at a lower level of understanding. And where life has ceased to function and has arrived at what one might call "total incapability," there is no understanding at all.

In Dianetics and Scientology, we have a great deal to do with this subject called understanding. Understanding has very specific component parts. These component parts are:

AFFINITY, REALITY and COMMUNICATION.

Affinity, Reality and Communication form an interdependent Triangle.

*"Understanding has very specific
component parts. These component parts are:
Affinity, Reality and Communication."*

It is easily discovered, on some inspection, that one cannot communicate in the absence of reality and affinity. Further, one cannot have a reality with something with which he cannot communicate and for which he feels no affinity. And similarly, one has no affinity for something on which he has no reality and on which he cannot communicate. Even more narrowly, one does not have affinity for those things on which he has no reality and which he cannot communicate upon. One has no reality on things which he has no affinity for and cannot communicate upon. And one cannot communicate upon things which have no reality to him and for which he has no affinity.

A graphic example of this would be anger. One becomes angry and what one says does not then communicate to the person at whom one might be angry. Even more crudely, the fastest way to go out of communication with a machine would be to cease to feel any affinity for it and to refuse to have any reality upon it.

We call this triangle the A-R-C TRIANGLE.

The precision definitions of these three items are as follows:

1. COMMUNICATION is the interchange of ideas or particles between two points.

    More precisely, the Formula of Communication is:

    Cause, Distance, Effect with Intention and Attention and a Duplication at Effect of what emanates from Cause.

    The Component Parts of Communication are:

    Consideration, Intention, Attention, Cause, Source-point, Distance, Effect, Receipt-point, Duplication, the Velocity of the impulse or particle, Nothingness or Somethingness. A non-Communication consists of Barriers. Barriers consist of Space, Interpositions (such as walls and screens of fast-moving particles) and Time.

2. REALITY is the degree of agreement reached by two ends of a communication line. In essence, it is the degree of Duplication achieved between Cause and Effect. That which is real is real simply because it is agreed-upon and for no other reason.

3. AFFINITY is the relative distance and similarity of the two ends of a communication line. Affinity has in it a mass connotation. The word, itself, implies that the greatest affinity there could be would be the occupation of the same space. And this, by experiment, has become demonstrated. When things do not occupy the same space, their affinity is delineated by the relative distance and the degree of duplication.[*]

These three items, AFFINITY, REALITY and COMMUNICATION, can be demonstrated to equate into UNDERSTANDING.

Above understanding is knowingness, without formula or design. And this might be considered to be a unit activity. Dropping down from a complete knowingness, we would arrive into the realm of understanding. For this is a "Third Dynamic" manifestation peculiar to two or more individuals.

Were you to be a clever mathematician, you could discover by symbolic logic how all mathematical formulas could be derived from this principle–that understanding is composed of affinity, reality and communication. No mathematics falling outside this triangle is a valid mathematics to Man. There is no additional factor in understanding except "significance." But this, of course, is the *idea* or *consideration* mentioned in number 1 above (COMMUNICATION).

It is a truism that if we could understand all life, we would then tolerate all life. Further–and more germane to *ability*–if one could occupy the position of any part of life, one would feel a sufficient affinity for life to be able to merge with it or separate from it at will.

---

*See the foldout chart at the back of this book which provides these definitions for continued reference with subsequent text.

When we say "life," all of us know more or less what we are talking about. But when we use this word "life" *practically,* we must examine its purposes and behavior and, in particular, the formulas evolved by life in order to have a game called life.

When we say "life," we mean understanding. And when we say "understanding," we mean affinity, reality and communication. To understand *all* would be to live at the highest level of potential action and ability. The quality of life exists in the presence of understanding–in the presence, then, of affinity, reality and communication. Life would exist to a far less active degree in the levels of misunderstanding, incomprehensibility, psychosomatic illness and physical and mental incapabilities. Because life is understanding, it attempts to understand. When it turns and faces the incomprehensible, it feels balked and baffled, feels there is a "secret" and feels that the secret is a threat to existence.

A secret is antipathetic to life. And therefore life, in searching for those things which would seem to reduce it, will hit upon various secrets it must discover. The basic secret is that a secret is an *absence of life.* And a total secret would be a *total unlivingness.*

Now let us look at this Formula of Communication and discover that we must have "a Duplication at Effect of what emanates from Cause." The classic example, here, is a telegram sent from New York City to San Francisco which says, "I love you." When it arrives in San Francisco, the machinery of communication has perverted it so that it says, "I loathe you." This failure of Duplication is looked upon as an error and would cause considerable problems and trouble. It could not then be considered to be a very good communication. Nothing wrong with the basic Intention. There was nothing wrong with the Attention which would be given the wire in San Francisco. The only thing that was wrong was a failure to "Duplicate at Effect of what emanated at Cause."

Now if life is understanding, it would find it very, very difficult to communicate with something which was non-understanding. In other words, life, faced with a non-understanding thing, would feel itself balked. For life, being understanding, could not then become non-understanding without assuming the role of being incomprehensible. Thus it is that the seeker after secrets, unless his way is carefully wended, is trapped into being a secret himself.

Where one has an Effect-point which is an incomprehensible thing and where one is occupying the Cause-point, in order to get any communication through to the Effect-point at all, it would be necessary for the one at Cause-point to somehow or another reduce his understandingness down toward incomprehensibility. The salesman knows this trick very well. He looks at his customer, recognizes his customer is interested in golf, and then pretends to be interested in golf himself in order to have the customer receive his sales talk. The salesman establishes points of agreement (and potential Duplication) and then proceeds into a communication.

Thus searchers after truth have often walked only into labyrinths of untruth – secrets – and have themselves become incomprehensible with conclusions of incomprehensibility. Thus we have the state of beingness of the philosophic textbooks of Earth. A wonderful example of this is Immanuel Kant, the "Great Chinaman of Königsberg," whose German participial phrases and adverbial clauses (and whose entire reversal of opinion between his first and second book) balks all our understanding, as it has the understanding of philosophic students since the late eighteenth century. But the very fact that it *is* incomprehensible has made it endure. For life feels challenged by this thing which, pretending to be understanding, is yet an incomprehensibility. This is the grave into which so many philosophers walk. This is the coffin into which the mathematician, seeking by mathematics the secrets of the universe, eventually nails himself.

But there is no reason why anyone should suffer simply because he looks at a few secrets. The test here is whether or not an individual possesses the power to *be* at his *own determinism*. If one can determine himself to be incomprehensible at will, he can of course then determine himself to be comprehensible again. But if he is obsessively and without understanding being determined into incomprehensibilities, then of course he is lost.

Thus we discover that the only trap into which life can fall is to do things without *knowing* it is doing them. Thus we get to a further delineation of the secret and we discover that the secret, or any secret, could exist only when life determined to face it without knowing and without understanding that it had so determined this action. The very best grade secret, then, would be something which made life also tend to forget that it was looking at a secret.

One can always understand that his ability can increase because in the direction of an increase of ability is further understanding. Ability is dependent entirely upon a greater and better understanding of that field or area in which one cares to be more able. When one attempts to understand less ability, he is of course looking at less comprehensibility, less understanding, and so does not then understand lessening ability anywhere near as well as he understands increasing ability. In the absence of understanding of ability, we get a fear of loss of ability, which is simply the fear of an unknown or a thought-to-be-unknowable thing. For there is less knownness and less understanding in less ability.

Because life does not want to face things which are less like life, it has a tendency to resist and restrain itself from confronting the less comprehensible. It is this resistance, alone, which brings about the "dwindling spiral" – the descent into less ability. Life does not *will* this descent into less ability (unless life is cognizant of the principles involved). Life *resists* itself into this less ability.

CHAPTER FOUR
ACCENT ON ABILITY

There is a primary rule working here:

THAT WHICH ONE FEARS, ONE BECOMES.

When one refuses to duplicate something and yet remains in its environment, his very resistance to the thing he refuses to duplicate will cause him eventually to become possessed of so many energy pictures of that thing which he refuses to duplicate that he will, to have any mass at all, find himself in possession of those energy pictures and – without actually noticing what has happened – is very likely to accept, at their level, those things which he refused to duplicate earlier. Thus we get the riddle of the engram, the facsimile, if we understand at the same time that life does not necessarily find it bad to have masses of energy around and is, indeed, unhappy unless it *does* have some energy. For if there is no energy, then there is no game.

Life has a motto that:

ANY GAME IS BETTER THAN NO GAME.

It has another motto:

ANY HAVINGNESS IS BETTER THAN NO HAVINGNESS.

Thus we find individuals clutching to them the most complex and destructive of facsimiles and mechanisms. They do not necessarily want these complexities. And yet they want the energy, or the game, which these complexities would seem to offer them.

If you would make anyone well, you must then concentrate upon an increase of ability, an increase of understanding. The only reason bad things come to life is because *understanding* has impressed further life *into* them. When an individual faces some secret, the fact that he is facing it and injecting life into it, alone, causes the secret to activate and have force and action. The only way a bad situation in existence can continue to have life is by taking life from nearby sources of communication.

The bad things of life, then, have life only to that degree that understanding is invested in them. We have an example in poliomyelitis, which was at one time an extremely minor and unheard-of illness. By various publications, by a great deal of advertising, by many invitations to combat this illness, it is made to take prominence and manifest itself in the society. The only life, actually, which poliomyelitis has, is the amount of life which can be invested in poliomyelitis. Yet poliomyelitis, one thinks, would exist and continue its way if it were ignored. If one were to go on ignoring poliomyelitis now that one knows about poliomyelitis – yes, this would be the case, the disease would continue to exist although everyone was studiously ignoring it. As a matter of fact, it would get worse. If, however, it were to be completely understood and if an ability on the part of individuals existed by which they could face it without having to resist it, then the matter would be solved.

One wonders why all the nurses and doctors in contagious wards do not immediately pick up the illness. And here we have another factor which is the same factor as understanding, but couched in a different way:

PEOPLE DO NOT ACQUIRE OBSESSIVELY THOSE THINGS WHICH THEY DO NOT FEAR.

An individual has to resist something, has to be afraid of something, has to be afraid of the consequences of something before it can have any adverse, obsessive effect upon him. At any time he could have a self-determined duplication of it. But this, not being obsessive, not being against his will, would of course not produce any ill symptom beyond the length of time he determined it.

Part of understanding and ability is CONTROL.

Of course, it is not necessary to control everything, everywhere, if one totally understands them.

However, in a lesser understanding of things and, of course, in the spirit of having a game, control becomes a necessary factor.

The anatomy of control is START, STOP and CHANGE.

This is fully as important to know as understanding itself and as the triangle which composes understanding (Affinity, Reality and Communication).

The doctors and nurses in a contagious ward have some feeling of control over the illnesses which they see before them. It is only when they begin to recognize their inability to handle these ills or these patients that they themselves succumb to this. In view of the fact that of recent centuries we have been very successful in handling contagious diseases, doctors and nurses then can walk with impunity through contagious wards. The fighters of disease, having some measure of control over the disease, are then no longer afraid of the disease and so it cannot affect them. Of course, there would be a level of body understanding on this which might yet still mirror fear, but we would have the same statement obtaining:

PEOPLE WHO ARE ABLE TO CONTROL SOMETHING DO NOT NEED TO BE AFRAID OF IT AND DO NOT SUFFER ILL EFFECTS FROM IT.

PEOPLE WHO CANNOT CONTROL THINGS CAN RECEIVE BAD EFFECTS FROM THOSE THINGS.

Here we have an example of what might happen in the realm of disease. How about human aberration?

We discover that the sanitariums of the world are all too often inhabited, in addition to patients, by those persons who were formerly at work in these institutions. It is a rather shocking thing to discover, in Ward 9, the nurse who was once supervisor of a mental hospital.

Now, here we had a condition where there was no control or understanding. People did not understand mental illness, aberration, insanity, neurosis. The first actual effort along this line which cut down the tally was Freudian analysis. And yet this, requiring much too long, was not an effective weapon. These doctors and nurses in institutions, who then are themselves patients in the same institution, knew definitely that they did not have any real control over insanity. Thus, having no control over it, they became subject to it.

They could not *start, stop* and *change* insanity.

The franticness of this state is represented by the medieval torture which has been utilized in such institutions as cures. By "cure," the people in charge of such institutions merely meant "quieter." The natural course of existence would lead them to think in terms of euthanasia and so they have—that it would be "best" to kill the patient rather than to have his insanity continue. And they have even accomplished this at the rate of 2,000 mental patients a year dead under electric shock machines. And they have accomplished it by a very high percentage dead under brain operations. The only "effectiveness" of electric shock and brain operations would be to render the patient less alive and more dead. And the end product achieved so many times of death would, of course, be "the only way to stop the insanity." These people, of course, could not envision the fact that immortality—and insanity in a future generation—would crop up as a problem. They had to conceive that if they killed the patient, or simply made him much quieter, they had then "triumphed" to some degree. The fact that Man, sane or insane, is not to be destroyed (according to law) weighs against this "solution."

With Dianetics, to use the study in a relatively narrow field of application, we have assumed some control over insanity, neurosis, aberration and can actually *start, stop* and *change* aberration.

CHAPTER FOUR
ACCENT ON ABILITY

In the First Book, *Dianetics: The Modern Science of Mental Health,* techniques were present which would place in view and then vanquish almost any mental manifestation known in the field of insanity and aberration. Where an auditor was unable to do anything for the insane or the neurotic, the fault (if fault there was) generally lay in the fact that the auditor was actually afraid. His fear was born entirely out of his insecurity in starting, stopping and changing the condition.

In modern instruction at Hubbard Professional College, there is little or no emphasis placed upon the case of the student. And yet when the student graduates, he is discovered to be in a very high tone. The entire concentration is upon giving the student the ability to handle any and all types of case. And he becomes sufficiently secure in his ability (if he is graduated) to walk, without any fear and with considerable calm, through areas of psychosis, neurosis and physical illness. He has been given the technologies by which these misbehaviors of life can be controlled. In view of the fact that he can start, stop and change them, he need no longer fear them and could, with impunity, work around the insane – if this were his mission.

The handling of psychosis, neurosis and psychosomatic illness does not happen to be the mission of the auditor. Indeed, these things get well only if they are more or less ignored. As long as the accent is upon ability, any malfunction will eventually vanish. The mission of the auditor is in the direction of ability. If he increases the general ability of the preclear in any and all fields, then of course any mis-abilities such as those represented by psychosis, neurosis and psychosomatic illness will vanish. The auditor, however, is not even covertly interested in these manifestations. Around him he sees a world which could be far more able. It is his business to make it so. While business in general does not recognize there is anything wrong with its abilities, it can recognize that its abilities can be better.

One well-trained auditor, working with Group Processing on the United States Air Force, could treble the number of pilots successfully graduated from the schools and could reduce the crash toll of high-speed planes by fully three-quarters. This is not a wild statement. It is simply an application of the research data already to hand.

The mission is greater ability, not an eradication of inability.

Just to "give more understanding to those around him" could be said to be a sufficient mission for a well-trained auditor. For by doing so, he would certainly increase their ability. By increasing their ability, he would be able to increase their life. The common denominator of all neurosis, psychosis, aberration and psychosomatic ill is "can't work." Any nation which has a high incidence of these is reduced in production, is reduced in longevity. ✳

And what does one do about "how bad it is"?

If one depends upon others or the environment to do something about it, he will fail. From his viewpoint, the only one who can put more life, more understanding, more tolerance and more capability into the environment is himself. Just by existing in a state of higher understanding, without even being active in the field of auditing, just by being more capable, an individual could resolve for those around him many of their problems and difficulties.

The accent is on *ability*.

*Amongst the unable is the criminal, who is _unable_ to think of the other fellow, _unable_ to determine his own actions, is _unable_ to follow orders, _unable_ to make things grow, is unable to determine the difference between good and evil, is _unable_ to think at all on the future — Anybody has some of these, the criminal has _all_ of them — Ɫ

CHAPTER

THE

FIVE

AUDITOR'S CODE

CHAPTER FIVE

THE AUDITOR'S CODE

THERE ARE SEVERAL CODES in Scientology and Dianetics. The only one which has to be obeyed, if we wish to obtain results upon a preclear, is the AUDITOR'S CODE 1954.

In the First Book, *Dianetics: The Modern Science of Mental Health,* we had an Auditor's Code which was derived more or less from an ideal, rather than from practical experience.

In the ensuing years, a great deal of auditing has been done and a great many errors have been made by auditors. And when we have taken the common denominator of what has caused preclears to make small or negative progress, we discover that these can be codified so as to inform the auditor who wishes to get results what to avoid in his processing.

When a psychoanalyst or psychologist uses Dianetics, he is very prone to be operating in his own frame of conduct. It is the conduct of the practitioner, almost as much as the processes, which makes Dianetics work.

In psychoanalysis, for instance, we discover that the basic failure of Freud's work in practice, and as used by analysts, fails chiefly because of two things done by the analyst in the consultation room. Whatever the value of Freud's libido theory, the effectiveness is reduced by the analyst's *evaluation* for the patient. The patient is not allowed to work out his own problems or come to his own conclusions. He is given ready-made interpretations.

In psychology, there is no operating code. For clinical psychology is not much practiced and is, indeed, outlawed in many states.

While psychiatry might have a "modus operandi," none of those conversant with this handling of the insane – the "function" of psychiatry – would call it "a code intended to induce a better state of beingness in a patient."

In education – which is, in itself, a therapy – we discover an almost total absence of codified conduct, beyond that laid down by school boards to regulate the social attitude of and restrain the possible cruelty in educators. Although education is very widespread and, indeed, is the practice best accepted by the society for the betterment of individuals, it yet lacks any tightly agreed-upon method or conduct-codification for the relaying of data to the student. Custom has dictated a certain politeness on the part of the professor or teacher. It is generally believed to be necessary to examine with rigor and thoroughness. Students are not supposed to whisper or chew gum. But education, in general, has no code designed to oil the flow of data from the rostrum to the student bench. On the contrary, a great many students would declare that any existing code was designed to stop any flow whatever.

Dianetics is in an interesting position in that it is *itself*. And although people may try to classify it with mental therapy, it is closer to the level of education so far as the society itself is concerned. Its goal is the improvement of the mind on a self-determined basis and its intended use is upon individuals and groups. Because it is an accumulation of data which is apparently the agreed-upon factors from which existence is constructed, and although the simple perusal of this data very often frees an individual, it is also disseminated on an individual and group basis (directly to individuals and groups) and is a form of self-recognition.

If you were to make the best progress along any highway, you would do well to follow its signs. In the Auditor's Code of 1954, we have a number of signposts. And if their directions are pursued, a maximum of result will result. If they are not pursued, one is liable to find the preclear "over in the ditch," in need of a tow truck in the form of a better auditor. Quite in addition to the command of the processes themselves, the difference between the Book Auditor and the Professional Auditor lies in the observance of this code.

A very great deal of time is invested in the auditor at Hubbard Professional College in demonstrating to him the effects of disobedience of this code and obedience of it—and in leading him to practice it closely. This supervision at the Hubbard Professional College is relatively simple. One takes a look at the class and finds somebody who is not in good shape. One discovers who audited him and one then knows what auditor is not following the Auditor's Code. The offending student is then taken aside and briefed once more.

A graduating auditor has to know this code by heart and, more importantly, has to be able to practice it with the same unconscious ease as a pilot flies a plane.

The Auditor's Code follows:

THE AUDITOR'S CODE
1954

1   Do not evaluate for the preclear.

2   Do not invalidate or correct the preclear's data.

3   Use the processes which improve the preclear's case.

4   Keep all appointments once made.

5   Do not process a preclear after 10:00 P.M.

6   Do not process a preclear who is improperly fed.

7   Do not permit a frequent change of auditors.

8   Do not sympathize with the preclear.

9   Never permit the preclear to end the session on his own independent decision.

10 Never walk off from a preclear during a session.

11 Never get angry with a preclear.

12 Always reduce every communication lag encountered by continued use of the same question or process.

13 Always continue a process as long as it produces change and no longer.

14 Be willing to grant beingness to the preclear.

15 Never mix the processes of Dianetics with those of various other practices.

16 Maintain two-way communication with the preclear.

If one were to sort out these various provisos, he would discover all of them important, but that three of them were more vitally concerned with processing than the others. And that these three, if overlooked, would inevitably and always result in case failure. These three are the difference between a good auditor and a bad auditor. They are numbers 12, 13 and 16.

In 12, we discover that the auditor should "Always reduce every communication lag encountered by continued use of the same question or process." Almost every case failure contains some of this. The difference between a Professional Auditor and a Book Auditor is most visible in this and the other two provisos mentioned. A good auditor would understand what a "communication lag" is (the length of time intervening between the asking of the question and the receiving of a direct answer to that question, regardless of what takes place in the interval). And he would be very careful to use only those processes on the preclear which the preclear could reasonably answer up to. And he would be very certain not to walk off from a communication lag into which the session had entered. A bad auditor would believe, when he had struck a communication lag, that he had simply found a blind alley and would hastily change to some other question.

In number 13, "Always continue a process as long as it produces change and no longer," we find the greatest frailty on the part of auditors. An auditor who is not in good condition, or who is not well trained, will "Q and A" with the preclear. When the preclear starts to change, the auditor will change the process. By Q and A, we mean that "the *answer* to the question is the *question*" and we indicate a duplication. Here we find an auditor possibly so much under the command of the preclear, rather than the reverse, that the auditor simply duplicates obsessively what the preclear is doing. The preclear starts to change, therefore the auditor changes. A process should be run as long as it produces change.

If the preclear is changing, that is what the auditor wants. If the auditor were to stop and change off to some other process just because the preclear had attained some change, we would discover some very sick preclears. Additionally, an auditor is liable to continue a process long after it has stopped producing change. He and the preclear get into a sort of a marathon (a machine-motivated grind) on the process "Opening Procedure by Duplication," which probably after ten hours produced no further alteration in the preclear. Yet this pair might go on to fifty hours with the process and would be quite disheartened to discover that for forty hours nothing had happened. This, however, is much less harmful as an action than the changing of the process simply because it is producing change.

The "Maintenance of a two-way communication" is the most touchy activity in auditing. An auditor, being the auditor and being concentrated upon controlling the preclear, all too often forgets to listen when the preclear speaks. Many an auditor is so intent upon the process that when it produces a change which the preclear thinks he should advise upon, the auditor ignores him. Ignoring the preclear at a time when he wishes to impart some vital information generally sends the preclear directly into apathy. At the same time, an auditor should not permit a preclear to keep on talking forever – as in the case of a lady, recently reported, who talked to the auditor for three days and three nights. The therapeutic value of this was zero, for the auditor was listening to a "machine," not to the preclear. One should understand, rather thoroughly, the difference between an *obsessive* or *compulsive* communication line and an *actual* communication. Listening to "circuits," of course, validates circuits. The auditor should pay attention to the rational, the usual, the agreed-upon and should leave very much alone the bizarre, the freakish, the compulsive and the obsessive manifestations of the preclear. The maintenance of a two-way communication is actually a process in itself and is the first, most basic process of Dianetics and continues on through all remaining processes.

Simply because we have pinpointed three of these is no reason to ignore the others. Every time there has been a "psychotic break" by reason of or during auditing, it has occurred when the processing was being done late at night, when the preclear was improperly fed, when the preclear had had a frequent change of auditors and when two-way communication had not been maintained and the effort on the part of the preclear to impart a vital change to the auditor was ignored. All these "psychotic breaks" were repaired. But because these factors were present, the patching up was rather difficult. Audit them early, audit them bright, listen to what they have to say about what's happening, make sure they are eating regularly and change auditors on a preclear as seldom as possible, and no "psychotic breaks" will occur.

If you are simply investigating Dianetics to discover whether or not it is workable, you should be aware of the fact that the Auditor's Code–following of–is an essential portion of Dianetics. Dianetics functions very poorly in the absence of the Auditor's Code. It is part of the process, not simply a polite way to go about handling people. Thus, if Dianetics is tested in the absence of the Auditor's Code, do not pretend that it has been tested at all.

Another phrase might have been added to this code, but it would be more germane to living than to auditing. And that phrase would be: "Maintain silence around unconscious or semiconscious people." (The reason for this is contained in *Dianetics: The Modern Science of Mental Health,* in the chapter Preventive Dianetics. Such statements become "engramic.") The addition of this to the Auditor's Code, however, is not practical. For the auditor often finds himself talking to a "groggy" preclear. Because the auditor is reducing every communication lag he encounters by the repetition of the question, the asking of a question or giving of a command to a semiconscious preclear is thus rendered relatively unaberrative. For, sooner or later, the question embedded in the unconsciousness will work loose and, indeed, the communication lag will not "flatten" until this occurs.

Thus, simply the reduction of the communication lag in itself eradicates such phrases. Thus, this is not part of the Auditor's Code.

However, when we encounter unconsciousness or semiconsciousness—as in moments immediately after the injury of a child, a street accident, an operation—we maintain silence, for we are not auditing the person. Mothers and fathers would spare themselves a great deal of later mental unrest on the child's part if they knew and would follow this injunction. And in many other ways, it is a very important one. A man can be killed by too much conversation around him while he is injured. No matter how deeply unconscious he may appear to be, something is always registering. The questioning by police at the scene of an accident, where the person being questioned is in a state of shock or where other accident victims are present, is probably the most aberrative conduct in this society. The questioning by police is quite restimulative, in any event, and many severe complications after accidents have been traced immediately to this activity on the part of the police. It might be very important for some ledger, somewhere, to know exactly who caused this. It is more important that the people involved in it live and be happy afterward. It is not that we do not like police. This is not the case. We simply believe that the police should be civilized too.

Simply memorizing this code is not enough. Memorizing it in order to practice it is indicated. But it is the *practice* of this code which is important. Observance of it is the hallmark of a good auditor and it signalizes the recovery of the case.

If an auditor is going to raise the ability of the preclear, his ability in the field of auditing must be considerable. That ability begins with the understanding and observance of the *Auditor's Code 1954.*

"*If an auditor is going to raise the ability of the preclear,
his ability in the field of auditing must be considerable.
That ability begins with the understanding
and observance of the* Auditor's Code 1954."

C H A P T E R

S I X

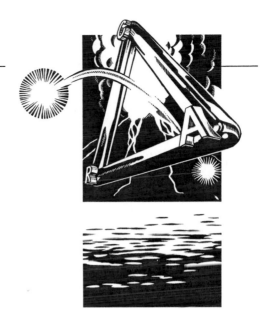

T R A P P E D

TRAPPED

N GREECE, Rome, England, Colonial America, France and Washington, a great deal of conversation is made on the subject of freedom. Freedom apparently is something that is very desirable. Indeed, freedom is seen to be the goal of a nation or a people.

Similarly, if we are restoring ability to the preclear, we must restore freedom. If we do not restore freedom, we cannot restore ability. The muscle-bound wrestler, the tense driver, the rocket jockey with a frozen reaction time, alike, are not able. Their ability lies in an increase of freedom, a release of tension and a better communication to their environment.

The main trouble with freedom is it does not have an anatomy. Something that is free is free. It is not free with wires, vias, bypasses or dams. It is simply free. There is something else about freedom which is intensely interesting: It cannot be *erased*. In *Dianetics: The Modern Science of Mental Health,* we learned that "pleasure moments" were not erasable. The only thing that was erasable was pain, discomfort, distortion, tenseness, agony, unconsciousness.

In more modern Scientological parlance, freedom cannot be "As-ised." It is something which is imperishable. You may be able to concentrate somebody's attention on something that is not free and thus bring him into a state of belief that freedom does not exist, but this does not mean that you have "erased" the individual's freedom. You have not. All the freedom he ever had is still there. Furthermore, freedom has no quantity. And by definition, it has no location in space or time. Thus we see the awareness of awareness unit as potentially the freest thing there could be. Thus Man's concentration upon freedom.

But if freedom has no anatomy, then please explain how one is going to attain to something which cannot be fully explained? If anyone talks about a "road to freedom," he is talking about a linear line. This, then, must have boundaries. If there are boundaries, there is no freedom.

This brings the interesting proposition to mind that the very best process, by theory, would be to have an individual "assume himself to be free." And then he would simply be asked to "assume himself to be free" again. Indeed, on many cases of a high-toned variety, this is a quite workable process. An individual is sick. He is usually in very good tone. The auditor simply asks him to assume that he is free and he will cease to be sick.

This magic, however, is limited to those people who have some concept of what "free" means. Talk to a person who works from eight o'clock until five–with no goals, with no future and no belief in the organization or its goals, who is being required by time payments, rent and other barriers of an economic variety, to invest all of his salary as soon as it is paid–and we have an individual who has lost the notion of freedom. His concentration is so thoroughly fixed upon barriers that "freedom" has to be in terms of "less barriers." Thus, in processing, we have to audit in the direction of less and less barriers in order to attain freedom.

"*Talk to a person who works from eight o'clock until five ...
and we have an individual who has lost the notion of freedom.
His concentration is so thoroughly fixed upon barriers
that 'freedom' has to be in terms of 'less barriers.'*"

If freedom is so very compelling and is so useful and is, in itself, something like a synonym for ability (even if not entirely), then it is our task to understand a little more about freedom, as itself, in order to accomplish its attainment. For unfortunately, it is not enough to the bulk of the human race simply to say "be free" and have the individual recover.

Life is prone to a stupidity, in many cases, in which it is not cognizant of a disaster until the disaster has occurred. The Middle Western farmer had a phrase for it: "Lock the door after the horse is stolen." It takes a disaster in order to educate people into the existence of such a disaster. This is education by pain, by impact, by punishment. Therefore, a population which is faced with a one-shot disaster that will obliterate the sphere would not have a chance to learn very much about the sphere before it was obliterated. Thus, if they insisted upon "learning by experience" in order to prevent such a disaster, they would never have the opportunity. If no atomic bomb of any kind had been dropped in World War II, it is probable there would be no slightest concern about atomic fission–although atomic fission might have developed right on up to the "planet buster" without ever being used against Man and then, as a "planet buster" being used on Earth, so destroying it.

If a person did not know what a tiger was and we desired to demonstrate to him that no tigers were present, we would have a difficult time of it. Here we have a "freedom from tigers" without knowing anything about tigers. Before he could understand an absence of tigers, he would have to understand a presence of tigers. This is the process of learning we know as "by experience."

In order to know anything (if we are going to use educational methods), it is necessary, then, to know as well its opposite. The "opposite of tigers" probably exists in Malayan jungles, where tigers are so frequent that the absence of tigers would be a novelty indeed. A country which was totally burdened by tigers might not understand at all the idea that there were no tigers in some parts of the world. And a great deal of argument would have to be entered into with the populace of a tiger-burdened area to get them to get any inkling of what an absence of tigers would be.

Many cases in processing have suddenly lost a somatic to discover themselves in a new and novel state. This somatic was so routine and so constant and so pervasive that they could not intellectually conceive of what life would be like without that particular somatic.

The understanding of freedom, then, is slightly complex, in that individuals who do not have it are not likely to understand it. And thus we find an individual, who knows nothing about exteriorization and knows everything about being in constant contact with the sensations of a body, failing to grasp the idea of the freedom resulting from exteriorization. These people do not even believe that exteriorization can exist and so combat it. They are so little experienced on the subject of freedom that this type of freedom is "known to be non-existent" to them.

The way to demonstrate the existence of freedom is to invite the individual to experience freedom. But if he does not know what freedom is, then he will not exteriorize. We have to hit some sort of a "gradient scale" on the matter. Or make him turn around and look squarely at the opposite of freedom.

But the opposite of freedom is slavery, everybody knows this.

Or is it?

I do not think these two things are a dichotomy. Freedom is not the "plus" of the condition where slavery is the "minus," unless we are dealing entirely with the political organism.

Where we are dealing with the individual, better terminology is necessary and more understanding of the anatomy of minus-freedom is required:

Minus-freedom is entrapment.

Freedom is the absence of barriers.

Less freedom is the presence of barriers.

Entirely minus-freedom would be the omnipresence of barriers.

A barrier is matter or energy or time or space.

The more matter, energy, time and space assume command over the individual, the less freedom that individual has. This is best understood as "entrapment," since "slavery" connotates an intention and entrapment might be considered almost without intention. A person who falls into a bear pit might not have intended to fall into it at all. And the bear pit might not have intended a person to fall upon its stake. Nevertheless, an entrapment has occurred. The person is in the bear pit.

If one wants to understand existence and his unhappiness with it, he must understand entrapment and its mechanisms.

In what can a person become entrapped? Basically and foremost, he can become entrapped in *ideas*. In view of the fact that freedom and ability can be seen to be somewhat synonymous, then ideas of disability are first and foremost in entrapment. I daresay, amongst men, the incident has occurred that a person has been sitting upon a bare plain in the total belief that he is entirely entrapped by a fence. There is that incident mentioned in *Self Analysis* of fishing in Lake Tanganyika, where the Sun's rays, being equatorial, pierce burningly to the lake's bottom. The natives there fish by tying a number of slats of wood on a long piece of line. They take either end of this line and put it in canoes and then paddle the two canoes toward the shallows of the lake, the slatted line stretching between. The Sun, shining downward, presses the shadows of these bars down to the bottom of the lake and thus a "cage of shadows" moves inward toward the shallows. The fish seeing this "cage" contract upon them, which is composed of nothing but the absence of light, flounder frantically into the shallows where they cannot swim and are thus caught, picked up in baskets and cooked. Yet there was nothing to be afraid of but shadows.

When we move out of mechanics, Man finds himself on unsure ground. The idea that *ideas* can be so strong and pervasive is foreign to most men.

For instance, a government attacked by the communist does not perceive that it is being attacked only by ideas. It believes itself to be attacked by guns, bombs, armies. And yet it sees no guns, bombs, armies. It sees only men, standing together, exchanging ideas. Whether these ideas are sound or not is beside the point. They are at least penetrative. No sixteen-inch armor plate could possibly stop an idea. Thus a country can be entrapped, taken and turned toward communism, simply by the spread of the communistic idea. A country that fails to understand this arms itself, keeps its guns cocked, its armies alert and then succumbs at last to the *idea* – now entered into the head of the armed forces which it so hopefully employed. The collapse of Germany in World War I was an instance of this. Its armies, its grand fleet, were all flying the red flag. Although Allied pressure and the conditions of starvation in Germany had much to do with this defeat, nevertheless it was keyed into being by this communist idea infiltrated into the minds of the men who originally were armed and trained to protect Germany. And communism, just as an idea, traps the *minds* of men. They find themselves organized into cells, they find their customs abandoned and a regimented, militant, biological, soulless tyranny their master. Here is an idea becoming a sort of trap.

So, first and foremost, we have the *idea*. Then, themselves the product of ideas, we have the more obvious mechanics of entrapment in *matter, energy, space* and *time*.

The most common barrier, which Man recognizes as such, would be a wall. This is so obviously a barrier that individuals quite commonly suppose all barriers to be composed of solid walls. However, almost any object can be made into a barrier. A less common use of an object as a barrier would be one which inhibited, by some sort of suction or drag, a departure from it. A solid lump of considerable magnetic properties will hold to it a piece of steel. Gravity is, then, a barrier of a kind. It holds the people or life units of Earth, to Earth.

Another barrier would be *energy.* A sheet of energy or something carrying energy, such as an electrical fence, can prove to be a formidable barrier. A cloud of radioactive particles, obstructing passage into another space, would also be a barrier. Tractor-type beams, as in the case of gravity but in the form of energy, could be seen to be a barrier of sorts.

Yet another barrier, easily understood, is that of *space.* Too much space will always make a barrier. Space debars an individual from progressing into another part of the galaxy. One of the finest prisons one could imagine would be one located on a small piece of matter surrounded by such a quantity of space that no one could cross it. Space is such an efficient barrier that people in the Southwest of the United States, committing crimes, discover their way everywhere blocked by the giganticness of space. In New York City it would be very easy for them, after the commission of a crime, to vanish. But in attempting to cross a space of such size as the Southwest, they become exposed everywhere to view – there being nothing else on which the police can fix their attention.

Quite another barrier, less well understood but extremely thorough, is the barrier of *time.* Time debars your passage into the year 1776 and prevents your repossession of things which you had in your youth. It also prevents you from having things in the future. Time is an exceedingly effective barrier. The absence of time can also be a barrier, for here an individual is unable to execute his desires and is so constricted by the pressure of time itself.

Matter, energy, space and time can all, then, be barriers.

An awareness of awareness unit, however, which is the personality and beingness of the person and which is composed of *quality*, not *quantity*, can be anywhere it wishes to be. There is no wall thick enough, nor any space wide enough, to debar the reappearance at some other point of an awareness of awareness unit. In that this *is* the individual (and not some ghost of the individual) and as the individual is himself an awareness of awareness unit (and not his machinery and his body), we see that as soon as one understands completely that he *is* an awareness of awareness unit, he no longer is restricted by barriers. Thus, those who would seek entrapment for individuals are entirely antipathetic toward the idea of exteriorization. And a person who knows nothing but barriers is apt to believe that a condition of no-barriers could not exist. Yet a condition of no-barriers can exist. And this is, itself, *freedom*.

Examining freedom, then, we have to examine why people do not attain it easily or understand it. They do not attain freedom because their attention is fixed upon barriers. They look at the wall, not the space on either side of the wall. They have "entities" and "demon circuits" which demand their attention. And, indeed, the body itself could be considered to be an attention-demanding organism. One might believe that its total function was to command interest and attention. It is so interesting that people do not conceive that just *behind them* lies all the freedom anybody ever desired. They even go so far as to believe that *that* freedom is not desirable and that if they could attain it, they would not want it.

One is reminded of prisoners who occasionally go so sufficiently "stir-crazy" as to demand, after their release from prison, confining walls and restricted spaces. Manuel Komroff once wrote a very appealing story on this subject–the story of an old man who had served twenty-five years in prison (or some such time) and who, on his release, asked for nothing more than the smallest room in his son's house, and was happiest when he could see someone on an opposite roof who had the appearance of a guard, and who actively put bars back on his window. One could consider a person who has been for a long time in a body to have such a fixation upon the barriers imposed by the body that once an auditor tries to remove them, the preclear puts them back quickly. You might say such a person is "stir-crazy." Yet the condition is remediable.

The anatomy of entrapment is an interesting one. And the reason why people get entrapped and, indeed, the total mechanics of entrapment are now understood in Scientology. A great deal of experimentation was undertaken to determine the factors which resulted in entrapment and it was discovered that the answer to the entire problem was "two-way communication."

Roughly, the laws back of this are:

FIXATION OCCURS ONLY IN THE PRESENCE OF ONE-WAY COMMUNICATION.

ENTRAPMENT OCCURS ONLY WHEN ONE HAS NOT GIVEN OR RECEIVED ANSWERS TO THE THING ENTRAPPING HIM.

Thus we see the A-R-C Triangle itself–and most importantly, the Communication factor of that Triangle–looming up to give us a roadway to freedom.

It could be said that:

ALL THE ENTRAPMENT THERE IS, IS THE WAITING ONE DOES FOR AN ANSWER.

CHAPTER SIX
TRAPPED

Here we find Man. Basically, he is an awareness of awareness unit which is capable of and active in the production of matter, energy, space and time as well as ideas. We discover that he is more and more fixated upon ideas, matter, energy, space and time and the processes and functions involving these. And we discover that these, being the product of the awareness of awareness unit, do not supply answers to the awareness of awareness unit unless the awareness of awareness unit supplies *itself* those answers.

Entrapment is the opposite of freedom. A person who is not free is trapped. He may be trapped by an idea. He may be trapped by matter. He may be trapped by energy. He may be trapped by space. He may be trapped by time. And he may be trapped by all of them. The more thoroughly the preclear is trapped, the less free he is. He cannot change, he cannot move, he cannot communicate, he cannot feel affinity and reality. Death, itself, could be said to be Man's ultimate in entrapment. For when a man is totally entrapped, he is dead.

It is our task in investigation and auditing to discover, for the individual and the group, the roadway to a greater freedom which is the roadway to a greater ability.

The processes the auditor uses today are designed entirely to secure greater freedom for the individual, for the group, for Mankind. Any process which leads to a greater freedom for all dynamics is a good process. It should be remembered, however, that an individual functions on all dynamics. And that the suppression by the individual of the Third or Fourth Dynamic leads to less freedom for the individual himself. Thus the criminal, becoming immorally free, harms the group and harms Mankind and, thus, becomes less free himself. Thus there is no freedom in the absence of affinity, agreement and communication. Where an individual falls away from these, his freedom is sharply curtailed and he finds himself confronted with barriers of magnitude.

The component parts of freedom, as we first gaze upon it, are then affinity, reality and communication – which summate into understanding. Once understanding is attained, freedom is obtained. For the individual who is thoroughly snarled in the mechanics of entrapment, it is necessary to restore to him sufficient communication to permit his ascendance into a higher state of understanding. Once this has been accomplished, his entrapment is ended.

None of this is actually a very difficult problem and the auditing done today is very simple. But where the auditing is done by a person who does not basically desire the freedom of the individual, a further entrapment is more likely to ensue than further freedom. The obsessively entrapped are, then, enemies of the preclear. For they will trap others.

A greater freedom can be attained by the individual. The individual does desire a greater freedom once he has some inkling of it. And auditing, according to the precision rules and codes of Dianetics and Scientology, steers the individual out of the first areas of entrapment to a point where he can gain higher levels of freedom – either by further auditing or by himself. The only reason we need a regimen with which to begin is to start an individual out of a mirror maze of such complexity that he, himself, in attempting to wend his way, only gets lost.

This is *Dianetics 55!*

"For the individual who is thoroughly snarled
in the mechanics of entrapment, it is necessary to restore
to him sufficient communication to permit his ascendance
into a higher state of understanding. Once this has been
accomplished, his entrapment is ended."

C H A P T E R

SEVEN

COMMUNICATION

COMMUNICATION

COMMUNICATION IS so thoroughly important today in Dianetics and Scientology (as it always has been on the whole track) that it could be said if you were to get a preclear into communication, you would get him well. This factor is not new in psychotherapy. But concentration upon it is new and interpretation of ability as communication is entirely new.

If you were to be in thorough and complete communication with a car and a road, you would certainly have no difficulty driving that car. But if you were only in partial communication with the car and in no communication with the road, it is fairly certain that an accident will occur. Most accidents do occur when the driver is distracted by an argument he has had, or by an arrest, or a white cross alongside the road that says where some motorist got killed, or by his own fears of accidents.

When we say somebody should be "in present time," we mean he should be in communication with his environment. We mean, further, that he should be in communication with his environment *as* it exists, not as it exist*ed*. And when we speak of "prediction," we mean that he should be in communication with his environment as it *will* exist, as well as *as* it exists.

If communication is so important, what *is* communication? It is best expressed as its Formula, which has been isolated, and by use of which a great many interesting results can be brought about in ability changes.

There are two kinds of communication, both depending upon the viewpoint assumed. There is "outflowing" communication and "inflowing" communication. A person who is talking to somebody else is communicating *to* that person (we trust), and the person who is being talked to is receiving communication *from* that person. Now, as the conversation changes, we find the person who has been talked to is now doing the talking and is talking *to* the first person, who is now receiving communication *from*.

A conversation is the process of alternating outflowing and inflowing communication. And right here exists the oddity which makes aberration and entrapment. There is a basic rule here:

HE WHO WOULD OUTFLOW MUST INFLOW;

HE WHO WOULD INFLOW MUST OUTFLOW.

When we find this rule overbalanced, in either direction, we discover difficulty.

A person who is only outflowing communication is actually not communicating at all, in the fullest sense of the word. For in order to communicate entirely, he would have to inflow as well as outflow. A person who is inflowing communication entirely is, again, out of order. For if he would inflow, he must then outflow. Any and all objections anyone has to social and human relationships are to be found, basically, in this rule of communication (where it is disobeyed). Anyone who is talking, if he is not in a compulsive or obsessive state of beingness, is dismayed when he does not get answers. Similarly, anyone who is being talked to is dismayed when he is not given an opportunity to give his replies.

Even hypnotism can be understood by this rule of communication. Hypnotism is a continuing inflow without an opportunity on the part of the subject to outflow. This is carried on to such a degree in hypnotism that the individual is actually trapped in the spot where he is being hypnotized and will remain trapped in that spot, to some degree, from there on. Thus, one might go so far as to say that a bullet's arrival is a heavy sort of hypnotism. The individual receiving a bullet does not outflow a bullet and thus he is injured. If he could outflow a bullet immediately after receiving a bullet, we could introduce the interesting question: "Would he be wounded?" According to our rule, he would not be. Indeed, if he were in perfect communication with his environment, he could not even receive a bullet injuriously. But let us look at this from a highly practical viewpoint.

As we look at two life units in communication, we can label one of them A and the other one of them B. In a good state of communication, A would outflow and B would receive. Then B would outflow and A would receive. Then A would outflow and B would receive. Then B would outflow and A would receive. In each case, both A and B would know that the communication was being received and would know what and where was the source of the communication.

All right, we have A and B facing each other in a communication. A outflows. His message goes across a Distance to B, who inflows. In this phase of the communication, A is Cause, B is Effect, and the intervening space we term the Distance. It is noteworthy that A and B are both life units. A true communication is between two life units. It is not between two objects, or from one object to one life unit. A, a life unit, is Cause. The intervening space is Distance. B, a life unit, is Effect. Now a completion of this communication changes the roles. Replied to, A is now the Effect and B is the Cause. Thus we have a cycle which completes a true communication.

The cycle is:

Cause, Distance, Effect with Effect then becoming Cause and communicating across a Distance to the original Cause which is now Effect.

And this we call a TWO-WAY COMMUNICATION.*

As we examine this further, we find out that there are other factors involved. There is A's Intention. This, at B, becomes Attention. And for a true communication to take place, a Duplication at B must take place of what emanated from A. A, of course, to emanate a communication, must have given Attention originally to B. And B must have given to this communication some Intention, at least to listen or receive. So we have both Cause and Effect having Intention and Attention.

Now there is another factor which is very important. This is the factor of Duplication. We could express this as "reality" or we could express it as "agreement." The degree of agreement reached between A and B, in this communication cycle, becomes their reality. And this is accomplished, mechanically, by Duplication. In other words, the degree of reality reached in this communication cycle depends upon the amount of Duplication. B, as Effect, must to some degree Duplicate what emanated from A, as Cause, in order for the first part of the cycle to take effect. And then A, now as Effect, must Duplicate what emanated from B for the communication to be concluded. If this is done, there is no aberrative consequence.

If this Duplication does not take place at B and then at A, we get what amounts to an unfinished cycle-of-action. If, for instance, B did not vaguely Duplicate what emanated from A, the first part of the cycle of communication was not achieved and a great deal of randomity, explanation, argument might result.

---

*See the foldout chart at the back of this book for the Formula of Communication, the Component Parts of Communication and the Two-way Cycle of Communication for continued reference in studying this text.

Then, if A did not Duplicate what emanated from B, when B was Cause on the second cycle, again, an uncompleted cycle of communication occurred with consequent unreality.

Now, naturally, if we cut down reality, we will cut down affinity. So where Duplication is absent, affinity is seen to drop. A complete cycle of communication will result in high affinity and will, in effect, erase itself. If we disarrange any of these factors, we get an incomplete cycle of communication and we have either A or B or both *waiting* for the end of cycle. In such a wise, the communication becomes aberrative.

The word "aberrate" means "to make something diverge from a straight line" (the word comes basically from optics). Aberration is simply something which does not contain straight lines. A confusion is a bundle of crooked lines. A mass is no more and no less than a confusion of mismanaged communications. The energy masses and deposits (the facsimiles and engrams) surrounding the preclear are no more and no less than unfinished cycles of communication, which yet wait for their proper answers at A and B.

An unfinished cycle of communication generates what might be called "answer hunger." An individual who is waiting for a signal that his communication has been received is prone to accept any inflow. When an individual has, for a very long period of time, consistently waited for answers which did not arrive–any sort of answer, from anywhere, will be pulled in to him, *by him,* as an effort to remedy his scarcity for answers. Thus, he will throw engramic phrases in the bank into action and operation against himself.

Uncompleted cycles of communication bring about a scarcity of answers. It does *not* much matter what the answers were, or would be, as long as they vaguely approximate the subject at hand. It *does* matter when some entirely unlooked-for answer is given, as in compulsive or obsessive communication, or when no answer is given at all.

Communication, itself, is aberrative only when the emanating communication at Cause was sudden and non sequitur to the environment. Here we have violations of Attention and Intention.

The factor of "interest" also enters here, but is far less important (at least from the standpoint of the auditor). Nevertheless, it explains a great deal about human behavior and explains considerable about circuits. A is interes*ted* and has the Intention of interes*ting* B. B, to be talked to, becomes interes*ting.* Similarly, B, when he emanates a communication, is interes*ted* and A is interes*ting.* Here we have, as part of the Communication Formula (but as I said, a less important part), the continuous shift from being interested to being interesting on the part of either of the terminals A or B. Cause is interes*ted.* Effect is interes*ting.*

Of some greater importance is the fact that the Intention to be received on the part of A, places upon A the necessity of being Duplica*table.* If A cannot be Duplicatable in any degree, then of course his communication will not be received at B. For B, unable to Duplicate A, cannot receive the communication.

As an example of this: A, let us say, speaks in Chinese, where B can only understand French. It is necessary for A to make himself Duplicatable by speaking French to B, who only understands French. In a case where A speaks one language and B another, and they have no language in common, we have the factor of "mimicry" possible and a communication can yet take place. A, supposing he had a hand, could raise his hand. B, supposing he had one, could raise his hand. Then B could raise his other hand and A could raise his other hand. And we would have completed a cycle of communication by *mimicry*. Communication by mimicry could also be called communication in terms of *mass*.

We see that reality is the degree of Duplication between Cause and Effect. Affinity is monitored by Intention and the particle sizes involved as well as the Distance. The greatest affinity there is, for anything, is to occupy its same space. As the Distance widens, affinity drops. Further, as the amount of mass or energy particles increases, so again does affinity drop. Further, as the Velocity departs from what A and B have considered optimum Velocity – either greater or lesser Velocity than what they consider to be the proper Velocity – affinity drops.

There is another fine point about communication and that is "expectancy."

Basically, all things are considerations. We *consider* that things are and so they *are*. The idea is always senior to the mechanics of energy, space, time, mass. It would be possible to have entirely different ideas about communication than these. However, these happen to be the ideas of communication which are in common in this universe and which are utilized by the life units of this universe. Here we have the basic "agreement" upon the subject of communication in the Communication Formula, as given above. Because ideas are senior to this, an awareness of awareness unit can get (in addition to the Communication Formula) a peculiar idea concerning just exactly how communication should be conducted and, if this is not generally "agreed-upon," can find himself definitely "out of communication."

Let us take the example of a modernistic writer who insists that the first three letters of every word should be dropped, or that no sentence should be finished, or that the description of characters should be held to a "cubist rendition." He will not attain agreement amongst his readers and so will become, to some degree, an "only one." There is a continuous action of natural selection, one might say, which weeds out strange or peculiar communication ideas.

People, to be in communication, adhere to the basic rules as given here. And when anyone tries to depart too widely from these rules, they simply do not Duplicate him and so, in effect, he goes out of communication.

We have seen an entire race of philosophers go out of existence since 1790. We have seen philosophy become a very unimportant subject, where once it was a very common coin amongst the people. The philosophers, themselves, put themselves out of communication with the people by insisting on using words of special definition which could not be assimilated with readiness by persons in general. The currency of philosophy could not be duplicated by those with relatively limited vocabularies. Take such jaw-cracking words as "telekinesis." While it probably means something very interesting and very vital, if you will think back carefully, no taxi driver has mentioned the word to you while you were paying your fare or even during the more verbose moments of the ride. Probably the basic trouble with philosophy was that it became Germanic in its grammar, an example set by Immanuel Kant. (And if you will recall that wonderful story by Saki, a man was once trampled to death while trying to teach an elephant German irregular verbs!) Philosophy shed some of its responsibility for a cycle of communication by rendering itself unduplicatable by its readers. It is the responsibility of anyone who would communicate that he speak with such vocabulary as can be understood. Thus, philosophy did not even begin, for some hundred and fifty years, a sound cycle of communication. And thus, is dead.

Now let us take up the individual who has become very "experienced" in life. This individual has a "time track" in particular. His time track is his own time track. It isn't anyone else's time track. The basic individualities amongst men are based upon the fact that they have different things happen to them and that they view these different things from different points to view. Thus, we have individualization and we have individual opinion, consideration and experience. Two men walking down the street witness an accident. Each one of them sees the accident from at least a slightly different point of view. Consulting twelve different witnesses of the same accident, you are likely to find twelve different accidents. Completely aside from the fact that witnesses like to tell you what they *think* they saw, instead of *what* they saw, there were actually twelve different points from which the accident was viewed and so twelve different aspects of the occurrences. If these twelve were brought together and if they were to communicate amongst themselves about this accident, they would then reach a point of agreement on what actually happened. This might not have been *the* accident. But it certainly is the agreed-upon accident, which then becomes the *real* accident. This is the way juries conduct themselves. They might or might not be passing upon the real crime, but they are certainly passing upon an agreed-upon crime.

In any war, it takes two or three days for enough agreement to occur to know what took place in a battle. Whereas there might have been a real battle, a real sequence of incidents and occurrences, the fact that every man in the battle saw the battle from his own particular point of view – by which we mean severely, "point from which he was looking," rather than his "opinions" – no one saw the battle in its entirety. Thus, time must intervene for enough communication on the subject of the battle to take place so that all have some semblance of agreement on what occurred. Of course, when the historians get to this battle and start writing different accounts of it out of the memoirs of generals, who were trying to explain away their defeats, we get a highly distorted account indeed. And yet, this becomes the agreed-upon battle as far as history is concerned. Reading the historians, one realizes one will never really know what took place at Waterloo, at Bennington, at Marathon. In that we can consider as a "communication" one soldier shooting at another soldier, we see that we are studying communications *about* communications. This scholarly activity is all very nice, but does not carry us very far toward the resolution of human problems.

We have seen these two words, Cause and Effect, playing a prominent role in the Communication Formula. We have seen that *first* Cause became, at the end of the cycle, *last* Effect. Furthermore, the intermediate point, *first* Effect, immediately changed to Cause in order to have a good communication cycle.

What, then, do we mean by Cause?

Cause is simply "the source-point of emanation of the communication."

What is Effect?

Effect is "the receipt-point of the communication."

In that we are only interested in life units, we see that we can readily ascertain Cause at any time. We are not interested in secondary or tertiary Cause. We are not interested in assisting Causes in any way. We are not interested in secondary and tertiary Effects. We are not interested in assisting Effects in any way. We consider any time that we look at a source-point of a communication that we are looking at Cause. In that the entire track is composed of this pattern of Cause and Effect, an individual is very prone, whenever he sees a possible Cause-point, to look for an earlier Cause-point and then an earlier one and an earlier one and an earlier one—and after a while takes to reading the Bible (which is very hard on the eyesight).

In view of the fact that all Cause is simply *elected* Cause, and all Effect is simply *elected* Effect, and that the primary echelon is the *idea* level of communication—that is Cause *which we elect to be Cause,* that is Effect *which elects to be Effect,* and there is no more that can be said about it.

Cause, in our dictionary here, means only "source-point."

Effect means only "receipt-point."

"What, then, do we mean by Cause?
Cause is simply 'the source-point of emanation
of the communication.' What is Effect?
Effect is 'the receipt-point of the communication.'"

We notice that the receipt-point, midway in the cycle of communication, shifts and becomes source-point. We could classify this shift, in this center of the cycle of communication, in some other fashion – but it is not necessary to do so. We would be getting too particular for our purposes.

Now we come to the problem of what a life unit must be *willing to experience* in order to communicate. In the first place, the primary source-point must be willing to be Duplicatable. It must be able to give at least some Attention to the receipt-point. The primary receipt-point must be willing to Duplicate, must be willing to receive, and must be willing to change into a source-point in order to send the communication, or an answer to it, back. And the primary source-point, in its turn, must be willing to be a receipt-point. As we are dealing basically with ideas and not mechanics, we see then that a state of mind must exist between a Cause and Effect-point whereby each one is willing to be Cause or Effect at will, is willing to Duplicate at will, is willing to be Duplicatable at will, is willing to change at will, is willing to experience the Distance between and, in short, *willing to Communicate.* Where we get these conditions in an individual or a group, we have sane people.

Where an unwillingness to send or receive communications occurs, where people obsessively or compulsively send communications without direction and without trying to be Duplicatable, where individuals in receipt of communications stand silent and do not acknowledge or reply, we have aberrative factors. And it is very interesting to note, from the standpoint of processing, that we have all the aberrative factors there are.

We do not need to know anything further about aberration than that it is a disarrangement of the cycle of communication. But to know that, of course, we have to know the Component Parts of Communication and the expected behavior.

Some of the conditions which can occur in an aberrated line are a failure to be Duplicatable before one emanates a communication, an Intention contrary to being received, an unwillingness to receive or Duplicate a communication, an unwillingness to experience Distance, an unwillingness to change, an unwillingness to give Attention, an unwillingness to express Intention, an unwillingness to acknowledge and, in general, an unwillingness to Duplicate. We might go so far as to say that the reason communication takes place, instead of occupying the same space and *knowing* (for communication introduces the idea of distance), is that one is unwilling to *be* to the degree necessary to *be anything*. One would rather communicate than be.

Thus we find that the inability to communicate is a gradient scale that goes down along with the inability to be. We get individuals winding up as only willing to be themselves, whatever that is, and thus becoming the "only one." To the degree that a person becomes the "only one," he is unwilling to communicate on the remaining dynamics. An individual who has become only himself is in a sad and sorry plight of being off the Second, Third and Fourth Dynamics, at least.

It might be seen by someone that the solution to communication is *not to communicate*. One might say that if he hadn't communicated in the first place, he wouldn't be in trouble now.

Perhaps there is some truth in this. But there is more truth in the fact that processing in the direction of "making communication unnecessary" or "reducing communication" is not processing at all, but murder. A man is as dead as he *can't* communicate. He is as alive as he *can* communicate. With countless tests I have discovered (to a degree which could be called conclusive) that the only remedy for livingness is further communicatingness. One must add to his ability to communicate.

Probably the only major error which exists in Eastern philosophy–and probably the one at which I balked when I was young–was this idea that one should "withdraw from life." It seemed to me that every good friend I had, amongst the priests and holy men, was seeking to pull back and cut off his communications with existence. Whatever the textbooks of Eastern philosophy may say, this was the practice of the people who were best conversant with Eastern mental and spiritual know-how. Thus I saw individuals taking fourteen or eighteen years in order to get up to a high level of spiritualistic serenity. I saw a great many men studying and very few arriving. To my impatient and possibly "practical" Western viewpoint, this was intolerable.

For a very great many years, I asked this question: "To communicate or not to communicate?" If one got himself in such thorough trouble by communication, then of course one should stop communicating. But this is not the case. If one gets himself into trouble by communicating, he should further communicate. More communication, not less, is the answer. And I consider this riddle solved after a quarter of a century of investigation and pondering.

"If one gets himself into trouble by communicating,
he should further communicate.
More communication, not less, is the answer."

CHAPTER

THE

APPLICATION

EIGHT

OF COMMUNICATION

CHAPTER EIGHT

THE APPLICATION
OF COMMUNICATION

I F YOU THINK we are talking about anything very esoteric or highly mathematical, kindly read the Communication Formula* again.

Just because we are speaking of the basic fundamentals of sanity, aberration, freedom, ability, truth, knowledge and secrets, is no reason why we have to be complicated. We expect the fundamentals of behavior to be complicated simply because so many highly complicated people have discussed the subject. If Immanuel Kant couldn't and if Adler addled communication, there is no reason why we should.

As we speak of the applications of communication, we are speaking of complexities of these fundamentals. And having isolated the fundamentals, we do not then see any complexity in the product of the basics.

---

*See the foldout chart at the back of this book for reference to the Formula of Communication and its Component Parts.

Let us say that we thoroughly understand that two plus two equals four. Now we write this on a piece of paper and put it on a table. It is still understandable. Now we write on another piece of paper "two plus two equals four" and put it on the same table. Now on a third piece of paper we write "two plus two equals four" and add it to those on the table. We take four tablets full of paper and on each sheet we write "two plus two equals four" and, tearing each sheet out, add these. Now we get some blocks of wood and we write "two plus two equals four" on these blocks of wood. We get some leather and charcoal and write "two plus two equals four" and add that to the table. Then we get some blackboards and on each one write "two plus two equals four" and put them on the table. And we get some colored chalk and write "two plus two equals four" in various colors on another blackboard and put it on the table. Then we have "two plus two equals four" bound in vellum and add that to the pile on the table. Then we get some building bricks and we scratch on them "two plus two equals four" and put them on the table. Now we get four gallons of ink and pour it over "two plus two equals four" and smear everything we have put on the table. Now we take a bulldozer and push the table out through the wall. We take a steamroller and run over the debris. We take some concrete and pour it over the whole and let it dry. And we still have not altered the fact that two plus two equals four.

In other words, no matter what mechanics we add to the Communication Formula, no matter what form we use to communicate, no matter how many types of words and meanings we place into the Communication Formula to become messages, no matter how we scramble meanings, messages, Cause-points and Effect-points—we still have the Communication Formula.

Here we have an individual. He has been living for a many-evented lifetime. He began life, let us say, with a perfect grasp of the Communication Formula. His experience has been consistent departures from the Communication Formula, only to the degree that he failed to emanate or failed to receive, twisted, perverted or failed to return communications. And at the end of that lifetime, all we would have to do to put him into excellent condition would be to restore–in its complete clarity–his ability to execute the Communication Formula. The only thing which has happened to him has been violation of the Communication Formula. He emanated something, it was not received. When it was received, it was not acknowledged. When it replied, he did not receive it. And thus he begins to look further and further afield for communications and becomes more and more complicated in his view of communications, becomes less and less Duplicatable, is less and less able to Duplicate, his Intentions swerve further and further, his Attention becomes more and more altered, what should have been straight lines wind up in a ball– and we have our preclear after a lifetime of living with Homo sapiens.

All we would have to do to get him into the most desirable clarity would be to restore his ability to perform the various parts of the Communication Formula and his ability to apply that Formula to anything in this or any universe. He would have to be willing to Duplicate anything. He would have to be willing to make himself Duplicatable. He would have to be able to tolerate Distance and Velocities and Masses. He would have to be able to form his own Intentions. He would have to be able to give and receive Attention. He would have to take or leave, at will, the Intentions of others. And, more important, he would have to *be* at any point and make it a Cause or Effect-point at will. If he were able to do this, he could not possibly be trapped. For here we are intimately walking into the deepest secret of the trap.

What is a secret? It is the answer which was never given. And this is all a secret is. Thus knowledge and use of the Communication Formula, within the framework of Dianetics and Scientology, resolves any and all secrets and even the belief in secrets.

The only thing which could be said to aberrate communication would be "restriction" or "fear of restriction." A person who is not communicating is one who has restricted communication. A person who is communicating compulsively is afraid of being restricted in his communication. A person who is talking on another subject than that to which Cause was giving his Attention has been so restricted on the subject of communication elsewhere, or has experienced such a scarcity of communication elsewhere, that he is still involved with communication elsewhere. This is what we mean by "not in present time."

When we look at "problems," without which humanity cannot seem to live, we discover that a problem is no more and no less than a confusion of communication lines – missing Cause or Effect-points, undeterminable Distances, misread Intentions, missing Attentions and failures in the ability to Duplicate and be Duplicatable. Move off the Communication Formula, in any direction, and a problem will result. A problem, by definition, is "something without an answer" (not because the two words are similar, but because all humanity has confused them). We find that "answer to a communication" and "answer to a problem" can, for our purposes, be synonymous.

When one has failed to get answers consistently to his communications, he begins to run into a scarcity for answers and he will get problems in order to have solutions. But he will not solve any of the problems because he already has a scarcity of answers. An auditor walks in on a preclear who has a scarcity of answers, finds the preclear has a circuit of problems, tries to resolve some of the problems of the preclear, discovers that the preclear creates new problems faster than old ones can be resolved. The one thing the preclear "knows" is that there aren't any answers – not to his particular kind of problems. He "knows" this to such a degree that he is unable to conceive of answers, which means to him that he is unable to conceive of solutions. He is like the old man in Manuel Komroff's story who, after his release from prison, yet created a cell of his own. He cannot look at freedom, he does not believe freedom exists, he cannot envision a world "without tigers." The remedy for this, of course, is to have him remedy his lack of answers by having him "mock-up" answers.

That confused look you see on a mathematician's face is the task he has set himself to procure symbolic answers to hypothetical abstracts (none of which, of course, are human answers). The longer he symbolizes, the more formulas he creates, the further he drifts from the human race. Answers are answers only when they come from living units. All else is a glut on the market. No mathematical formula ever gave anybody any answer to anything, unless it was to the problem of communication itself. But this, I invite your attention, was not involved with and was not derived from mathematics as we know them. The Communication Formula was derived from an observation of and working with life. It could be derived only because one had entirely abandoned the idea that energy could tell anyone anything. Life is not energy. Energy is the byproduct of life.

Your recluse is one who has become so thoroughly convinced that there are no obtainable answers from anyone that he does not any longer believe that life itself exists. He is the only living thing alive, in his opinion. Why? Because he is the only thing which communicates. I daresay every recluse, every "only one," every obsessively or compulsively communicating individual has so thoroughly associated with "life units" which were so *dead* that it became "very plain" that no one else was alive.

The attitude of the child toward the adult contains the opinion that "adults have very little life in them." A child, with his enthusiasms, is in his family everywhere surrounded by communication blocks of greater or lesser magnitude. His questions do not get answered. The communications which are addressed to him are not posed in a way which can be Duplicated.

In other words, the adult does not make himself Duplicatable. Freud and his confreres were entirely in error in believing that the child is totally self-centered. It is not the child who is totally self-centered. He believes that he is in communication with the total world. Investigation of children demonstrates that they are very heavy on the First, Second, Third and Fourth Dynamics. The child is so convinced of his ability to communicate that he will touch a hot stove. Life has no terrors for him. He has not yet "learned by experience" that he cannot communicate. It's the adult who has drawn back into the "only one." And one believes that the inspiration of this continuous belief on the part of the psychologist and psychoanalyst–that "the child is entirely self-centered and has only his own world"–must be the expression of an opinion held by the psychoanalyst and psychologist out of his own bank. As one grows, one goes less and less into communication with the environment until he is, at last, entirely out of it. Only he is out of it in the wrong direction–dead.

Where you see aberration, where you would wish to detect aberration, you must look for violations in the Communication Formula. People who consistently and continuously violate portions of the Communication Formula can be suspected of being just that–dead. The further one departs from the Communication Formula, the more death exists for them. The more concentrated they become on secrets, the more they question intentions, the less they are likely to assume the point of view called Cause or the point of view called Effect.

One should not go so far as to say that life *is* communication. It is, however, a native condition of life to be able to communicate. Life, the awareness of awareness unit, the ability to have unlimited quality with no quantity or to produce quantity, is capable of communication. And here, again, we are consulting ability. Ability, first and foremost could be conceived to be the ability to be and also the ability to vary beingness. And this means the ability to communicate. One has to be able to be in order to communicate. One has to be able to vary one's beingness in order to return communications.

There is the manifestation, then, known as the "stuck flow." This is one-way communication. The flow can be stuck incoming or it can be stuck outgoing. The part of a communication cycle which goes from primary Cause to Effect may be the flow that is stuck. Or it might be the other, from B back to A, that is stuck.

Here we have several possible methods of achieving a stuck flow and several conditions of flow—four to be exact:

1. The flow can be stuck from primary Cause to primary Effect, from the viewpoint of primary Cause.

2. The flow can be stuck from primary Cause to primary Effect, from the viewpoint of primary Effect.

3. The flow can be stuck from Effect turned-Cause to final Effect, from the viewpoint of Effect turned-Cause.

4. The flow can be stuck from Effect-turned-Cause to final Effect, from the viewpoint of final Effect.

These four stuck flows can become—any of them or a combination of them—the anatomy of the "communication lag" of the case. A person can hear, but cannot answer. A person can cause a communication to begin, but cannot receive an acknowledgment. A primary Cause can be totally engrossed in keeping the flow from arriving at primary Effect. And so forth.

A failure to complete a cycle of communication will leave some part of that communication in suspense. It will leave it, in other words, silent. And this will stick on the track, it will float in time, it will restimulate, it will attract and hold attention long after it has occurred.

Unconsciousness, itself, results from receipt of too much, too heavy communication. It can similarly, but less often, result from the emanation of too much, too heavy, communication – as in the case of blowing up a large balloon, where one becomes dizzy after the expulsion of too much breath. Theoretically, one sending a large mass toward another one might fall unconscious as a result of sending too much mass away from himself too suddenly. And we find this can be the case. This is degradation because of loss. One gives away too much or loses too much and the departure of the mass, or even the idea, can bring about a drop in consciousness. In view of the fact that an awareness of awareness unit can create at will, this is not a very dangerous situation. One can receive too much communication, too suddenly, such as a cannonball. Unconsciousness will result from this. Most engrams are composed of too much incoming mass and too much outgoing mass, so as to make a confusion into which any answer, any phrase interjected can then be effective – since there is a scarcity of phrases and a plus in masses. One could even go so far as to say that the only reason a mass interchange is ever effective in the line of unconsciousness is that it does not have enough "reasons" with it. I suppose if one explained carefully enough to a soldier why he had to be shot, the arrival of the bullet would not make him unconscious or hurt him. But, again, this is theoretical (since very little reason goes on in war and thus it has never been subjected to a clinical experiment).

The resolution of any stuck flow is remedying the scarcity of that which stuck the flow. This might be "answers," it might be "original communications," it might be "chances to reply."

The Communication Formula at work is best understood through the "communication lag."

"A failure to complete a cycle of communication
will leave some part of that communication in suspense.
It will leave it, in other words, silent. And this will
stick on the track, it will float in time, it will restimulate,
it will attract and hold attention long after it has occurred."

CHAPTER

TWO-WAY

NINE

COMMUNICATION

CHAPTER NINE

TWO-WAY COMMUNICATION

A CYCLE OF COMMUNICATION and TWO-WAY COMMUNICATION are actually two different things. If we examine closely the anatomy of communication, we will discover that a cycle of communication is not a two-way communication in its entirety.

(over)

If you will inspect Graph A below, you will see a cycle of communication:*

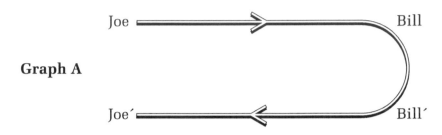

Graph A

Here we have Joe as the originator of a communication. It is his primary impulse. This impulse is addressed to Bill. We find Bill receiving it. And then Bill originating an answer or acknowledgment, as Bill′, which acknowledgment is sent back to Joe′. Joe has said, for instance, "How are you?" Bill has received this. And then Bill (becoming secondary Cause) has replied to it as Bill′, with "I'm okay," which goes back to Joe′ and thus ends the cycle.

Now, what we call a two-way cycle of communication may ensue, as in Graph B below:

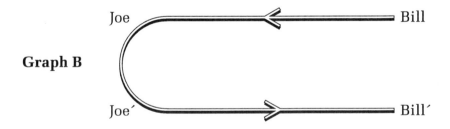

Graph B

Here we have Bill originating a communication. Bill says, "How's tricks?" Joe receives this. And then as Joe′ (or secondary Cause) answers, "Okay, I guess," which answer is then acknowledged in its receipt by Bill′.

---

*See the foldout chart at the back of this book, which contains these graphic illustrations for reference throughout this chapter.

In both of these Graphs, we discover that the acknowledgment of the secondary Cause was expressed, (in Graph A) by Joe′ as a nod or a look of satisfaction and, again, (in Graph B) Joe″'s "Okay, I guess" is actually acknowledged by Bill′ with a nod or some expression signifying the receipt of the communication.

If both Joe and Bill are "strong, silent men" (highly aberrated), they would omit some portion of these cycles. The most flagrant omission, and the one most often understood as "communication lag" by the auditor, would be for Joe (in Graph A) to say, "How are you?" and for Bill to stand there without speaking. Here we have Joe causing a communication and Bill′ failing to continue the cycle. We do not know or inquire and we are not interested in whether or not Bill, as the receipt-point, ever did hear it. We can assume that he was at least present and that Joe spoke loudly enough to be heard and that Bill's Attention was somewhere in Joe's vicinity. Now, instead of getting on with the cycle of communication, Joe is left there with an incompleted cycle and never gets an opportunity to become Joe′.

There are several ways in which a cycle of communication could not be completed and these could be categorized as:

1. Joe failing to emanate a communication.

2. Bill failing to hear the communication.

3. Bill′ failing to reply to the communication received by him.

4. Joe′ failing to acknowledge, by some sign or word, that he has heard Bill′.

We could assign various "reasons" to all this. But our purpose here is not to assign reasons why they do not complete a communication cycle. Our entire purpose is involved with the non-completion of this communication cycle.

Now, as in Graph A, let us say we have, in Joe, a person who is compulsively and continually originating communications, whether he has anybody's Attention or not and whether or not these communications are germane to any existing situation. We discover that Joe is apt to be met, in his communicating, with an inattentive Bill who does not hear him. And thus, an absent Bill' who does not answer him. And thus, an absent Joe' who never acknowledges.

Let us examine this same situation in Graph B. Here we have, in Bill, an origination of a communication. We have the same Joe with a compulsive outflow. Bill says, "How are you?" and the cycle is not completed because Joe, so intent upon his own compulsive line, does not become Joe' and never gives Bill a chance to become Bill' and acknowledge.

Now let's take another situation. We find Joe originating communications and Bill a person who never originates communications. Joe is not necessarily compulsive or obsessive in originating communications. But Bill is aberratedly inhibited in originating communications. We find that Joe and Bill, working together, then get into this kind of an activity: Joe originates communication, Bill hears it, becomes Bill', replies to it and permits Joe a chance to become Joe'.

This goes on quite well, but will sooner or later hit a jam on a two-way cycle which is violated because Bill never originates communication.

A two-way cycle of communication would work as follows: Joe, having originated a communication and having completed it, may then wait for Bill to originate a communication to Joe, thus completing the remainder of the two-way cycle of communication. Bill does originate a communication, this is heard by Joe, answered by Joe' and acknowledged by Bill'.

Thus we get the normal cycle of a communication between two "terminals." For in this case, Joe is a terminal and Bill is a terminal and communication can be seen to flow between two terminals.

The cycles depend on Joe originating communication, Bill hearing the communication, Bill becoming Bill' and answering the communication, Joe' acknowledging the communication. Then, Bill originating a communication, Joe hearing the communication, Joe' answering the communication and Bill' acknowledging the communication. If they did this, regardless of what they were talking about, they would never become in an argument and would eventually reach an agreement—even if they were hostile to one another. Their difficulties and problems would be cleared up and they would be, in relationship to each other, in good shape.

A two-way communication cycle breaks down when either terminal fails, in its turn, to originate communications.

We discover that the entire society has vast difficulties along this line. They are so used to "canned" entertainment and so inhibited in originating communications (by parents who couldn't communicate and by education and other causes) that people get very low on communication origin. Communication origin is necessary to start a communication in the first place. Thus we find people talking mainly about things which are forced upon them by exterior causes. They see an accident, they discuss it. They see a movie, they discuss it. They wait for an exterior source to give them the occasion for a conversation. But in view of the fact that both are low on the origin of communication—which could also be stated as "low on imagination"—we discover that such people, dependent on exterior primal impulses, are more or less compulsive or inhibitive in communication and thus the conversation veers rapidly and markedly and may wind up with some remarkable animosities or misconclusions.

Let us suppose that lack of prime Cause impulse on Joe's part has brought him into obsessive or compulsive communication. And we find that he is so busy outflowing that he never has a chance to hear anyone who speaks to him and, if he did hear them, would not answer them. Bill, on the other hand, might be so very, very, very low on primal Cause (which is to say, low on communication origination) that he never even moves into Bill' or, if he does, would never put forth his own opinion, thus unbalancing Joe further and further into further and further compulsive communication.

As you can see by these Graphs, some novel situations could originate. There would be the matter of obsessive answering as well as inhibitive answering. An individual could spend all of his time answering, justifying or explaining – all the same thing – no primal communication having been originated at him. Another individual (as Joe' in Graph A or Bill' in Graph B) might spend all of his time acknowledging, even though nothing came his way to acknowledge. The common and most noticed manifestations, however, are "obsessive" and "compulsive origin" and "nonanswering acceptance" and "nonacknowledgment of answer." And at these places we can discover stuck flows.

As the only crime in the universe seems to be *to* communicate, and as the only saving grace of an awareness of awareness unit *is* to communicate, we can readily understand that an entanglement of communication is certain to result. What we should understand – and much more happily – is that it can now be resolved.

That which we are discussing here is *minimally* theory and *maximally* derived from observation. The main test of this is whether or not it resolves cases. You can be assured that it does.

Flows become stuck, on this twin cycle of communication, where a scarcity occurs in:

1. Origination of communication.

2. Receipt of communication.

3. Answering a communication given.

4. Acknowledging answers.

Thus it can be seen that there are only four parts which can become aberrated (in both Graph A and Graph B), no matter the number of peculiar manifestations which can occur as a result thereof.

These observations of communication are so vital that a considerable difference amongst case results comes about between an auditor who does acknowledge whatever his preclear answers and an auditor who does not.

Let us take auditor G. And we discover that he is running "Opening Procedure of 8-C" on a preclear, but that at the end of two hours of Opening Procedure of 8-C the preclear has benefited very little. Then let us take auditor K. This auditor does fifteen minutes of Opening Procedure of 8-C and gets very good results on the preclear. The difference between auditor G and auditor K is only that auditor G never acknowledges any answer or statement or communication origin on the part of the preclear. He simply continues doggedly with the process. Auditor K, on the other hand, is willing to let the preclear originate a communication and always acknowledges whenever the preclear concludes the action called for in a command or when the preclear volunteers a verbal answer. In other words, G did not answer or acknowledge, but ran the process with mechanical perfection. And K both answered and acknowledged, as well as originated orders. The fact that the scarcest thing there is, is the origin of orders or communications, and the fact that G was at least doing this, is enough to cause G to get some improvement in the preclear. But he will not get anything like the improvement obtained by auditor K.

Silence is nowhere desirable except *only* in permitting another to communicate or waiting for another to acknowledge. The auditing of silence will wind the preclear in a perfect "fishnet" of aberration. The total process which remedies this is remedying the scarcity, by whatever means, of the four parts of a two-way communication.

"The auditing of silence will wind the preclear
in a perfect 'fishnet' of aberration. The total process
which remedies this is remedying the scarcity,
by whatever means, of the four parts
of a two-way communication."

CHAPTER

COMMUNICATION

T E N

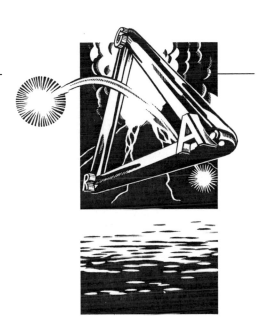

L A G

COMMUNICATION LAG

THE EXACT DEFINITION of a communication lag is "the length of time intervening between the posing of the question, or origination of a statement, and the exact moment that question or original statement is answered."

If you will look very closely at this definition, you will discover that nothing is said whatever about what goes on between the asking of the question, or the origination of the communication, and its being answered. What goes on in between is "lag." It does not matter if the preclear stood on his head, went to the North Pole, gave a dissertation on botany, stood silent, answered some other question, thought it over, attacked the auditor or began to string beads. Any other action but answering, and the time taken up by that action, is communication lag.

An auditor has to understand this very thoroughly.

Usually he interprets a communication lag as "the length of time it takes the preclear to answer the question" and loosely applies this as "the length of time between the asking of the question and the first moment the preclear starts to speak." This is not communication lag. For the preclear may start to speak on some other subject, may desire more information, may *almost* answer the question and still not actually answer the question.

If you will look around at people, you will find them possessed of a great many communication lag mechanisms. In their effort not to be an Effect or in their effort not to be Cause, in their aberrations about compulsive communication and inhibitive communication, and in indulging in impulsive, compulsive and inhibitive communication, they manage to assemble quite a number of interesting mechanisms. But all these mechanisms are communication lag.

Here is an example of communication lag:
Joe: "How are you, Bill?"
Bill: "You look fine, Joe."

Here, the question was never answered at all and would go on as a communication lag from there until the end of the universe.

Here is another example:
Joe: "How are you, Bill?"
Bill: (after twenty seconds of study) "Oh, I guess I'm all right today."

As this is the commonest form of communication lag, it is the most readily observed.

Less well known is the following communication lag:
Joe: "How are you, Bill?"
Bill: "What do you want to know for?"

Again, this question goes on unanswered until the end of the universe.

The most maddening kind of communication lag is:

Joe: "How are you, Bill?"

Bill: *Silence* from there on out.

This is dramatized when people anxiously inquire of an unconscious person *"how he is?"* and they become entirely frantic. They are simply looking at a communication lag which they believe will become total. And their anxiety is simply their multiple suffering on the subject of communication lag.

Here is another type of communication lag:

Joe: "How are you, Bill? I was saying to Ezra the other day that I have seen a lot of sick men in my time, but you certainly look pretty bad, Bill. Now, how are you? I've been down to see the doctor and he was telling me there's a lot of these colds and things going around...."

In other words, Joe never gives Bill an opportunity to reply. And this is the other side of communication lag.

An auditor's understanding of the subject of communication lag is brief if he believes that it is the lag between the originator of the communication and the person to whom it is addressed. On our Graph A (Chapter Nine*), this would be from Joe to Bill'. There is a "return lag" and that is from Bill' to Joe'. And as above, there is the lag between Joe and Joe, where Joe simply keeps on talking without ascertaining if there is any Bill' there. You could also call this return lag an "acknowledgment lag." Joe to Joe is not a communication at all. Actually Joe to Bill', without a completion of the cycle, is the same thing. Joe' never acknowledges the communication and so the return lag is actually Joe to Joe. The proper sequence of such a communication is Bill' to Joe'. In other words, Joe' (to make a complete cycle of communication) must acknowledge in some manner, verbal or gesture, that Bill' has said something.

---

*See foldout chart at the back of this book containing the Graphs from Chapter Nine.

Joe to Joe as a communication lag (which is to say, no acknowledgment) has, as its initial root, an absence for Joe of Bill to Bill' (in Graph B). In other words, Joe has been called upon to originate communication so consistently that he now does so compulsively and obsessively, since there has been an entire scarcity of other people originating communications.

Now let us look at a highly specialized type of communication lag. Here we have Joe to Bill to Bill' to Joe' (as in Graph A). Then we have Joe waiting for Bill (in Graph B) to originate a communication. If Bill does not and only silence ensues, Joe then originates another communication. In other words, we have no two-way communication.

The two-way cycle of communication is not quite as important in auditing as it would be in life. For in auditing, the auditor, perforce, is originating communications in order to get the preclear up to the point where he can originate communications. One does not remedy life by approximating it exactly in the auditing room. The process is so designed that it will accomplish a rehabilitation in life without, to a marked degree, having to live it. As an example of this, the auditor does not expect the preclear to turn around and originate some process to make the auditor well. But the auditor does expect to get audited by somebody, sooner or later, or expects to be at a level where he can rise above this need of a communication interchange in order to live.

The place auditors have the most trouble with, in communication lag, is the "return lag." Auditors seldom acknowledge the execution of the command on the part of the preclear. As in Opening Procedure of 8-C (a process which is one of the Six Basic Processes today), the auditor sends the preclear over to touch the wall. When the preclear has touched the wall, the auditor is quite prone to give another command without acknowledging the fact that the preclear has touched the wall. It is an amazing thing what the lack of acknowledgment will do to slow down a case recovery. Many times when an auditor is doing this (*is* acknowledging), he is doing it in such a perfunctory fashion that the preclear does not recognize it as an acknowledgment, but as a prelude to a new command. A good auditor makes very, very sure that the preclear knows the acknowledgment has occurred.

As an example, the auditor says:

"Go over to the wall and touch it."

The preclear does so. The auditor says:

"Very good."

And with a definite pause after this acknowledgment, says:

"Now go over to that wall and touch it."

In other words, the auditor who is a good auditor makes sure that the preclear knows that a complete cycle of communication has occurred on this particular auditing command.

Another failure on the part of auditors is to fail to let the preclear originate a communication. The auditor tells the preclear:

"Go over to that wall and touch it."

The preclear does so, but stops midway in the gesture and gasps, then completes the gesture. The bad auditor will fail to note and inquire after this gasp. This is actually the origin of a communication on the part of the preclear. He does not verbalize it. He does not express it any further than some physical gesture or a look of dismay. And even these might be slight. But this is usually as far as he can go in originating a communication. The auditor who fails to pick this up, fails to inform the preclear thus that the preclear is permitted to originate a communication.

This gasp, this gesture should at once be noted by the auditor with:

"What's happened?"

or

"What's the matter?"

or

"Something happen?"

This gives the preclear the opportunity to originate a second cycle of communication.

Remember that the gesture or the gasp was actually a communication. The preclear probably will not acknowledge the auditor's statement, beyond starting out on the origin of a new communication. But the fact that he does originate a statement on the subject of *"What is the matter"* is, in itself, an acknowledgment of the fact that he has heard the auditor. This is so vital that many cases have stumbled, tripped and bogged, simply because the auditor did not encourage the preclear to make a statement as to something which had occurred. Actually, the more often an auditor can do this, the better auditor he is and the more good will be done by auditing.

Now, of course, there is an opposite side to this, where the auditor can give credence to an obsessive or compulsive outflow on the part of the preclear to such an extent that the auditing is entirely interrupted. An example of this occurred recently, where a preclear outflowed at an auditor three days and three nights without the auditor recognizing entirely that this was simply obsessive communication in action. But this is not communication. This is not pertinent to the situation. And the definition of "compulsive" or "obsessive communication" is "an outflow which is not pertinent to the surrounding terminals and situation." In other words, compulsive or obsessive communication is an outflow which is not "in reality" with the existing reality.

"… *compulsive or obsessive communication*
is an outflow which is not 'in reality'
with the existing reality."

We see, then, that an auditing session really does include a two-way cycle of communication. But it does not include it, ever, unless the auditor invites the preclear to comment upon what is going on as he does processes.

(Just as a side comment here, the way to handle an obsessive or compulsive communication is to wait for a slight break in the flow and interject an auditing command. Remember that an obsessive outflow is actually not a communication. A communication is on the subject and is in agreement with the environment. It is also in agreement with what is occurring.)

Now it doesn't happen to matter what process is being done, the basic of that process is two-way communication. In auditing, as in living, communication *is* existence. In the absence of communication, we have silence. And where we have silence, we have no time. Time is manifested in communication lag to the extent that the preclear has been subjected to silences or such a thing as an obsessive or compulsive outflow which had nothing to do with communicating on the subject at hand – which is, again, a sort of silence (somebody talking obsessively or continually about things which might or might not exist and to no one in particular without expecting any cycle of communication to take place).

A communication lag is handled, by an auditor, by repetition of the question or command which elicited a communication lag.

Here is an example:

Bill: "How are you, Joe?"
Joe: *Silence, silence, silence* – Finally a grunt.

Bill: "How are you, Joe?"
Joe: *Silence, silence* – "Okay, I guess."

Bill: "How are you, Joe?"
Joe: "I'm all right, I tell you!"

Bill: "How are you, Joe?"
Joe: *Silence* – "I'm okay."

Bill: "How are you, Joe?"
Joe: "All right, I guess."

Bill: "How are you, Joe?"
Joe: "All right."

Bill: "How are you, Joe?"
Joe: "Oh, I'm all right."

This is an example of "flattening" a communication lag. At first we have silence and no very intelligible reply. Then we have silence and a reply. And then other manifestations, each one of which demonstrates a changing interval of time, until the last couple of commands – three, in actual auditing practice – where the same interval of time was present. Flattening a communication lag requires only that the preclear answer after a uniform interval of time, at least three times. This uniform interval of time could, for practical purposes, be as long as ten seconds. Thus we get lengths of time required to answer an auditing question, as follows:

Answer requires thirty-five seconds,
Answer requires twenty seconds,
Answer requires forty-five seconds,
Answer requires twenty seconds,
Answer requires ten seconds,
Answer requires ten seconds,
Answer requires ten seconds.

To all intents and purposes – with these three last ten-second intervals – the auditor could consider that he has to some degree flattened this particular auditing command because he is getting a consistent response. However, with such a long lag as ten seconds, the auditor will discover that if he asked the question two or three more times, he would recover a changing interval once more.

This is the mechanical formula of flattening a communication lag: Give the *order* (as in Opening Procedure of 8-C) or ask the *question* (as in Straightwire) and then continue to give that same order or ask that same question until the preclear executes it, after a short interval, three times the same.

There is an entirely different manifestation for a completely flattened communication lag. We get "extroversion." The preclear ceases to put his attention on his mind, but puts his attention on the environment. We see this happen often in the Opening Procedure of 8-C, where the preclear has the room suddenly become bright to him. He has extroverted his attention. He has come free from one of these communication tangles, out of the past, and has suddenly looked at the environment. This is all that has happened. On a thinkingness level, this happens quite often. The preclear is doing the process very well and then begins to remember odds and ends of appointments he has, or some such thing. Just because he does this is no reason the auditing session should be ended. It simply demonstrates an extroversion. You have, in one way or another, pulled the preclear out of a communication tangle and put him into present time when he extroverts.

Communication lag, as a subject, could be a very large one. We have all manner of communication lags in evidence around us. Probably the most interesting one is the shock reaction after an accident, which one occasionally sees. At times it takes the body thirty-six hours to find out and reply to the fact that it has received an impact. It is quite common for a body to suddenly manifest the impact half an hour after it. This is communication lag. There are many humorous angles to communication lag. Sometimes you ask somebody, "How are you?" and you get a reply from his social machinery. He says, "I'm fine." Then two or three hours later, he is liable to say to you, "I feel terrible." This is the preclear, himself, answering. This is the awareness of awareness unit awakening to this communication lag.

CHAPTER TEN
COMMUNICATION LAG

This universe could be called "a consistent and continual communication lag." One is trapped in it to the degree that he is lagging. If there were no remedy for communication lag, I would never bring up the subject. However, there is. And it is a remedy which is easily undertaken in auditing today.

Entrapment is actually communication lag. One has waited for communications which never arrived or has expected something to answer, so long and so often, that he becomes fixated upon something or in something and so does not believe he can escape from it. The first and foremost factor in communication lag, of course, is time. And the next factor is waiting, which is also dependent upon time.

As has been commented earlier, the only things which float on the time track are the moments of silence when no communication occurred. These are "no-time" moments and so have no time in which they can live and so they float forward on the time track. It is an oddity that an engram behaves in such a way as to put all its silent moments in present time, with the preclear, and leave its talking or action moments back on the track. When we took a person back to birth and ran out birth, we took out the action moments. If we did not take out, as well, the silent moments in birth, we did not take out the very things which pinned themselves to the preclear in present time. In other words, the birth engram did not move at all, but the silent moments in birth might have a tendency to come up into present time. These silent moments in engrams and facsimiles do, themselves, compose the matter extant in the preclear. This matter is not so much composed of action moments as silent moments.

Thus we see that an individual, the longer he lives in this universe, the more communication lag he runs into, the more upset he is about existence, the greater his communication lag, the more he is silent.

Of course, obsessive or compulsive communication is just one grade above silence. It is the last frantic effort to keep things from going entirely quiet. It is not communication and is, actually, silence of a sort–particularly since very few people listen to it.

Now, we are studying about communication and we are communicating about communication and you have every opportunity here to get yourself beautifully snarled. So I would ask you to look around your environment and check a number of manifestations of communication lag. You are not controlled by the subject. You can easily control it. The dangerous thing is not to know the answers and simply go on in these consistent and continual communication lags imposed upon us by the lack of communication in this universe.

It is of great interest to note that imagination, as a function of existence, becomes drowned in an absence of communication origin. An individual can become so dependent upon others or entertainments in originating communications, that he himself does not. Indeed, it is very unpopular in this society, at this time, to originate communications. One should always say that somebody else thought of it first, or that it goes back to the ancient Ugluks, or that it's happened many times before, or that one has just dug up the information after it has been buried, or one is really taking direction from the archangel Smearel, rather than stand up and plead guilty to originating a communication. Unless one can originate communications, one's imagination is in bad shape. The reverse does not happen to be true. The imagination is not that thing which is first imperiled and then results in failure to originate communication. Failure of communication origin, then, results in failure of imagination. So the rehabilitation of communication origin rehabilitates, as well, the imagination. This is very good news, indeed, for anyone in the creative arts particularly. But who is not in the creative arts?

CHAPTER TEN
COMMUNICATION LAG

In examining the whole subject of communication, one discovers that there are very few people around him, in this day and age, who are actually communicating. And there are a lot of people who think they are communicating, who are not. (The AMA would like to believe that I am in the latter category.)

C H A P T E R

ELEVEN

PAN-DETERMINISM

PAN-DETERMINISM

AN ENTIRELY NEW CONCEPT in Dianetics and Scientology is that of PAN-DETERMINISM.

In Book One we talked about Self-determinism. Self-determinism meant, in essence, control by the awareness of awareness unit of that which it conceived to be its identity. Some effort in Book One was made to move Self-determinism out into the remaining dynamics.

Pan-determinism is a word which describes determinism all along the dynamics. Actually, Self-determinism attempted to do this and our earlier idea of Self-determinism was a sort of Pan-determinism.

We have to remember here that the dynamics involved in Dianetics are the first four, the dynamics involved in Scientology are the last four, of the total set of eight.

The Eight Dynamics are as follows:

THE EIGHT DYNAMICS

DYNAMIC ONE is the urge toward survival as self.

DYNAMIC TWO is the urge toward survival through sex or children and embraces both the sexual act and the care and raising of children.

DYNAMIC THREE is the urge toward survival through the group and as the group.

DYNAMIC FOUR is the urge toward survival through all Mankind and as all Mankind.

DYNAMIC FIVE is the urge toward survival through life forms, such as animals, birds, insects, fish and vegetation, and is the urge to survive as these.

DYNAMIC SIX is the urge toward survival through the physical universe and has as its components Matter, Energy, Space and Time (from which we derive the word MEST).

DYNAMIC SEVEN is the urge toward survival through spirit and would include the manifestations or the totality of awareness of awareness units, thetans, demons, ghosts, spirits, godlings and so forth.

DYNAMIC EIGHT is the urge toward survival through the Supreme Being or, more exactly, Infinity. It is called Dynamic Eight because it is Infinity (∞) turned up on its side.

The urge toward survival through self, sex, children, groups and Mankind are the proper province of Dianetics.

THE EIGHT DYNAMICS

Now let us examine this concept of Pan-determinism. Pan-determinism would be the willingness to determine or control self and dynamics other than self, up to the eight listed above. Like Self-determinism, Pan-determinism is self-elected (or self-determined) in that one does it knowingly and directly, not from obsession, compulsion or inhibition. An Un-determined individual, of course, does not exist. But an Other-determined individual definitely can exist. Where we have Self-determinism (and we interpret Self-determinism as "determinism on the First Dynamic"), we have only willingness to control self and no willingness to control anything beyond self. If this is the case in Self-determinism, we have as Other-determinism sex, children, groups, Mankind and (going on into Scientology) animal life, vegetation, the physical universe, spirits and God – or whatever else might compose Infinity.

In view of the fact that Self-determinism was interpreted in this fashion, it left an individual in the state of mind of being willing to be determined on all other dynamics and by all other dynamics except his own "personal dynamic." In view of the fact that a "personal dynamic" cannot exist and in view of the fact that all auditing is the Third Dynamic and that an individual as we see him (a man) is actually a composite – and is not a First Dynamic, but a Third Dynamic – we see we are in difficulties with this definition of Self-determinism and continued use of Self-determinism. It is necessary, then, to investigate further and to assign more precision to this concept of "willingness to control."

When we say "control," we do not mean the "control case," where control is obsessive, or Other-determined, or where the individual is controlling things out of compulsion or fear. We simply mean "willingness to start, stop and change." The anatomy of control is just that – starting, stopping and changing things. Now, it is not necessary for a person to start, stop and change things just to demonstrate that he can control them. He must, however, to be healthy and capable, be able to start, stop and change things.

Here we come immediately to what we mean by "ability." It would be the ability to start, change and stop things. And if we have an *ability* to start, stop and change things, we of course must have a *willingness* to start, stop and change things. Those people who are unwillingly behaving in some direction, so as to start, stop and change things, are very sick people. And in this category (this last category) we discover the bulk of the human race at this writing.

The basic difference between aberration and sanity, between inability and ability, between illness and health, is the knowingness of causation by self, opposed to unknown causation by others or other things. An individual who knows he is doing it is far more capable than one who is doing it, but supposes something else is doing it. Psychosis is, itself, simply an inversion of determinism. A psychotic is entirely Other-determined. A sane man is, in good measure, Self-determined. Pan-determinism would mean "a willingness to start, change and stop on any and all dynamics." That is its primary definition. A further definition, also a precision definition, is "the willingness to start, change and stop two or more forces, whether or not opposed." And this could be interpreted as two or more individuals, two or more groups, two or more planets, two or more life species, two or more universes, two or more spirits, whether or not opposed. This means that one would not necessarily fight, he would not necessarily "choose sides."

This is in total controversy to some of the most cherished beliefs of Man. But may I point out to you, quickly, that Man is not an entirely sane person? And thus, some of his beliefs must be somewhat aberrated. There is such a thing as "courage," but there is not such a thing as "sanity totally opposed."

People who are afraid of control are liable to be afraid of Pan-determinism. But if they will see this as a *willingness* to start, change and stop any dynamic, they will see that a person must be assuming the responsibility for any of the dynamics.

A conqueror, in his onslaught against society, is fighting Other-determinisms. He is starting, changing and stopping things because of an *unwillingness* to associate with or support other races or customs than his own. Therefore, what he is doing can be interpreted as bad.

In support of this, we get all of the earlier religious teachings. But these have been grossly misinterpreted. These have been interpreted to mean that a person should not fight in any way, or defend anything, or have anything, or own anything. This is not true. A person who is willing to be other individualities, besides himself, does not necessarily harm these other individualities. Indeed, we cannot make the complete distinction of "other than himself," since we are saying, in this, that he clings to something he calls "self" and supports and defends it without being willing to identify himself with others. (One of the most maddening debaters is one who moves at will between the viewpoints of himself and those who have elected him as an enemy.)

There is an important Scale Down From Pan-determinism. It does not lead along a dwindling dynamic path, but it could of course. One could simply see, as Pan-determinism dwindling, the falling off of one dynamic after another until one is down to First Dynamic. But that is not a particularly workable picture and an auditor does not use it.

The SCALE DOWN FROM PAN-DETERMINISM is:

Pan-determinism

Fighting

Must and Must Not Happen Again

Repair

Association

These are actually processes:

At the bottom we find an unwillingness to Associate with anything;

Just above this is an unwillingness to Repair anything, but a willingness to Associate somewhat;

Above this is a willingness to Associate and to Repair somewhat, but no willingness to let certain things Happen Again;

Above this is a willingness to Fight things; and

Above this is Pan-determinism.

These are arranged in this fashion because this is the ladder a preclear climbs if he is run on a certain type of process. This is something like the old Emotional Scale–which went Apathy, Grief, Fear, Anger, Antagonism, Boredom, Conservatism and Enthusiasm–only in this case it is a scale of behavior manifestations. Where an individual who is unwilling to Associate with various things is certainly a long way from being Pan-determined and definitely is not even Self-determined, he has to come up a ways before he is willing to Repair anything. But in this frame of mind, he can Repair quite generally, but is unwilling or unable to create *or* destroy. (An oddity here is that a person who is unwilling to Associate is only able to destroy. And a person has to be very far up this scale before he can create. In fact, he has to be up around Pan-determinism to adequately create.) Above this level of Repair, we find an individual "frozen" in many incidents, which he is preventing from occurring once more, and is holding the facsimiles or engrams of these incidents so that he will have a model and so know what Mustn't Occur. And above this level, we discover an individual Fighting or being willing to Fight almost anything. And above this level, we discover an individual Pan-determined, willing or able to *be* almost anything, and so may be at peace with things and does not have to Fight things.

An individual at a Pan-determinism level can *create.*

An individual at Association, as I have said, can only *destroy.*

An individual at Repair and Must and Mustn't Happen Again is making a very heavy effort—and I do mean effort—to *survive.*

Let us take, for our example of Pan-determinism, the Second Dynamic. Here we find such a thorough effort to have Other-determinism that Freud picked this out as the only aberrative factor. It is not the only aberrative factor. But in view of the fact that it is a desired inflow, it can be considered (with many other things) to have some aberrative value. Let us look at it from terms of Self-determinism and Pan-determinism. Here we have an individual, believing himself to be a *man,* who believes that his only sexual pleasure can be derived from remaining very solidly a man and having sexual relationships with a woman and being very sure that he is not the woman. On the other hand, we find the *woman,* determined to be herself and experience as herself and to experience a sexual inflow from a man. In the case of the man, as in the case of the woman, we have an unwillingness to be the other sex. This is considered natural. But do you know that when this is entirely true, when we have complete determinism to be self and not to be to any slightest degree the other person, there is no sexual pleasure interchange of any kind whatsoever? We get the condition known as satyrism and nymphomania. We get a tremendous anxiety to have a sexual flow.

Probably the only reason you can see the universe at all is because you are still willing to be some part of it. Probably the only reason you can talk to people is because you can also be the other person you are talking to. Probably the only reason you can really let people talk to you is because you are willing to let the other person be you, somewhat, and he is willing to let you be him, to some degree.

In view of the fact that space itself is a "mock-up" (is a state of mind), it can be seen that individuality depends to some degree upon the law that "no two things must occupy the same space." When we get this law in action, we have a universe. Until this law goes into action, there is no universe and one would be hard put to differentiate entirely. Two things *can* occupy the same space to the degree that you are willing to believe they can. It is a very easy thing to talk to an audience if you are perfectly willing to be an audience. It is a very difficult thing to talk to an audience if you are unwilling to be the audience. Similarly, it is very difficult to be an audience if you are unwilling to be on the stage. One could conceive that a person who had a considerable amount of stage fright would be incapable of enjoying the performance of actors. And so it is. We discover the person who is in the audience and has, himself, considerable stage fright, writhing and feeling embarrassed for every actor who makes the slightest slip or mistake. In other words, we find this person compulsively "being on the stage" although he is in the audience.

Things of this nature have led more than one philosopher to assume that we were all from the same mold or that we were all the same thing. This is a very moot question. Processing demonstrates, rather adequately, that we are all really individuals and that we are not the same individual. And, indeed, people who believe we *are* all the same individual have a very rough time of it. But, evidently, we could all *be* the same individual–at least if we were entirely sane.

The physical universe is a sort of a "hypnotic trance," where the individual believes himself to be capable of viewing from various points. The illusion is rendered very excellent by the fact that other individuals believe that they are viewing the same things from the same points as they occupy. We are all, as awareness of awareness units, basically different. We are not the same "pool of life." And we are all, evidently, differently endowed (no matter what the Communist Party would like to believe).

One of the most significant differences from man to man is the degree to which he is willing to be Pan-determined. The man who has to forcefully control everything in his vicinity, including his family, is not being Self-determined, usually, much less Pan-determined. He is not *being* his family. If he were being his family, he would understand why they were doing what they were doing. And he would not feel that there was any danger or menace in their going on executing the motions or emanating the emotions which they do. But anchored down as one person, rather obsessed with the damage that can be done to him or those around him, an individual is apt to launch himself upon a course of heavy, solid, "super-control" of others. Now let us take the person who is Self-determined and Pan-determined, in the same situation. And we discover that he would have enough *understanding,* in the vicinity of his family and of his family, and with this understanding would be willing to *be* and experience *as* the remainder of the family. And we would find out that he actually could control the family with considerable ease.

The oddity of it is that force can only control down into "entheta" – to "enturbulation" – but that a Pan-determinism controls upward into greater happiness and understanding, since there is more A-R-C present. You have seen individuals around whom a great deal of peace and quiet obtained. Such individuals, quite commonly, hold into sanity and cheerfulness many others in their environment who are not basically stable or Self-determined at all. The individual who is doing this is not doing it out of obsession. He is doing it simply by knowing and being. He understands what people are talking about because he is perfectly willing to be these people. When he falls away from understanding what they are talking about, he has also fallen away from being willing to be them. Willingness to *understand* and willingness to *be* are, for our purposes, synonymous.

Now, how does this Pan-determinism tie into communication?

We have seen that difficulties arose, on the cycle of communication and on the two-way cycle of communication, when origins of communication, answers and acknowledgments were scarce. This must be, then, that the individual–becoming aberrated through communication–must have conceived the necessity of an Other-determinism. In other words, one has to fall away from Pan-determinism to get into any of the traps of communication at all.

It is a very fortunate thing for us that Pan-determinism exists. Otherwise, there would be absolutely no way whatsoever out of this maze of miscommunications that a person gets into. The only way out of it would be to have other people come around and do enough talking, and go to enough movies, and seek out another Self-determinism which would communicate and make it communicate–until one was sane. However, it doesn't happen to work out, in an unlimited sense, in this way. The oddity is that it works out in "mock-up" processing. Further, it works out best in mock-up, for in mock-up we introduce the idea of Pan-determinism.

When we ask somebody to *"get the idea that* (somebody else) *is present"* (who is not) and then have him make this "person" give him answers, we discover after a while that some major aberrations have blown out of our preclear. In the first part, the preclear is actually remedying the scarcity of *answers* – or if these were being processed, *origins* or *acknowledgments* – and is so disentangling communication lines. The "sense" of what he would mock the person up as "saying" would have nothing to do with it. The communication could be almost pure gibberish as long as it was an answer. This would straighten out the bank to a very marked degree. The other factor which enters into this is Pan-determinism. We are making the individual actually mock-up somebody else and make somebody else say something. In other words, we are making our preclear take over the control – the start, change and stop – of another communication medium.

And with further test and experiment, we discover that we can do this for all the dynamics. And when we have done it for all the dynamics, we have brought our preclear up to a point of where he is willing to monitor communications on all the dynamics. And when he is willing to do this—and get origins, answers and acknowledgments along all the dynamics—we find that we have a very serene person who can do the most remarkable things.

Anything you have read about concerning the potential abilities of the Clear (and a lot more) come true when we follow this course. So it is a very fortunate thing for us that Pan-determinism exists. Otherwise, there would be no processing anybody.

Remember, when you are explaining this to people, that it is *willingness* to control on any and all dynamics. And that it is not *obsessive* or *compulsive* control to own, protect or hide on any dynamic. All the ills of Earth come from an obsession to own, control, protect and hide on other dynamics than self. The true enlightenments of this world have come from willingness to *be* along any of the dynamics.

One of the things which gives truth to Pan-determinism is the savageness with which the aberrated attempt to drive an individual away from anything resembling Pan-determinism. This is simply an obsessive action on the part of people to climb up to Pan-determinism by force. Pan-determinism cannot be climbed by force. The ladder to that height is not made of pikes and spears, spankings and police forces. It is made of *Understanding—Affinity, Reality* and *Communication.*

"Pan-determinism cannot be climbed by force.
The ladder to that height is not made of pikes
and spears, spankings and police forces. It is made of
Understanding–Affinity, Reality and Communication."

CHAPTER

THE SIX
BASIC

T W E L V E

PROCESSES

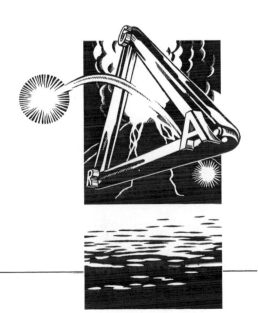

CHAPTER TWELVE

THE SIX BASIC PROCESSES

TODAY'S AUDITOR MUST be conversant with SIX BASIC PROCESSES and must be able to get results with these processes before he can expect to get results with higher levels of auditing. These six processes form a roadway for more than the auditor. We discover that they compose a Tone Scale. This Tone Scale is as follows:

At its lowest and highest reaches, whether by mimicry, words or mock-up, we have Two way Communication.

Next above this, occupying the position from about 1.1 to 1.8, we have Elementary Straightwire.

Above this, from 1.8 to 2.5, we have Opening Procedure of 8-C.

Above this, from 2.6 to 3.0, we have Opening Procedure by Duplication.

Above this, from 3.1 to 3.5, we have Remedy of Havingness.

And above this, from 3.6 to 4.0, we have Spotting Spots in Space.

CHART OF PROCESSES

WHERE THEY ARE ON THE A-R-C SCALE:*

Exteriorized

Process	Value
Spot Spots in Space	4.0
Spot Spots in Space	3.6
Remedy of Havingness	3.5
Remedy of Havingness	3.1
Opening Procedure by Duplication	3.0
Opening Procedure by Duplication	2.6
Opening Procedure 8-C	2.5
Opening Procedure 8-C	
Elementary Straightwire	1.8
Elementary Straightwire	1.1
Two-way Communication	1.0
Two-way Communication	– 8.0

Process	Value
"One-shot Clear"	4.0
"One-shot Clear"	2.5

*See *Chart of Human Evaluation* as given in *Science of Survival*.

An auditor, in auditing these Six Basic Processes, becomes sufficiently capable in observing and communicating that he can handle or can bring the preclear up to the point where he can handle the "subjective process" which remedies Communication, or the other one which is the "One-shot Clear."

The problem of psychosis never rightly belonged in Dianetics, but it has been solved there. Opening Procedure of 8-C and the Mimicry techniques, as given in the Professional Auditor's Bulletins, resolve psychosis. They resolve it rapidly and care for it adequately and we have no real worry on that score. The only reason we would enter the field of psychosis at all would be to find out how far south our techniques worked. These Six Basic Processes also resolve psychosomatic illness and do other remarkable things.

As covered much more fully in *The Creation of Human Ability*, these Six Basic Processes form the background to all processes. Through them, we find two-way communication everywhere. It can be said, with honesty, that there is no auditing without two-way communication.

TWO-WAY COMMUNICATION

The process Two-way Communication, itself, could be subdivided into verbal and non-verbal processes. The verbal processes would include questions about the present time environment and the preclear's life, interests and so forth, and would get a direct answer to every question, no matter how long the communication lag was. In other words, a two-way communication would be entered upon so as to actually bring the preclear to talk to the auditor. In the case of people who have great difficulties in this line, we have non-verbal techniques – such as Mimicry – wherein the auditor mimics the preclear and persuades the preclear to mimic the auditor. Various processes are used, such as passing a ball back and forth between them, nodding, shaking hands, sitting down, standing up, walking across the room and back and sitting down – all of which are effective.

Much of this book, *Dianetics 55!* is on the *subject* of two-way communication. And the totality of *auditing* is bringing a preclear into excellent two-way communication. And it is conceived a little difficult, by instructors, to relay the *process* called Two-way Communication. However, it is actually simplicity itself. For all that is necessary is to get the preclear to actually volunteer communications and answer the communications volunteered to him. There is always something the preclear will talk about.

Mimicry, particularly when used on psychotics, is a precision subject. Mimicry is not a new process. It is almost as old as psychotherapy. But it is spotty when used without an intimate knowledge of "validation." It can be said that "that which one validates, comes true." The only force or strength life has, is that which derives directly from the upper echelon of understanding. When life gets down to a point where it is incomprehensible, it cannot relay any understanding. Understanding this is essential for an auditor. He must realize that he gives power to everything he validates. We made something important out of the engram. And by validating engrams, we actually (where they were audited poorly) gave force and power to engrams. Thus it is with the psychotic. To mimic the strange, peculiar, bizarre and unusual things he does, is to give force and strength to those things. It cannot be said with sufficient emphasis that the auditor must *never* mimic the strange, bizarre and unusual manifestations of the psychotic. The only way that the auditor can make Mimicry work, consistently and continually and rapidly, is by validating what the environment considers the agreed-upon, the usual, the routine, the ordinary. Perhaps a psychotic is twisting his hands madly and occasionally nodding slightly. The auditor, in mimicking him, would not twist his hands but would nod slightly – since a nod is the agreed-upon manifestation in the environment, not the twisting of hands. If the auditor does this, the preclear will begin to nod more and twist his hands less. If the auditor were to begin to mimic the psychotic by twisting hands, he would discover that the psychotic would probably stop twisting his hands but would do something else much more bizarre. And if the auditor then mimicked this much more bizarre thing, the psychotic would simply go on to something even wilder or might become entirely motionless. For the one fear the psychotic has is becoming predictable. The psychotic is under the control of "entities" (demon circuits). He does have a grain of sanity present, otherwise he would not be able to function at all. Therefore, those things that he does which are sane must be mimicked and so reinforced. If an auditor knows this thoroughly and practices it smartly, he will discover that psychotics can be brought into two-way communication and moved immediately into Opening Procedure of 8-C – the proper process on psychotics. (8-C, while not a psychotic process, does work on psychotics. However, in working Opening Procedure of 8-C on the psychotic, the auditor must be very careful not to go beyond Part (a) for a long, long time.)

ELEMENTARY STRAIGHTWIRE

From the process known as Two-way Communication, we move on to the process known as Elementary Straightwire. Elementary Straightwire has two basic commands. One of these commands is used continually, over and over and over and over, until the communication lag is entirely flat on it. Then the other command is used, over and over and over, until the communication lag is entirely flat. At which time it will be discovered that the first command will now give communication lags and so it is used, over and over and over. And then the second one is used, over and over and over. In other words, what we do here is to use this process of Elementary Straightwire with just two commands, continuingly, one command at a time, flattening each communication lag encountered. While doing this, of course, one maintains a two-way communication. He acknowledges the fact that the preclear has recalled something and is, in general, alert to receive from the preclear an originated communication, answer it and give further orders.

The two commands of Elementary Straightwire are:

"Give me something you wouldn't mind remembering,"

"Give me something you wouldn't mind forgetting."

This can be varied with:

"Tell me something you wouldn't mind remembering,"

"Tell me something you wouldn't mind forgetting."

This Elementary Straightwire is a standard form. If it is varied, it should be varied toward simplicity.

A simple form of Straightwire is:

"Remember something," over and over, again and again and again and again and again.

Do not use, however, *"Forget something,"* since this is far too rough for the preclear.

Another, even simpler form, is to apply *"Remember something"* to the dynamics, such as:

"Remember a man,"

"Remember a group."

The only error that can be made in Elementary Straightwire is to get too fancy (for one does not believe that an auditor who has advanced this far in auditing would make an error in communication).

There is an entire gamut which we call "the next-to-the-last list in Self Analysis" (published in *Self Analysis*), which has many times been known to break a person from a neurotic to a sane state. This is:

"Can you recall a time that is really real to you?"

"Can you recall a time when you were communicating well to someone?"

"Can you recall a time when someone was communicating well to you?"

"Can you recall a time when you felt affinity for someone?"

"Can you recall a time when someone felt affinity for you?"

By keeping this in the understanding or affinity line, a case advances more rapidly than if mis-emotion and other factors are addressed.

OPENING PROCEDURE OF 8-C

Opening Procedure of 8-C is one of the most effective and powerful processes ever developed and should be recognized and used as such.

The main error which is made with the Opening Procedure of 8-C is not to do it long enough. It takes about fifteen hours of Opening Procedure of 8-C in order to bring a person into a completely relaxed and Self-determined state of mind regarding *orders*. Opening Procedure 8-C is a precision process.

Part (a) of Opening Procedure of 8-C is:

"Do you see that (object)?" (the auditor pointing).

When the preclear signifies that he does, the auditor says:

"Walk over to it."

When the preclear has walked over to it, the auditor says:

"Touch it."

When the preclear does, the auditor says:

"Let go," and designates another object (a wall, a lamp), calls them by name or not, and goes through the same procedure once more.

It is important that the auditor specifically acknowledge each time the preclear has executed the command given. When the preclear has seen the object, when he has walked over to it, when he has touched it, when he has let it go–each time, the auditor signifies that he has perceived and does acknowledge this action on the part of the preclear.

This Step (a) is used until the preclear does it easily, smoothly, without the slightest variation or introduction of any physical communication lag, and has demonstrated completely that he has no upset feeling about the auditor or objects in the room.

When (a) has been run for a length of time necessary to bring the case uptone, Part (b) is run. Part (b) introduces the idea of *decision*. It is notable that the "One-shot Clear" must be very strong on this "power of decision." It is also notable that a person in extremely bad condition has no power of decision.

The commands of Part (b) are:

"Pick a spot in this room."

And when the preclear has:

"Walk over to it."

And when the preclear does:

"Put your finger on it."

And when the preclear has:

"Let go."

Each time, the auditor acknowledges the completion of the command by the preclear, signifying *"All right"* or *"Okay"* or *"Fine,"* making it very plain that he has noticed and approves of and is acknowledging the action of the preclear in following each specific command. He approves of these, one at a time, in this fashion.

The preclear is run on this until he demonstrates no physical communication lag of any kind in making up his mind what to touch, how to touch it, and so forth.

Part (c) of Opening Procedure of 8-C introduces further *decision.*

It goes as follows:

The auditor says:
"Pick a spot in this room."

And when the preclear has, the auditor says:
"Walk over to it."

When the preclear does, the auditor says:
"Make up your mind when you are going to place your finger on it and do so."

When the preclear has done this, the auditor says:
"Make up your mind when you are going to let go and let go."

The auditor, each time, acknowledges the completion of one of these orders to the preclear.

In doing Opening Procedure of 8-C, the preclear must not be permitted to execute a command before it is given. And a two-way communication must be maintained.

As I have said, Opening Procedure of 8-C is a very powerful process. If all auditors knew was how to do Opening Procedure 8-C – and could do this very well – we would, right there, have psychotherapy licked. But we are not trying to lick psychotherapy. It has never been a major problem to us. We are trying to bring people a long way further north than psychotherapy ever dreamed of. And Dianetics and Scientology are not psychotherapies, they are processes which increase the abilities of people.

OPENING PROCEDURE BY DUPLICATION

Opening Procedure by Duplication has as its goal the separating of time, moment from moment. This is done by getting a preclear to duplicate his same action, over and over again, with two dissimilar objects.

In England, this process is called "Book and Bottle," probably because these two familiar objects are the most used in doing Opening Procedure by Duplication.

The first step of Opening Procedure by Duplication is to familiarize the preclear with both objects, as to their reality and his ability to own them. One makes him handle them and feel them and acquaint himself with them – makes him describe them as objects he is experiencing in present time, not as something related into the past. A little time spent on this can be quite beneficial.

The auditor then begins what will become to the preclear, before he is through with this, some of the most hated phrases anyone could conceive – but which, by the time the preclear is finished with this, become just like any other phrases.

Many people believe that Opening Procedure by Duplication induces hypnosis. This is because, in running it, hypnotism runs off. The preclear, while the hypnotism is running off, may feel quite hypnotized. It is the exact reverse of hypnotism. Hypnotism is an effort to persuade the individual to do nothing, to sit still and to accept fully the inflow. Opening Procedure by Duplication contains two-way communication and, indeed, does not work unless two-way communication is done with it.

The main liability in doing two-way communication on Opening Procedure by Duplication is that the auditor, in introducing two-way communication to it, may stray considerably from the pattern laid down. He must not do this. Although he is maintaining two-way communication, he must adhere very sharply to the process.

He can make the preclear tell more about them. He can make the preclear describe various things which are manifesting themselves to the preclear. He can be insistent the preclear really knows he has just picked this up. But he must stay with this sequence of auditing commands and may not vary from them even vaguely. He can interject other conversation, but not other auditing commands, into Opening Procedure by Duplication.

The auditing commands are:

"Do you see that book?" says the auditor, pointing.

When the preclear signifies that he has, the auditor says:

"Walk over to it."

When the preclear does, the auditor says:

"Pick it up."

When the preclear does, the auditor says:

"Look at it."

When the preclear does (usually he was looking at it, but now looks at it more closely) the auditor says:

"Give me its color."

When the preclear does, the auditor says:

"Give me its weight."

When the preclear does, the auditor says:

"Give me its temperature."

When the preclear has, the auditor says:

"Put it back exactly as you found it."

This action sequence having been completed, the auditor points to the bottle:

"Do you see that bottle?"

When the preclear does, the auditor says:
"Walk over to it."

When the preclear does, the auditor says:
"Pick it up."

When the preclear has, the auditor says:
"Look at it."

When the preclear does, the auditor says:
"Give me its color."

When the preclear has, the auditor says:
"Give me its weight."

When the preclear has, the auditor says:
"Give me its temperature."

When the preclear has, the auditor says:
"Put it back exactly as you found it."

Then the auditor says, pointing at the book:
"Do you see that book?"

And so on, back and forth, using this exact sequence of commands.

The auditor can interject:
"Describe it more fully."

The auditor can sometimes – but not more often than once every fifteen minutes – point to the book, have the preclear go through the full sequence with the book, and then point to the book again and have the preclear once more go through the full sequence with the book. This will break down the "automatic machinery" a preclear is bound to set up to compensate for this process. We want to keep the preclear doing it, not his machines. By asking the preclear to describe the object or describe its temperature more fully (in its proper sequence in these commands), machines are also broken down and the alertness and awareness of the preclear is increased.

The auditor must not omit letting the preclear give him the preclear's reactions. The preclear will pause, seem to be confused. It is up to the auditor, at that moment, to say, *"What happened?"* And to find out what happened. And then to continue with the process, having acknowledged the communication of the preclear. An auditor must never be afraid to let a preclear emanate a communication. And an auditor must never fail to acknowledge the completion of an auditing action, no matter how minute.

REMEDY OF HAVINGNESS

The Remedy of Havingness is an extremely effective process, for it remedies the ability of the preclear to "have" or "not-have" at will. Sometimes auditors interpret this process as "inflow only." That is because the physical universe is an inflow universe and it is all too easy for an auditor to assign to auditing (and all other actions) inflow characteristics only.

The modus operandi of the Remedy of Havingness is to have the preclear mock-up something, pull it in, or mock-up something and throw it away. It does not matter what you have him mock-up. The item can have significance or not, as the case may be. Preclears who are low in tone (if this is run on them – and it should not be) have a tendency to make everything they mock-up very *significant*. It is not the significance, it is the *mass* which counts.

However, to keep the preclear interested or to assist his mocking-up, an auditor may designate specific things and does so.

It will be found that the "acceptance level" and "expectance level" of the preclear very definitely monitor what he mocks-up and what he can pull in and what he can throw away. As covered in the Professional Auditor's Bulletins, Acceptance Level Processes can be combined with Remedy of Havingness.

The commands of Remedy of Havingness are as follows:

"Mock-up a (planet, man, brick),"

"Make a copy of it,"

"Make a copy of it,"

"Make a copy of it."

And when the preclear has from five to fifteen copies:

"Push them all together,"

"Now pull them in on you."

When the preclear has done this for some time, the last command is varied by saying:

"Throw them away and have them disappear in the distance."

In other words, we have the preclear mock-up something. When he has, we have him make a copy of it, make another copy and another copy and another copy, one at a time, push them together and pull them in or throw them away. We keep up this process for some time, until we are very certain that he can actually throw things away or pull them in on himself at will. This is the Remedy of Havingness. Remedy of Havingness does not mean "stuffing the preclear with energy." It means "remedying his ability to have or not-have energy." Run with particular significances, such as money, women, etc., one could remedy specific scarcities on the part of the preclear. But remember, they may be so scarce at first that he will have to "waste" a large quantity of them before he can "have" one.

On an awareness of awareness unit, exteriorized, we run Remedy of Havingness a little differently.

We say:

"Put up eight anchor points."

We describe to him how we want these put up. We want them put up in such a way as to form the corners of a cube. In other words, these eight anchor points are not to be in a group in front or behind the preclear, but they are to be distributed around him.

When the preclear has done this, we say:

"Pull them into you."

We keep this up for a long time.

We also have the preclear, exteriorized, mock-up eight anchor points and send them away from him. A preclear exteriorized can be very unhappy about his lack of havingness and this last process is used to remedy this upset.

Remedy of Havingness is an exteriorization technique. If it is run on an individual long enough, say eight or ten hours, he will probably exteriorize at the end of that time. If you kept on running it as an exteriorized process (given in the second part above), he would then have his visio clear up and he would finally get into very excellent condition. This is quite a process. However, remember, this process depends upon the preclear following the auditor's orders. Unless the auditor has guaranteed this by Opening Procedure of 8-C and Opening Procedure by Duplication, the chances of the preclear actually following his orders–although pretending to do so–are very slim.

(We have discovered, in old-time Dianetics, that the breakdown was in the failure of the preclear to follow the auditor's orders. Preclears would pretend to follow an auditor's orders, but actually would not.)

SPOTTING SPOTS IN SPACE

The process known as Spotting Spots in Space is not to be attempted on somebody who is having a difficult time. And when it is attempted, it should be accompanied with Remedy of Havingness. One makes a person spot spots in space for a short time, then remedy havingness, then spot spots in space, then remedy havingness, then spot spots in space.

These two processes, Remedy of Havingness and Spotting Spots in Space, actually belong together. However, the preclear eventually emerges up into a higher band where he can spot spots in space without remedying his havingness.

The auditing commands are:

"Spot a spot in the space of this room."

When the preclear has, the auditor says:

"Spot another spot," etc.

When the preclear gets well into the process in this fashion, we say:

"Spot a spot in the space of this room,"
"Walk over to it."

When he has:

"Put your finger on it."

When he does:

"Let go."

The auditor should ask a preclear, when he starts this process, if:

"The spot has any mass, color, temperature or any other characteristic?"

    or

"How big is it?"

The auditor asks this to make sure this preclear is actually spotting a spot – a simple location – not a spot that has mass or temperature or characteristics. A location is simply a location. It does not have mass, it does not have color, it does not have temperature. When we ask the preclear to spot a spot, at first his spots are liable to have mass and temperature. We do not object to this. We simply ask him frequently, once we have discovered that his spots do have this, *"how* (his) *spots are getting along?"* And we remember, on such a preclear, that we must remedy havingness. Eventually, he will move out to a point where he is simply spotting locations.

USE OF SIX BASIC PROCESSES

These are the Six Basic Processes that an auditor must know. They are, all of them, very powerful processes. And each and any one of them can accomplish the goals which were envisioned in *Dianetics: The Modern Science of Mental Health*. The essence of these processes is to do them as given, to do them "purely," all the while maintaining a two-way communication with the preclear. Auditors get into minor variations on this set of processes. But these processes were evolved first from theory by myself, were developed in practice by myself – and were then given to many auditors to do, and many auditors were trained in them – and then these processes were refined and inspected and refined and inspected, until they represent a very broad agreement. And we have found that these commands, as you have them here, are the best commands which can be used in processing a preclear.

The failure of an auditor to duplicate, his unwillingness to duplicate, his upset about duplication in general, will quite often lead him up the blind alley of varying a process compulsively or obsessively. When he does, he can expect to lessen the results. Auditing today, by the experience of a very large number of auditors, is a very severe discipline on the individual. It is not an art. And it never will be an art. It is a precision science. In the old days, all this talk about "art" and "intuition" and "instinctiveness" cost a lot of preclears the benefit of auditing. Auditing in the long ago was tremendously complicated, but it was nonetheless precise. Now that it is very simple, it is still very precise.

Amongst these processes, an understanding of communication lag and Opening Procedure of 8-C were chosen as the two processes to be taught to a very large area which contained a large number of auditors. This area had been noteworthy, heretofore, for the strange results "obtained" by auditors and the strange techniques which were used in it. A couple of auditors were sent into this area to teach everybody communication lag and Opening Procedure of 8-C. (Actually, these two auditors were originally from this area.) They did so. And several lives have been reported saved to date. And a great many cases have been salvaged. And the entire science is looking up in that particular area – simply because the area was taught nothing but communication lag and the Opening Procedure of 8-C and did nothing, thereafter, but this. Out in the outskirts of this area, a couple of auditors varied Opening Procedure by Duplication and were reported to be having "very good luck" with the variation. But these two auditors were not part of the crew who were taught Opening Procedure of 8-C and communication lag. And the results they were obtaining were very junior to the results being obtained by their own fellows very close by.

It could be said that the only real danger in auditing was "failure." Auditing is the *start, change and stop of aberration,* or the *creation of ability.* Today, creation of ability takes prominence to a point where aberration drops out of sight and is forgotten. But the auditor who does not obtain results is demonstrating to himself that he cannot control human aberration and human ability. And the demonstration of his failure, to himself, is sufficient to make him slightly incapable in handling his own difficulties. Thus it is a tremendously important thing that we have processes which, when used exactly as given and used with skill, produce uniformly good results on preclears. An auditor, using these on preclears, gets better and better and better and better, even when he doesn't have any auditing himself – a thing which was not the story of 1950. When you can control aberration in others, when you can increase the ability of others, you certainly do not worry about your own. An auditor who has consistent failures will eventually drop back to "self-auditing." But these processes will cure even that. Self-auditing, of course, is the manifestation of going around running concepts or processes on one's self. One is doing this because he has been made afraid, through his failure on others, of his ability to control his own engrams, facsimiles, thoughts and concepts. And he seeks to control them through auditing. It is not necessary for an individual to audit himself in order to control his own machinery.

Before anyone should adventure in the direction of testing the "One-shot Clear," or doing anything about exteriorizing the awareness of awareness unit and so making a Clear, he should be entirely conversant with these processes. Actually, any of these processes run long enough would probably result in an exteriorization.

There are faster ways to achieve an exteriorization than these processes. But these processes are preliminary to that. The preclear who cannot follow the auditor's orders will not sit there and do a "subjective" (which is to say, an out-of-sight, in his own mind) process without varying it. The trouble with the preclear is that he cannot duplicate. He cannot follow the orders of the auditor.

And when the auditor tells him to run a concept or a thought, the preclear probably pays token nod to this and runs entirely something else. A very close E-Meter review of a number of preclears who were not advancing under "subjective processes," disclosed that each and every one of them had never run what the auditor told them to run. They were afraid of obeying the auditor, they were afraid of what the auditor was doing, they were afraid of his skill. Opening Procedure of 8-C remedies this fear and brings the inability and unwillingness of the preclear out into the open where it belongs.

In Opening Procedure by Duplication, we very often get a preclear "blowing the session" where the auditor has run an insufficient quantity of Opening Procedure of 8-C. When a preclear "blows a session" on Opening Procedure by Duplication, the auditor has missed. He has not run enough Opening Procedure of 8-C. How much is enough Opening Procedure of 8-C? Until the person is in very good condition as Homo sapiens.

Remember that whether the command is physical or mental, the auditor must observe communication lag. In Opening Procedure of 8-C, he simply repeats the process commands all the way through – and then again and again and again – and in such a way flattens any lag which shows up. He does not repeat the command on which the preclear got the lag. It is easier to do this way. It is a more orderly process when it is done this way. By very close theory, the actual command on which the preclear lagged should be repeated again, but this is not done.

These are the Six Basic Processes which we must know before we can constitute ourselves auditors today. These are the processes which are getting results. These are the processes which are making able men and able women.

These processes can be varied into specific uses, where ability is concerned. One of the uses of these, for instance, would be to raise the ability of a pilot to fly a plane, or a person to drive a car, simply by having him approach, *"touch"* and *"let go"* of various parts of the object to be controlled. The exact procedure (as given above of Opening Procedure of 8-C) is run, except that the object to be controlled is used.

Typists have learned to type better, people have learned to drive cars better and many other abilities have been recovered, simply by running 8-C.

One could envision a pianist who was getting tired, run-down or upset by his music, coming into full awareness of it once more simply by running 8-C on his instrument or instruments.

If we wanted to increase the ability of a salesman, it would only be necessary to run any of the above processes (in their proper position on the Tone Scale) to increase his ability. Abilities increase, in general, when these are run.

When does one run what process?

One should have a copy of the Chart of Human Evaluation, from *Science of Survival,* and know that chart well in order to understand exactly where one starts. In general practice, however, an auditor simply starts with Two-way Communication. And when he is getting answers to his questions and is talking rather freely with his preclear, he goes into Elementary Straightwire. And from Elementary Straightwire, he goes into Opening Procedure of 8-C.

There is a variation on Two-way Communication. If you have a difficulty in getting a preclear started in Two-way Communication, it is a very easy thing to get him talking about *problems.* And from problems, to run this one:

"What problem could you be to yourself?"

"What problem could you be to others?" running one and then the other, each time, until the preclear understood he could be an "infinity of problems."

Many people are so thoroughly scarce on problems that they will not let any go until they know that they can create problems for themselves. When a case is stalling, he is generally finding it very hard to give up a pet problem because he "knows" he can't have any more. Of course, all this is basically situated on *answers*. He can't have any answers, so he has to have problems. Then from problems, he finally gets to a point where he can't even have these.

Anyone desiring to be a good auditor should follow this chapter very closely, should provide himself with a copy of *The Creation of Human Ability* and should also procure *Science of Survival* – and study them. The best way to become an auditor is to be trained as an auditor. We have found this so much the case that while we still offer an examination to anyone who wishes to take it (to the grade of Hubbard Certified Auditor or Hubbard Dianetic Auditor), we never expect them to pass it. For they never have, even though it is on the most simple elements as you see before you. There is no substitute for good training.

*"The best way to become an auditor
is to be trained as an auditor."*

CHAPTER

THE
PROCESSING OF

THIRTEEN

COMMUNICATION

CHAPTER THIRTEEN

THE PROCESSING OF COMMUNICATION

F YOU WILL EXAMINE the Six Basic Processes, you will discover that they are COMMUNICATION PROCESSES.

The efficacity of Opening Procedure of 8-C derives from the fact that it places into the realm of knowingness, communication with the physical universe. The physical universe does not give us back answers. But the Opening Procedure of 8-C remedies, to a marked degree, the liability of this no-answer situation by making the individual *aware* of the fact that walls are simply walls, that chairs are chairs, and floors floors, and ceilings ceilings.

Opening Procedure by Duplication is processing another facet of communications, *terminals* – the object (terminal) at Cause interchanging flow with the object (terminal) at Effect.

Elementary Straightwire is simply a communication with the past and securing of answers from the past. In other words, using the *past* as a terminal.

Havingness, in itself, describes the mass at a terminal or *masses*.

And Spotting Spots in Space improves the tolerance of an *absence* of a communication terminal.

These Six Basic Processes, as designed, bring an individual up a gradient scale of *tolerance* for more and more communication. Once a preclear has been pressed through these, he is ready for the direct processing of Communication. He is not ready for the direct processing of Communication until he has been put through these Six Basic Processes.

The ability of an individual depends upon his ability to communicate. The first and foremost of mechanical abilities is this communication ability. An individual who cannot communicate with something will become the victim of that something. That which a person withdraws from in this universe becomes, to a marked degree, his master. That which one fears becomes one's master. If an individual were willing to communicate with anything and everything in the entire universe, he would then be free in the entire universe. Additionally, he would have an unlimited supply of distances and terminals. A barrier, perforce, is something which an individual cannot communicate beyond. When we see space as a barrier, its total operation as a barrier is the inability of the individual to be at the other extreme end of that space or outside that space. When we see energy as a barrier, we simply see it as something which will not permit the egress or ingress of an individual. When we see mass, walls or time as a barrier, we mean "imagined impossibility of communication." If you do not imagine that you cannot communicate, then there cannot be a barrier.

At the same time, we are placed up against this conundrum: In the absence of communication, in the absence of interchanges of communication, in the absence of other terminals, flows and terminals to which others can communicate, an awareness of awareness unit is not, by its own consideration, *living*. Livingness is communication. Communication is livingness. We add to this the variant degrees of affinity. We add to it agreements and obtain reality. But still, these are only significances entered into communication.

Any and all types of significances can be entered into communication in order to "give a reason for" communication. These "reasons for" are simply reasons for a game, reasons to have communication.

In the light of the concept of Pan-determinism, we see that an individual has to assume that he cannot *know* what another is talking about if he wishes to communicate with and depend upon the communications of that other. In other words, he has to pretend that he cannot communicate. An individual who has some sort of barrier around him must pretend that he cannot communicate beyond that barrier. Actually, this is nothing more nor less than a pretense. These barriers are the shadows through which the fish would not move. They could have swum through these shadows except for the fact that they did not believe they could penetrate beyond the shadows. It could be said that *belief*, alone, is the reason for any entrapment.

However, there are the mechanics of entrapment. And we discover that an entrapment must be a communication barrier. An individual becomes entrapped in something because he does not believe he can communicate outside of it. Or he becomes fixated on a terminal *as* a terminal himself. To be very precise:

THE REASON WHY AN INDIVIDUAL IS ENTRAPPED HAS TO DO WITH SCARCITY OF COMMUNICATION.

An individual is still waiting, still looking toward something, expecting it to communicate to him. It has not. And he has eventually turned his attention slightly off of this onto something else which he expects to communicate to him. And when this does not, he expects communication and so finds it elsewhere. But each time he sets up one of these expectancy lines, he is to that tiny degree trapped against the terminal from which he was expecting, but did not get a communication.

"The reason why an individual is entrapped
has to do with scarcity of communication.
An individual is still waiting, still looking toward
something, expecting it to communicate to him."

Thus we have the entire bundle known as the reactive mind, the entire anatomy of "ridges" and any other enturbulative mechanism, and even problems themselves, being a seemingly endless chain of communication scarcities.

What are the specific scarcities in a communication line? There is no scarcity of silence. Anyone has far too much silence. Silence might be conceived to be the native state of a "thetan" (an awareness of awareness unit), but it is not. For obviously, a thetan is alive only to the degree that he is communicating his action–concentrated only to the degree that he is living. We discover that the tiniest cells of the body consider themselves to be "the very mirrors of truth" when they are the most silent. There is an interesting and peculiar test here, where the auditor has the preclear mock-up, in any area which contains a somatic, a great many *answers* or *originated communications* from these "dead cells." And we discover this somatic-ridden area coming to life, waking up, becoming active once more. This, in itself, is a specific for all types of somatics. All one has to do is have the preclear mock-up answers in these dead cell areas. An Ultimate Truth (which is studied to a far greater extent in *The Creation of Human Ability*) is a nothingness. But this Ultimate Truth is not life. Life is composed of this pretense that one cannot communicate, that one must communicate. It is composed of this intricate tangle of communications and self-erected barriers which give us a game. When we get too deeply immersed in this game, when answers get entirely too scarce, we forget that we were the ones who interposed the idea that no answers were to be given.

Silences do not process. There is entirely too much silence on the track. Remember that: *It does not process.* You can fill silence, but silence itself is death. And when you process silence, you process the preclear down toward death, not upward toward life. The way to process him upward toward life is by supplying his scarcity of communication.

We find the preclears who are in the worst condition are the preclears who are the most silent, the most out of communication. These are closest to death, closest to aberration. The way to get them alive again is to supply some of the scarcity of communication.

REMEDY OF SCARCITY OF COMMUNICATION

For a preclear who is in very poor shape–or in common practice, any preclear you encounter–you would use first the Six Basic Processes in order to bring the individual up to something approaching a livable communication stratum. And then you would go immediately into the Remedy of Scarcity of Communication by having him mock-up, himself, even if just as ideas, the various parts of the two-way cycle of communication.

The parts of a communication cycle which have to be remedied are:

1. Originated communications.

2. People to communicate to, or other awareness of awareness units to communicate to.

3. Answers.

4. Acknowledgments.

And additionally, but not as important:

5. Arrivals.

6. Departures.

It is not necessary that the preclear have the ability to mock-up, or to put out and hear back sound. In other words, sonic and visio are not necessary to this process. The entirety necessary is the *idea* of communication. You might say, you have him mock-up a "verbalizing idea."

The preclear will sort through, himself, Parts 2, 3, 4, 5 and 6, if the preclear is simply told to:

"Mock-up some people speaking."

He will, in rotation, get people answering, people acknowledging, people greeting him and people saying goodbye to him.

Because the preclear is usually far down the Tone Scale on origin and ideas, and because "necessity level" Other-determined forces have been necessary to get him into communication, it is likely that he will not himself spot the origination of communication (Part 1) and the auditor will have to call his attention to this.

Remember, this is not done on a preclear who has not first been put through his paces on the Six Basic Processes. For an auditor sitting there, asking a preclear to mock-up answers or acknowledgments or originated communications, could not otherwise be sure that the preclear is doing this at all. Further, the preclear's attention is very likely to stray into various portions of his own bank, for his bank starts to come to pieces under the impact of all of these communications.

The preclear must be kept at his job. His mocking-up of communications must be kept in a simplicity and out of "deep significances." And if his attention seems to fixate upon flows and he begins to "wrestle with mass," the auditor should get him back into mocking-up communications as fast as possible.

What degree of originality is required of the preclear in mocking-up any of these originative communications, answers or acknowledgments?

The answer to this is none. No variety is necessary whatsoever. Simply the idea of communication, with some sort of a specific idea being communicated, is all that is necessary.

Having a preclear, silent himself, mock-up before him something saying:

"Hello,"
and saying *"Hello"* again,
and saying *"Hello"* again.

And then having him mock this up behind him saying:

"Hello,"
and saying *"Hello,"*
and saying *"Hello,"*
and saying *"Hello,"* would be quite adequate for an originated communication.

Having the preclear mock-up any banality, such as:

"All right,"

    or

"Okay," serves very well for both answers and acknowledgments.

We are not at all concerned with the significance of the communication. We do not want long and involved communications. The preclear will try to get off into them. He will also try to get into his prenatal bank, his early childhood and eight lives ago.

We do not want him to do this. We want him to go on mocking-up originated communications, answers, acknowledgments. We are validating ability. We are not trying to get rid of inabilities in his *past.* We are trying to increase his ability to communicate in the *present* and originate communications and take a Pan-determinism of all communicating terminals. We are not trying to get him to run out anything in the past. I know that an old Dianeticist is going to have a very hard time restraining himself from running out the prenatal which immediately appears after the preclear has made something say *"Hello"* to him fifteen or twenty times.

It is the auditor's job, today, to make the preclear go on having the preclear (or something) say, *"Hello"* or *"Okay"* or *"I did it,"* and to ignore that engram. The number of engrams which will blow into view and beg to be run are countless. The auditor is not interested in these.

Of course, if the preclear wants to tell the auditor about these, the auditor must permit the preclear to originate the communication and must answer it–simply to get the preclear to originate communications. He should not let the preclear go on and on and on, discussing what has occurred, once the preclear has told him the essentials of it.

The auditor wants to get the preclear back on to mocking-up originating communications, answers and acknowledgments. The auditor is also making the preclear mock-up something to communicate to (number 2 above) while he is doing this–a point which is cared for automatically and which is not addressed, actually and actively, in auditing. Naturally, if there is a spot in the air out there saying, *"Hello"* or *"Okay"* or *"I did it,"* the preclear is assuming that there is something alive there that can say *"Hello"* to him.

All manner of thinkingness machines, large black masses, white and green fire, purple spheres, falling stars, shooting rockets may appear in the preclear's bank while he is undergoing this process. The auditor is not interested in this phenomenon. He is merely interested in getting the preclear to mock-up further communications.

It does not matter if the preclear says these communications, himself aloud, or simply does them quietly to himself. The necessity here is not sound. Sound is a byproduct of communication, is a carrier wave of communication and is not itself communication.

Some interesting variations can be worked on this. They are not advised and, indeed, they violate the terms of this process. But they demonstrate how much power this process has.

One has the preclear say aloud:

"*Okay, Mama,*" a few hundred times.

He will be amazed at the amount of variation which will occur, the communication lags, the impatience, the anger, the amount of data which will jump up about Mama. But this data that is jumping up is simply the bank which is triggered to agree with what the preclear is doing at this moment. In other words, that is stimulus-response.

Restimulation is stimulus-response, as is covered in great detail in *Dianetics: The Modern Science of Mental Health.* We could clear away an ally, we could do almost anything we wanted to do in Book One, with this process of Remedying the Scarcity of Communications.

Another point immediately arises as to whether or not the havingness has to be remedied on the preclear. It has not been found necessary to remedy havingness on the preclear if one is actually remedying the scarcity of communication. This is a great oddity. For the preclear's bank, being composed of tangled and unfinished communication lines, starts to come apart the moment that you begin to remedy the scarcity of originated communications, answers and acknowledgments. Some of these black masses, which the preclear has fondly held before his face, blow into forever. And yet the preclear does not need his mass remedied. The reason why he had to have mass was to compensate for the lack of communication. Where you have had a lack of communication, you are liable to have a mass.

As an example of this, an individual loses an ally and then keeps close by him a ring which belonged to that ally. The ring is a substitute communication terminal for the ally. After a while, one begins to believe that he really has to have mass. He doesn't have to have mass at all.

The Remedy of the Scarcity of Communication cures a person of having to have mass, having to eat obsessively, or do anything else obsessively.

Along with the remedy of originated communications, the preclear's imagination rises quite markedly. And thus, he is able to imagine new games and new ways of communication with sufficient rapidity to compensate for the old games which you are taking away from him. Actually, the preclear, being a preclear, *is* a game–perhaps even the last last-ditch game in which the individual could engage.

When the auditor has the preclear run acknowledgments, the wording is:

"I did it."

This will remedy responsibility difficulties. All "automaticity" comes about through lack of acknowledgments (absent players, secret players).

In view of the fact that Pan-determinism is control on all dynamics–and in view of the fact that control is start, change and stop–one can have the preclear *stop* making things communicate for a moment, and then *change* the communication, and then *start* anew. This gives the preclear practice in starting, changing and stopping.

The auditing commands which would go with this are simply:

"Mock-up some answers,"

"Mock-up some original communications,"

"Mock-up some acknowledgments," with enough guiding talk to give the preclear the idea that you do not want new, startling, difficult action–but only the simple placing of communication ideas, such as *"Hello,"* in the vicinity of the preclear, over and over and over and over.

EXACT AUDITING COMMANDS

The exact auditing commands to process Communications are:

ORIGINATED COMMUNICATIONS

Auditor: *"Have somebody out there* (indicating a spot in the air) *start saying 'Hello' to you."*

The preclear does so, is himself silent.

When the process is long run:

Auditor: *"Start saying 'Hello' to a live spot out there."*

The preclear aloud, or as himself, does so.

ANSWERS

Auditor: *"Have a spot out there start saying 'Okay' to you."*

The preclear does this many times.

Auditor: *"Start saying 'Okay' to a spot out there."*

ACKNOWLEDGMENTS

Auditor: *"Have a spot out there start saying 'I did it.'"*

When the preclear has many, many times:

Auditor: *"Start saying 'I did it' to a spot out there."*

The command that turns on a somatic, repeated often enough, will turn it off.

When in doubt, remedy havingness.

This is the processing of Communication directly. Remember that it is done after one has already done the Six Basic Processes. Remember that a two-way communication is maintained with the preclear while it is being done. And remember that the preclear must be audited in full understanding and practice of the Auditor's Code 1954. If you do this, you will have *Clears.*

*"The way to process him upward toward life is
by supplying his scarcity of communication."*

C H A P T E R

T H E

FOURTEEN

ONE-SHOT CLEAR

THE ONE-SHOT CLEAR

THE GOAL of the ONE-SHOT CLEAR has been with us since the earliest days of Dianetics.

By One-shot Clear, we meant "one phrase or one action given once, or repeated, which would bring into being the Clear as described in Chapter Two of *Dianetics: The Modern Science of Mental Health*."

It should be understood by this time that the Clear described in *Dianetics: The Modern Science of Mental Health* is actually the "thetan exterior" of Scientology (the exteriorized awareness of awareness unit*). The way to clear somebody is to get him out of the influence of his reactive bank and his analytical machinery. When a person is so cleared, his level of knowingness is sufficient to overcome the need of machinery and the need of stimulus-response mechanisms as contained in his reactive mind.

---

*In Scientology, the *awareness of awareness unit* is called a *thetan* –from the Greek symbol *theta* (θ).

Long since, we have had a One-shot Clear for 50 percent of the human race. All we say to the individual is *"Be three feet back of your head."* If he *is,* he orients himself, he knows that he is not his body, he knows he does not have to be up against his reactive mind, he has been gotten out of the trap.

Of course, there are many other things which you could do to further increase his ability and orient him in this position, but this is not immediately in our province in Dianetics. When an individual is so exteriorized, he also can look over the body and patch up pinched nerves, black areas, rearrange the "anchor points" which create and hold the space of the body, and so repair a body quite excellently. However, it is not the purpose of exteriorization simply to get a person to square away the machine known as a body.

"Be three feet back of your head" is a strange and interesting combination of words. Evidently, this simple combination has not been known before by Man. It is notable that one does not say, *"Move three feet back of your head,"* since an awareness of awareness unit doesn't *move*—it *appears* and *disappears* from locations.

If one uses this One-shot Clear technique, he should be advised that he must not ask or expect of the newly exteriorized person a number of strange or impossible things. He must not ask him to go chasing around finding things. He must not ask him to prove that he is exteriorized. The individual says so—that's the end of it.

In Scientology, of course, on "Route 1" as contained in *The Creation of Human Ability,* we go on to improve the ability of this exteriorized awareness of awareness unit up to a point which we call "Operating Thetan." We do this by running many drills and exercises which improve his perception. However, the process of Answers, or even the Six Basic Processes, can be run on the individual after he is exteriorized and his exteriorization will markedly increase and he will get into even better condition as an exteriorized person.

CHAPTER FOURTEEN
THE ONE-SHOT CLEAR

If you were to say, *"Be three feet back of your head"* to somebody–and he *was*–the next thing to do would be to go into Elementary Straightwire, then into Opening Procedure of 8-C, then Opening Procedure by Duplication, then Remedy of Havingness, then Spotting Spots in Space and then Answers (or as the last chapter gives forth, Remedy of Scarcity of Communication). If you did these things, just as given in this book, you would have something like a stable Clear. You would pay no attention to the fact that he was Clear.

As a matter of fact, if you were to run any of these Six Basic Processes long enough–and certainly if you were to run Answers for any length of time after you have run these Six Basic Processes–you would have somebody exteriorized.

It is a peculiar thing that there is no argument about exteriorization. Any argument which has been in existence was born out of the psychiatrist's observation of "compulsive exteriorization" by an individual who so detested his body that he stayed outside of it. Psychiatrists have been known to give people electric shocks and other "treatments" to get them to get back inside their body. This level of punishment, trying to get a person to accept something under duress, does not work. But then, nothing in psychiatry ever worked (except bank accounts).

This "compulsive exteriorization" is a manifestation which we call, in Scientology, "doing a bunk" (in other words, running away). You will occasionally encounter this, but you will not encounter it if you run the Six Basic Processes before you go in for exteriorization.

There is, astonishingly enough, a "One-command Clear" for the remaining 50 percent (even if it has to be repeated many times). I have been developing and testing this for some time and have kept it back on the shelf against the time when we had enough competent auditors to use a process intelligently.

This is a One-shot Clear technique, in that one uses one command and so achieves clearing. And after clearing to the stage of exteriorization has been accomplished, one simply goes on using the same type of command. It is a highly effective process, a very violent process. Theoretically, it would work on any level of case. In actual practice, psychotic, neurotic cases, or people badly out of communication, receive it with considerable difficulty and it is not recommended for them. But it would work on them if it could be communicated to them. (On such people use Opening Procedure of 8-C only.)

The basis for this process is the observation that the MEST universe is a game.

One can have a game and know it. He can be in a game and not know it. The difference is his determinism.

Games require space and havingness. A game requires other players. Games also require skill and knowingness that they are games.

Havingness is the need to have terminals and things to play for and on.

When a game is done, the player keeps around tokens. These are hopes the game will start again. When that hope is dead, the token, the terminal, is hidden. And it becomes an automaticity–a game going on below the level of knowingness. Truthfully, one never stops playing a game once started. He plays old games in secret–even from himself–while playing or not playing new ones.

The only *real* game one can have is in present time. All others are in the past or the future. Anxiety for a game takes one into the past.

The command is:

"Invent a game."

And when the preclear has, again:

"Invent a game."

Then:

"Have somebody else invent a game."

Having established the fact that an auditing session is in progress and established some slight communication with the preclear, the auditor says:

"Invent a game."

When the communication lag on this is flat, the auditor then uses the command:

"Have somebody else invent a game."

This is the only phrase he utters. But he, of course, engages in two-way communication with the preclear when the preclear has something to say to him.

An auditor has to be a good auditor in order to use this process. Just because it is a simple "one-command" process is no reason why it will work for an auditor who is not cognizant with the Auditor's Code, cognizant of a two-way communication, and hasn't some experience in more basic levels of processing.

We use this process as a remedy for the scarcity of games and we use it in full awareness of the processes involved in two-way communication.

It is a murderous process and requires five or ten hours, in rough cases, to bring about an understanding of existence.

This is not necessarily a recommended process. It is a workable process, it does function, it is fast.

But remember that it has the frailty of the ability of the auditor himself. It has the frailty of failing when a two-way communication is not maintained with the preclear. It will fail if the preclear, in volunteering information, finds no attention from the auditor. It will fail if the auditor does not acknowledge the fact that the preclear has done this. But, if these things are considered, it will work.

This process can be abused by the preclear. He can wander from it. He can sit there in the auditing chair doing other things. But we depend upon the skill of the auditor to see that the preclear is not doing other things and that he is actually doing the process.

The preclear will "pick his bank clean" rather than invent, he will have doubts that he *is* inventing. But we persevere – and we win.

"The preclear will 'pick his bank clean' rather than invent,
he will have doubts that he is inventing.
But we persevere—and we win."

C H A P T E R

FIFTEEN

A-R-C PROCESSING

A-R-C PROCESSING

I F WE EXAMINE COMMUNICATION, we will discover that all communication lag is the introduction of matter, energy, space and time into communication. The more it has been introduced into communication, the less communication there is.

As an example of this, let us say that a star in some other galaxy explodes. And then let us trace the length of time necessary for a small amount of that explosion's particles to reach Earth across great space. Almost countless light-years elapse before this communication line has been completed. This is a very, very long communication (not necessarily a communication *lag*, since the progress of the particles is not interrupted). There are no vias. Actually, MEST itself does not have a communication lag, it is totally a communication lag.

The more this sort of thing enters into communication, the worse off is the preclear. Thus we conceive the subject of MEST, itself, is the aberrative factor.

As we examine barriers, we find that they are matter, energy, space and time. We discover that we can overcome the barriers of matter–we can climb the walls or go through them. We can, somehow or other, brave or get on the other side of energy barriers. We discover that even space has limitations, even when it appears as limitless as the space of this universe (and the space of this universe appears as big as a person supposes it is big, whereas actually it is, to a thetan who can get outside of it, about the size of a matchbox to a child). The one barrier which we could discover difficult to get around is *time.*

The basic definitions and understanding of matter, energy, space and time are not particularly germane in this place. They are taken up on a much higher theoretical level in Scientology. But the essence of time is that it is measured, or marked, by the motion of particles in space. Space and energy particles are necessary to have mechanical time. But what is time, basically? Time is actually *consideration.* There is time because one considers there is time.

You must examine the physical universe very closely to discover that the reason it is always here is because it is–each and every particle of it, each cubic inch of space of it–in *forever.* The physical universe is not moving through time. It is stuck in time. Each and every part of it is fixed in a "now" which lasts forever. The only real changes which take place in the physical universe are those introduced into it by life. We can argue about this if we want to, but we are interested here in a concept which leads toward a workable process.

We discover that time exists for the individual to the degree that the individual *makes* time. Time is an Other-determined thing to nearly everyone alive. He depends on clocks, he depends on the rising and setting of the Sun, he depends on all manner of mechanisms to tell him what is the time. Actually, the more a person is told what the time is, the more he gets into a dependency upon some other consideration and so he drops into "forever." When he stops considering that he is making time, when he stops making time by considerations, he is dropping himself into a foreverness. He has less and less motion. He has less and less determinism. Time is a very insidious barrier because its apparency would tell an individual that time is created by the movement of things. Actually, it is not. It is created by a consideration that things are moving.

REMEDY OF THE BARRIER OF TIME

The Remedy of the Barrier of Time produces an astonishing effect upon a preclear. This process is the essence of simplicity. It has one command.

The command is:

"Make some time."

This is all the command there is. One does not advise or teach the preclear how to make some time. One accepts whatever the preclear decides "makes time" as the answer. One maintains two-way communication with the preclear and answers comments which the preclear has on it. One carefully does not evaluate for the preclear and tell him how to make some time. One does not set an example of making time. One simply has the preclear make some time.

This process, on some cases, has to be run many hours before the preclear comes into partial control of the barrier of time. When he does this, he of course comes into some control of his engram bank and his considerations.

The making of time, naturally, puts into motion all those silent or motionless masses which are hanging to the preclear and which actually pin together his reactive bank.

This is an enormous joke upon the preclear–by himself and the universe–that he *makes* all the time he will ever perceive. He cannot possibly get out of phase with "forever" if he is in contact with the *foreverness* of space and energy masses of which this universe is composed. When he starts to protest against the universe at large, he starts to protest against the foreverness which includes all time. And so he withdraws into earlier times when he was making time, in order to have some himself.

"Make some time," is a process of astonishing ramifications.

But remember, time is a barrier. One could also say:

"Make some space,"

"Make some energy,"

"Make some objects,"

"Make some terminals," and have gains in a preclear.

But these are barriers. Although a game requires barriers, the preclear already has too many in the past, too few in the present.

Barriers are not life.

THREE CARDINAL RULES IN PROCESSING

We must use three cardinal rules in processing:

1. Process toward the truth.

2. Process toward ability.

3. Process toward life.

Auditing commands must emphasize truth, ability, life.

Don't process toward "entheta," chronic somatics, difficulties. Ignore them.

The only thing wrong with the preclear is that his attention is fixed on barriers–MEST. His freedom depends upon putting his attention on freedom or present time.

Here are two auditing commands. Which is correct?

1. *"Find some things you can't do."*

2. *"Find some things you can do."*

The second is correct. The first will almost spin a preclear. Why? Because it concentrates on a lie. A preclear can do anything!

A preclear has a bad leg. Which is the right process?

1. *"Touch the back of your chair."*

2. *"Recall a time when somebody hurt his leg."*

The first is correct. It is *faster*. Why? Because it processes toward ability.

We have a preclear who is apathetic. Which process is the right one?

1. *"Who used to have headaches?"*

2. *"Feel the floor beneath your feet."*

The second is correct because it processes toward life, not illness.

That which the auditor concentrates upon in auditing comes *true*. Hence, the processing of MEST gives us new *barriers*. The processing of life gives new *life*.

Processing barriers gives us *limited* processes. Processing life gives us *unlimited* processes.

Life is composed of *Affinity, Reality, Communication*. These make *understanding*.

A-R-C PROCESSING

Modern A-R-C Processing processes Communication, as given earlier in this volume.

A-R-C Processing includes the following powerful processes:

1. *"Tell me something you might communicate with,"*
   "Tell me something that would communicate with you."

2. *"What might you agree with?"*
   "What might agree with you?"

3. *"Tell me something you would like,"*
   "Tell me something that might like you."

These are present time, not past or future processes. They produce very strong reactions. They solve *very* rough cases. They are summed in a simple process which does not dispense with them:

"Tell me something (someone) you could understand,"

"Tell me something (someone) who could understand you."

Note - Of course a very basic process which resolves chronic somatics, eye difficulties, any specific item is to have the affected part or bad area of energy say "hello" and "okay" and "all right" until it is in good condition — not that an auditor should address specific conditions — LRH

C H A P T E R

SIXTEEN

EXTERIORIZATION

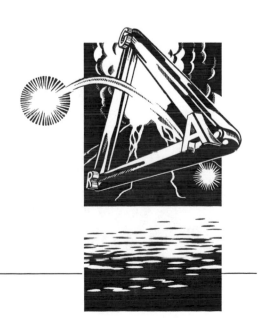

EXTERIORIZATION

THE AUDITOR will be confronted with a great many problems in Exteriorization once he has exteriorized his preclear.

The things *to* do and *not* to do are as follows:

1. Do not require the awareness of awareness unit to again put its attention on the body.

2. Do not make a person prove that he is exteriorized.

3. Do not make a newly exteriorized person discover, find things, read the future or do other nonsensical tricks.

4. Maintain the Auditor's Code more severely than before.

5. Continue the process on which the preclear exteriorized.

If the auditor knows these things, he will not get the preclear and himself into trouble.

The auditing command, *"Be three feet back of your head,"* sometimes gets the auditor into more trouble than he is equipped to handle.

The preclear may do a "compulsive exteriorization" ("do a bunk") and drop his body limp in the chair and give from that body no sign that he is hearing any of the auditing commands given by the auditor. One such case was pleaded with for half an hour by an auditor–along the lines that the preclear should remember her husband, should think of her children, should come back and live for the sake of her friends–and found no response from the preclear. Finally, the auditor said, "Think of your poor auditor," at which moment the preclear promptly returned.

A limited "compulsive exteriorization" is the preclear going out of the body and getting plastered against the ceiling or falling in terror upward into the sky (an inverting of gravity). This manifestation is equally upsetting.

If a preclear has been given the command, *Be three feet back of your head,* and if he "does a bunk" or if he "falls out of the body upward," all the auditor has to do is get in two-way communication with the preclear. Actually, he should have, as an auditor, an excellent command of the Chart of Human Evaluation of *Science of Survival.* He would then not tell a preclear below 2.0 on the Tone Scale to *"Be three feet back of your head."* For when they do, at these lower levels of the Tone Scale, it is on a compulsive or obsessive level. And all the preclear can think of is to try and get away.

Another remedy, if this untoward and strange occurrence happens, is to ask the preclear to:

"Reach from your position to your body,"
"Withdraw from the body,"
"Reach for the body,"
"Withdraw from the body,"

or

"Decide to run away, and run away," several times.

Chapter Sixteen
Exteriorization

Remember, such things as this occur only when the auditor has not placed his preclear on the Tone Scale before he began to audit him.

The way to get away from these *entirely* is to audit the Six Basic Processes on the preclear. And then audit either or both of the One-shot Clear processes, or Remedying Scarcity of Communication and A-R-C Processing, until the preclear exteriorizes. And then simply go right on auditing the process which exteriorized the preclear.

Remember that a preclear exteriorized is simply an awareness of awareness unit which has been taken out of a trap. And the awareness of awareness unit has not changed any from the basic individual, but now recognizes itself to be out of the trap and is quite happy about it.

A very funny manifestation occurs on some very low-toned preclears. When they talk about exteriorization, they say "I'm over there." This, of course, is impossible. An individual is always "here." It is *here* where you *are*. Lord knows what this individual who says "I'm over there" has exteriorized—a circuit, a mock-up, some such thing. He, himself, definitely is not.

Another manifestation we have is "buttered all over the universe." A preclear who is buttered all over the universe is one who does not know where he is. And if we ask him many, many times, over and over and over, each time making him get a spot with certainty:

"Can you find a spot where you are not?" we will gradually narrow down his area.

What has actually happened, in such a case, is that the preclear has used "remote viewpoints" and has left remote viewpoints located all over *everywhere*—to such a degree that the preclear thinks he is *anyplace,* rather than where he *is*.

The main thing one has to know about exteriorization is that it takes place.

If one uses the Six Basic Processes, remembers the Auditor's Code and the two One-shot Clear processes, he is then quite safe on exteriorization. For it will occur only when it occurs. And the thing to do after it occurs is to do the same process one has been doing when it occurs. Of course, one should acknowledge the fact of the preclear's mentioning it and one should certainly permit the preclear to discuss it. But one should continue with the process which exteriorized him unless, of course, one is very well trained in exteriorization exercises.

As exteriorization drilling, as an activity, is most germane to the realm of Scientology, further knowledge of it and about it is written up in *The Creation of Human Ability.* Here is given the Route 1 steps which should be run after an exteriorization takes place.

The creation of a Clear, undertaken in 1950, actually was this manifestation of exteriorization happening at some random moment and not being adequately cared for after it occurred. Nobody remarked upon the fact that he was a distance from the body because most of the people who were thus exteriorized had very good visio on their own banks, but very poor visio on the immediate environment. A little more exteriorization work and any one of these Clears would have suddenly found themselves out into the room, looking at the room directly without the aid of eyes.

We wanted Clears in 1950. We still want Clears. This is the way to make them, the way to make them stable, the way to make anybody you process far more able.

The byword on this is not to address specific errors or difficulties, but to validate abilities and process immediately toward the acquisition of further and further and higher abilities.

Chapter Sixteen
Exteriorization

We are not in there to pay attention to all the bad things in the world, since these are composed only of the imaginings of the individual. Let us increase the ability of the individual to create, to be, to perceive and increase his ability to associate all along the dynamics.

If we should do this, it would be a far, far better world.

A P P E N D I X

FURTHER STUDY
BOOKS & LECTURES BY L. RON HUBBARD

The materials of Dianetics and Scientology comprise the largest body of information ever assembled on the mind, spirit and life, rigorously refined and codified by L. Ron Hubbard through five decades of research, investigation and development. The results of that work are contained in hundreds of books and more than 3,000 recorded lectures. A full listing and description of them all can be obtained from any Scientology Church or Publications Organization. (See *Guide to the Materials.*)

The books and lectures below form the foundation upon which the Bridge to Freedom is built. They are listed in the sequence Ron wrote or delivered them. In many instances, Ron gave a series of lectures immediately following the release of a new book to provide further explanation and insight of these milestones. Through monumental restoration efforts, those lectures are now available and are listed herein with their companion book.

While Ron's books contain the summaries of breakthroughs and conclusions as they appeared in the developmental research track, his lectures provide the running day-to-day record of research and explain the thoughts, conclusions, tests and demonstrations that lay along that route. In that regard, they are the complete record of the entire research track, providing not only the most important breakthroughs in Man's history, but the *why* and *how* Ron arrived at them.

Not the least advantage of a chronological study of these books and lectures is the inclusion of words and terms which, when originally used, were defined by LRH with considerable exactitude. Far beyond a mere "definition," entire lectures are devoted to a full description of each new Dianetic or Scientology term—what made the breakthrough possible, its application in auditing as well as its application to life itself. As a result, one leaves behind no misunderstoods, obtains a full conceptual understanding of Dianetics and Scientology and grasps the subjects at a level not otherwise possible.

Through a sequential study, you can see how the subject progressed and recognize the highest levels of development. The listing of books and lectures below shows where *Dianetics 55!* fits within the developmental line. From there you can determine your *next* step or any earlier books and lectures you may have missed. You will then be able to fill in missing gaps, not only gaining knowledge of each breakthrough, but greater understanding of what you've already studied.

This is the path to knowing how to know, unlocking the gates to your future eternity. Follow it.

DIANETICS: THE ORIGINAL THESIS • Ron's *first* description of Dianetics. Originally circulated in manuscript form, it was soon copied and passed from hand to hand. Ensuing word of mouth created such demand for more information, Ron concluded the only way to answer the inquiries was with a book. That book was Dianetics: The Modern Science of Mental Health, now the all-time self-help bestseller. Find out what started it all. For here is the bedrock foundation of Dianetic discoveries: the *Original Axioms,* the *Dynamic Principle of Existence,* the *Anatomy of the Analytical* and *Reactive Mind,* the *Dynamics*, the *Tone Scale,* the *Auditor's Code* and the first description of a *Clear.* Even more than that, here are the primary laws describing *how* and *why* auditing works. It's only here in Dianetics: The Original Thesis.

DIANETICS: THE EVOLUTION OF A SCIENCE • This is the story of *how* Ron discovered the reactive mind and developed the procedures to get rid of it. Originally written for a national magazine–published to coincide with the release of Dianetics: The Modern Science of Mental Health–it started a wildfire movement virtually overnight upon that book's publication. Here then are both the fundamentals of Dianetics as well as the only account of Ron's two-decade journey of discovery and how he applied a scientific methodology to the problems of the human mind. He wrote it so you would know. Hence, this book is a must for every Dianeticist and Scientologist.

DIANETICS: THE MODERN SCIENCE OF MENTAL HEALTH • The bolt from the blue that began a worldwide movement. For while Ron had previously announced his discovery of the reactive mind, it had only fueled the fire of those wanting more information. More to the point–it was humanly impossible for one man to clear an entire planet. Encompassing all his previous discoveries and case histories of those breakthroughs in application, Ron provided the complete handbook of Dianetics procedure to train auditors to use it everywhere. A bestseller for more than half a century and with tens of millions of copies in print, Dianetics: The Modern Science of Mental Health has been translated in more than fifty languages, and used in more than 100 countries of Earth–indisputably, the most widely read and influential book about the human mind ever written. And that is why it will forever be known as *Book One.*

DIANETICS LECTURES AND DEMONSTRATIONS • Immediately following the publication of *Dianetics,* LRH began lecturing to packed auditoriums across America. Although addressing thousands at a time, demand continued to grow. To meet that demand, his presentation in Oakland, California, was recorded. In these four lectures, Ron related the events that sparked his investigation and his personal journey to his groundbreaking discoveries. He followed it all with a personal demonstration of Dianetics auditing–the only such demonstration of Book One available. *4 lectures.*

FURTHER STUDY

DIANETICS PROFESSIONAL COURSE LECTURES—*A SPECIAL COURSE FOR BOOK ONE AUDITORS* • Following six months of coast-to-coast travel, lecturing to the first Dianeticists, Ron assembled auditors in Los Angeles for a new Professional Course. The subject was his next sweeping discovery on life—the *ARC Triangle,* describing the interrelationship of *Affinity, Reality* and *Communication.* Through a series of fifteen lectures, LRH announced many firsts, including the *Spectrum of Logic,* containing an infinity of gradients from right to wrong; *ARC and the Dynamics;* the *Tone Scales of ARC;* the *Auditor's Code* and how it relates to ARC; and the *Accessibility Chart* that classifies a case and how to process it. Here, then, is both the final statement on Book One Auditing Procedures and the discovery upon which all further research would advance. The data in these lectures was thought to be lost for over fifty years and only available in student notes published in Notes on the Lectures. The original recordings have now been discovered making them broadly available for the first time. Life in its highest state, *Understanding,* is composed of Affinity, Reality and Communication. And, as LRH said, the best description of the ARC Triangle to be found anywhere is in these lectures. *15 lectures.*

SCIENCE OF SURVIVAL—*PREDICTION OF HUMAN BEHAVIOR* • The most useful book you will ever own. Built around the *Hubbard Chart of Human Evaluation,* Science of Survival provides the first accurate prediction of human behavior. Included on the chart are all the manifestations of an individual's survival potential graduated from highest to lowest, making this the complete book on the Tone Scale. Knowing only one or two characteristics of a person and using this chart, you can plot his or her position on the Tone Scale and thereby know the rest, obtaining an accurate index of their *entire* personality, conduct and character. Before this book the world was convinced that cases could not improve but only deteriorate. Science of Survival presents the idea of different states of case and the brand-new idea that one can progress upward on the Tone Scale. And therein lies the basis of today's Grade Chart.

THE SCIENCE OF SURVIVAL LECTURES • Underlying the development of the Tone Scale and Chart of Human Evaluation was a monumental breakthrough: The *Theta-MEST Theory,* containing the explanation of the interaction between Life—*theta*—with the physical universe of Matter, Energy, Space and Time—*MEST.* In these lectures, delivered to students immediately following publication of the book, Ron gave the most expansive description of all that lies behind the Chart of Human Evaluation and its application in life itself. Moreover, here also is the explanation of how the ratio of *theta* and *en(turbulated)-theta* determines one's position on the Tone Scale and the means to ascend to higher states. *4 lectures.*

SELF ANALYSIS • The barriers of life are really just shadows. Learn to know yourself – not just a shadow of yourself. Containing the most complete description of consciousness, Self Analysis takes you through your past, through your potentials, your life. First, with a series of self-examinations and using a special version of the Hubbard Chart of Human Evaluation, you plot yourself on the Tone Scale. Then, applying a series of light yet powerful processes, you embark on the great adventure of self-discovery. This book further contains embracive principles that reach *any* case, from the lowest to the highest – including auditing techniques so effective they are referred to by Ron again and again through all following years of research into the highest states. In sum, this book not only moves one up the Tone Scale but can pull a person out of almost anything.

ADVANCED PROCEDURE AND AXIOMS • With new breakthroughs on the nature and anatomy of engrams – "Engrams are effective only when the individual himself determines that they will be effective" – came the discovery of the being's use of a *Service Facsimile:* a mechanism employed to explain away failures in life, but which then locks a person into detrimental patterns of behavior and further failure. In consequence came a new type of processing addressing *Thought, Emotion* and *Effort* detailed in the "Fifteen Acts" of Advanced Procedure and oriented to the rehabilitation of the preclear's *Self-determinism.* Hence, this book also contains the all-encompassing, no-excuses-allowed explanation of *Full Responsibility,* the key to unlocking it all. Moreover, here is the codification of *Definitions, Logics,* and *Axioms,* providing both the summation of the entire subject and direction for all future research. *See Handbook for Preclears, written as a companion self-processing manual to Advanced Procedure and Axioms.*

> **THOUGHT, EMOTION AND EFFORT** • With the codification of the Axioms came the means to address key points on a case that could unravel all aberration. *Basic Postulates, Prime Thought, Cause and Effect* and their effect on everything from *memory* and *responsibility* to an individual's own role in empowering *engrams* – these matters are only addressed in this series. Here, too, is the most complete description of the *Service Facsimile* found anywhere – and why its resolution removes an individual's self-imposed disabilities. *21 lectures.*

HANDBOOK FOR PRECLEARS • The "Fifteen Acts" of Advanced Procedure and Axioms are paralleled by the fifteen Self-processing Acts given in Handbook for Preclears. Moreover, this book contains several essays giving the most expansive description of the *Ideal State of Man*. Discover why behavior patterns become so solidly fixed; why habits seemingly can't be broken; how decisions long ago have more power over a person than his decisions today; and why a person keeps past negative experiences in the present. It's all clearly laid out on the Chart of Attitudes–a milestone breakthrough that complements the Chart of Human Evaluation–plotting the ideal state of being and one's *attitudes* and *reactions* to life. *In self-processing, Handbook for Preclears is used in conjunction with Self Analysis.*

THE LIFE CONTINUUM • Besieged with requests for lectures on his latest breakthroughs, Ron replied with everything they wanted and more at the Second Annual Conference of Dianetic Auditors. Describing the technology that lies behind the self-processing steps of the *Handbook*–here is the *how* and *why* of it all: the discovery of *Life Continuum*–the mechanism by which an individual is compelled to carry on the life of another deceased or departed individual, generating in his own body the infirmities and mannerisms of the departed. Combined with auditor instruction on use of the Chart of Attitudes in determining how to enter every case at the proper gradient, here, too, are directions for dissemination of the Handbook and hence, the means to begin wide-scale clearing. *10 lectures.*

SCIENTOLOGY: MILESTONE ONE • Ron began the first lecture in this series with six words that would change the world forever: "This is a course in *Scientology*." From there, Ron not only described the vast scope of this, a then brand-new subject, he also detailed his discoveries on past lives. He proceeded from there to the description of the first E-Meter and its initial use in uncovering the *theta line* (the entire track of a thetan's existence), as entirely distinct from the *genetic body line* (the time track of bodies and their physical evolution), shattering the "one-life" lie and revealing the *whole track* of spiritual existence. Here, then, is the very genesis of Scientology. *22 lectures.*

THE ROUTE TO INFINITY: TECHNIQUE 80 LECTURES • As Ron explained, "Technique 80 is the *To Be or Not To Be* Technique." With that, he unveiled the crucial foundation on which ability and sanity rest: *the being's capacity to make a decision*. Here, then, is the anatomy of "maybe," the *Wavelengths of ARC*, the *Tone Scale of Decisions,* and the means to rehabilitate a being's ability *To Be* … almost *anything. 7 lectures. (Knowledge of Technique 80 is required for Technique 88 as described in Scientology: A History of Man–below.)*

SCIENTOLOGY: A HISTORY OF MAN • "A cold-blooded and factual account of your last 76 trillion years." So begins A History of Man, announcing the revolutionary *Technique 88* – revealing for the first time the truth about whole track experience and the exclusive address, in auditing, to the thetan. Here is history unraveled with the first E-Meter, delineating and describing the principal incidents on the whole track to be found in any human being: *Electronic implants, entities, the genetic track, between-lives incidents, how bodies evolved* and *why you got trapped in them* – they're all detailed here.

TECHNIQUE 88: INCIDENTS ON THE TRACK BEFORE EARTH • "Technique 88 is the most hyperbolical, effervescent, dramatic, unexaggeratable, high-flown, superlative, grandiose, colossal and magnificent technique which the mind of Man could conceivably embrace. It is as big as the whole track and all the incidents on it. It's what you apply it to; it's what's been going on. It contains the riddles and secrets, the mysteries of all time. You could bannerline this technique like they do a sideshow, but nothing you could say, no adjective you could use, would adequately describe even a small segment of it. It not only batters the imagination, it makes you ashamed to imagine anything," is Ron's introduction to you in this never-before-available lecture series, expanding on all else contained in History of Man. What awaits you is the whole track itself. *15 lectures.*

SCIENTOLOGY 8-80 • The *first* explanation of the electronics of human thought and the energy phenomena in any being. Discover how even physical universe laws of motion are mirrored in a being, not to mention the electronics of aberration. Here is the link between theta and MEST revealing what energy *is*, and how you *create* it. It was this breakthrough that revealed the subject of a thetan's *flows* and which, in turn, is applied in *every* auditing process today. In the book's title, "8-8" stands for *Infinity-Infinity*, and "0" represents the static, *theta*. Included are the *Wavelengths of Emotion, Aesthetics, Beauty and Ugliness, Inflow and Outflow* and the *Sub-zero Tone Scale* – applicable only to the thetan.

SOURCE OF LIFE ENERGY • Beginning with the announcement of his new book – Scientology 8-80 – Ron not only unveiled his breakthroughs of theta as the Source of Life Energy, but detailed the *Methods of Research* he used to make that and every other discovery of Dianetics and Scientology: the *Qs* and *Logics* – methods of *thinking* applicable to any universe or thinking process. Here, then, is both *how to think* and *how to evaluate all data and knowledge*, and thus, the linchpin to a full understanding of both Scientology and life itself. *14 lectures.*

FURTHER STUDY

🎙 **THE COMMAND OF THETA** • While in preparation of his newest book
and the Doctorate Course he was about to deliver, Ron called together
auditors for a new Professional Course. As he said, "For the first time with
this class we are stepping, really, beyond the scope of the word *Survival*."
From that vantage point, the Command of Theta gives the technology
that bridges the knowledge from 8-80 to 8-8008, and provides the first full
explanation of the subject of *Cause* and a permanent shift of orientation
in life from *MEST* to *Theta*. *10 lectures.*

SCIENTOLOGY 8-8008 • The complete description of the behavior and potentials
of a *thetan,* and textbook for the Philadelphia Doctorate Course and The Factors:
Admiration and the Renaissance of Beingness lectures. As Ron said, the book's
title serves to fix in the mind of the individual a route by which he can rehabilitate
himself, his abilities, his ethics and his goals – the attainment of *infinity* (8) by the
reduction of the apparent *infinity* (8) of the MEST universe to *zero* (0) and the increase
of the apparent *zero* (0) of one's own universe to *infinity* (8). Condensed herein are
more than 80,000 hours of investigation, with a summarization and amplification
of every breakthrough to date – and the full significance of those discoveries form
the new vantage point of *Operating Thetan.*

🎙 **THE PHILADELPHIA DOCTORATE COURSE LECTURES** • This renowned
series stands as the largest single body of work on the anatomy, behavior
and potentials of the spirit of Man ever assembled, providing the very
fundamentals which underlie the route to Operating Thetan. Here it is in
complete detail – the thetan's relationship to the *creation, maintenance* and
destruction of universes. In just those terms, here is the *anatomy* of matter,
energy, space and time, and *postulating* universes into existence. Here,
too, is the thetan's fall from whole track abilities and the *universal laws* by
which they are restored. In short, here is Ron's codification of the upper
echelon of theta beingness and behavior. Lecture after lecture fully expands
every concept of the course text, Scientology 8-8008, providing the total
scope of *you* in native state. *76 lectures and accompanying reproductions
of the original 54 LRH hand-drawn lecture charts.*

🎙 **THE FACTORS: ADMIRATION AND THE RENAISSANCE OF BEINGNESS** •
With the *potentials* of a thetan fully established came a look outward
resulting in Ron's monumental discovery of a *universal solvent* and the
basic laws of the theta *universe* – laws quite literally senior to anything:
*The Factors: Summation of the Considerations of the Human Spirit and
Material Universe.* So dramatic were these breakthroughs, Ron expanded
the book Scientology 8-8008, both clarifying previous discoveries and
adding chapter after chapter which, studied with these lectures, provide a
postgraduate level to the Doctorate Course. Here then are lectures containing
the knowledge of *universal truth* unlocking the riddle of creation itself.
18 lectures.

THE CREATION OF HUMAN ABILITY – *A HANDBOOK FOR SCIENTOLOGISTS* • On the heels of his discoveries of Operating Thetan came a year of intensive research, exploring the realm of a *thetan exterior*. Through auditing and instruction, including 450 lectures in this same twelve-month span, Ron codified the entire subject of Scientology. And it's all contained in this handbook, from a *Summary of Scientology* to its basic *Axioms* and *Codes*. Moreover, here is *Intensive Procedure,* containing the famed Exteriorization Processes of *Route 1* and *Route 2* – processes drawn right from the Axioms. Each one is described in detail – *how* the process is used, *why* it works, the axiomatic technology that underlies its use, and the complete explanation of how a being can break the *false agreements* and *self-created barriers* that enslave him to the physical universe. In short, this book contains the ultimate summary of thetan exterior OT ability and its permanent accomplishment.

PHOENIX LECTURES: FREEING THE HUMAN SPIRIT • Here is the panoramic view of Scientology complete. Having codified the subject of Scientology in Creation of Human Ability, Ron then delivered a series of half-hour lectures to specifically accompany a full study of the book. From the *essentials* that underlie the technology – *The Axioms, Conditions of Existence* and *Considerations and Mechanics,* to the processes of *Intensive Procedure*, including twelve lectures describing one-by-one the thetan exterior processes of *Route 1* – it's all covered in full, providing a conceptual understanding of the *science of knowledge* and *native state OT ability*. Here then are the bedrock principles upon which everything in Scientology rests, including the embracive statement of the religion and its heritage – *Scientology, Its General Background*. Hence, this is the watershed lecture series on Scientology itself, and the axiomatic foundation for all future research. *42 lectures.*

DIANETICS 55! – *THE COMPLETE MANUAL OF HUMAN COMMUNICATION* • *(This current volume.)* With all breakthroughs to date, a single factor had been isolated as crucial to success in every type of auditing. As LRH said, "Communication is so thoroughly important today in Dianetics and Scientology (as it always has been on the whole track) that it could be said if you were to get a preclear into communication, you would get him well." And this book delineates the *exact,* but previously unknown, anatomy and formulas for *perfect* communication. The magic of the communication cycle is *the* fundamental of auditing and the primary reason auditing works. The breakthroughs here opened new vistas of application – discoveries of such magnitude, LRH called Dianetics 55! the *Second Book* of Dianetics.

THE UNIFICATION CONGRESS: COMMUNICATION! FREEDOM & ABILITY • The historic Congress announcing the reunification of the subjects of Dianetics and Scientology with the release of *Dianetics 55!* Until now, each had operated in their own sphere: Dianetics addressed Man *as Man* – the first four dynamics, while Scientology addressed *life itself* – the Fifth to Eighth Dynamics. The formula which would serve as the foundation for all future development was contained in a single word: *Communication*. It was a paramount breakthrough Ron would later call, "the great discovery of Dianetics and Scientology." Here, then, are the lectures, as it happened. *16 lectures and accompanying reproductions of the original LRH hand-drawn lecture charts.*

SCIENTOLOGY: THE FUNDAMENTALS OF THOUGHT – *THE BASIC BOOK OF THE THEORY AND PRACTICE OF SCIENTOLOGY FOR BEGINNERS* • Designated by Ron as the *Book One of Scientology.* After having fully unified and codified the subjects of Dianetics and Scientology came the refinement of their *fundamentals.* Originally published as a résumé of Scientology for use in translations into non-English tongues, this book is of inestimable value to both the beginner and advanced student of the mind, spirit and life. Equipped with this book alone, one can begin a practice and perform seeming miracle changes in the states of well-being, ability and intelligence of people. Contained within are the *Conditions of Existence, Eight Dynamics, ARC Triangle, Parts of Man,* the full analysis of *Life as a Game,* and more, including exact processes for individual application of these principles in processing. Here, then, in one book, is the starting point for bringing Scientology to people everywhere.

> **HUBBARD PROFESSIONAL COURSE LECTURES** • While Fundamentals of Thought stands as an introduction to the subject for beginners, it also contains a distillation of fundamentals for every Scientologist. Here are the in-depth descriptions of those fundamentals, each lecture one-half hour in length and providing, one-by-one, a complete mastery of a single Scientology breakthrough – *Axioms 1-10; The Anatomy of Control; Handling of Problems; Start, Change and Stop; Confusion and Stable Data; Exteriorization; Valences* and more – the *why* behind them, *how* they came to be and their mechanics. And it's all brought together with the *Code of a Scientologist,* point by point, and its use in actually creating a new civilization. In short, here are the LRH lectures that make a *Professional Scientologist* – one who can apply the subject to every aspect of life. *21 lectures.*

ADDITIONAL BOOKS CONTAINING SCIENTOLOGY ESSENTIALS

WORK

THE PROBLEMS OF WORK–*SCIENTOLOGY APPLIED TO THE WORKADAY WORLD* • Having codified the entire subject of Scientology, Ron immediately set out to provide the *beginning* manual for its application by anyone. As he described it: life is composed of seven-tenths work, one-tenth familial, one-tenth political and one-tenth relaxation. Here, then, is Scientology applied to that seven-tenths of existence including the answers to *Exhaustion* and the *Secret of Efficiency.* Here, too, is the analysis of life itself – a game composed of exact rules. Know them and you succeed. Problems of Work contains technology no one can live without, and that can immediately be applied by both the Scientologist and those new to the subject.

LIFE PRINCIPLES

SCIENTOLOGY: A NEW SLANT ON LIFE • Scientology essentials for every aspect of life. Basic answers that put you in charge of your existence, truths to consult again and again: *Is It Possible to Be Happy?, Two Rules for Happy Living, Personal Integrity, The Anti-Social Personality* and many more. In every part of this book you will find Scientology truths that describe conditions in your life and furnish *exact* ways to improve them. Scientology: A New Slant on Life contains essential knowledge for every Scientologist and a perfect introduction for anyone new to the subject.

AXIOMS, CODES AND SCALES

SCIENTOLOGY 0-8: THE BOOK OF BASICS • The companion to *all* Ron's books, lectures and materials. This is *the* Book of Basics, containing indispensable data you will refer to constantly: the *Axioms of Dianetics and Scientology; The Factors;* a full compilation of all *Scales* – more than 100 in all; listings of the *Perceptics* and *Awareness Levels;* all *Codes* and *Creeds* and much more. The senior laws of existence are condensed into this single volume, distilled from more than 15,000 pages of writings, 3,000 lectures and scores of books.

SCIENTOLOGY ETHICS:
TECHNOLOGY OF OPTIMUM SURVIVAL

INTRODUCTION TO SCIENTOLOGY ETHICS • A new hope for Man arises with the first workable technology of ethics–technology to help an individual pull himself out of the downward skid of life and to a higher plateau of survival. This is the comprehensive handbook providing the crucial fundamentals: *Basics of Ethics & Justice; Honesty; Conditions of Existence; Condition Formulas* from Confusion to Power; the *Basics of Suppression* and its handling; as well as *Justice Procedures* and their use in Scientology Churches. Here, then, is the technology to overcome any barriers in life and in one's personal journey up the Bridge to Total Freedom.

PURIFICATION

CLEAR BODY, CLEAR MIND–*THE EFFECTIVE PURIFICATION PROGRAM* • We live in a biochemical world, and this book is the solution. While investigating the harmful effects that earlier drug use had on preclears' cases, Ron made the major discovery that many street drugs, particularly LSD, remained in a person's body long after ingested. Residues of the drug, he noted, could have serious and lasting effects, including triggering further "trips." Additional research revealed that a wide range of substances–medical drugs, alcohol, pollutants, household chemicals and even food preservatives–could also lodge in the body's tissues. Through research on thousands of cases, he developed the *Purification Program* to eliminate their destructive effects. Clear Body, Clear Mind details every aspect of the all-natural regimen that can free one from the harmful effects of drugs and other toxins, opening the way for spiritual progress.

REFERENCE HANDBOOKS

WHAT IS SCIENTOLOGY?

The complete and essential encyclopedic reference on the subject and practice of Scientology. Organized for use, this book contains the pertinent data on every aspect of the subject:

• The life of L. Ron Hubbard and his path of discovery

• The Spiritual Heritage of the religion

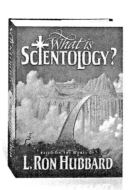

• A full description of Dianetics and Scientology

• Auditing–what it is and how it works

• Courses–what they contain and how they are structured

• The Grade Chart of Services and how one ascends to higher states

• The Scientology Ethics and Justice System

• The Organizational Structure of the Church

• A complete description of the many Social Betterment programs supported by the Church, including: Drug Rehabilitation, Criminal Reform, Literacy and Education and the instilling of real values for morality

Over 1,000 pages in length, with more than 500 photographs and illustrations, this text further includes Creeds, Codes, a full listing of all books and materials as well as a Catechism with answers to virtually any question regarding the subject.

You Ask and This Book Answers.

THE SCIENTOLOGY HANDBOOK

Scientology fundamentals for daily use in every part of life. Encompassing 19 separate bodies of technology, here is the most comprehensive manual on the basics of life ever published. Each chapter contains key principles and technology for your continual use:

• Study Technology

• The Dynamics of Existence

• The Components of Understanding– Affinity, Reality and Communication

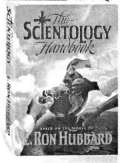

• The Tone Scale

• Communication and its Formulas

• Assists for Illnesses and Injuries

• How to Resolve Conflicts

• Integrity and Honesty

• Ethics and Condition Formulas

• Answers to Suppression and a Dangerous Environment

• Marriage

• Children

• Tools for the Workplace

More than 700 photographs and illustrations make it easy for you to learn the procedures and apply them at once. This book is truly the indispensable handbook for every Scientologist.

The Technology to Build a Better World.

ABOUT L. RON HUBBARD

Io really know life," L. Ron Hubbard wrote, "you've got to be part of life. You must get down and look, you must get into the nooks and crannies of existence. You have to rub elbows with all kinds and types of men before you can finally establish what he is."

Through his long and extraordinary journey to the founding of Dianetics and Scientology, Ron did just that. From his adventurous youth in a rough and tumble American West to his far-flung trek across a still mysterious Asia; from his two-decade search for the very essence of life to the triumph of Dianetics and Scientology—such are the stories recounted in the L. Ron Hubbard Biographical Publications.

Presenting the photographic overview of Ron's greater journey is *L. Ron Hubbard: Images of a Lifetime.* Drawn from his own archival collection, this is Ron's life as he himself saw it.

While for the many aspects of that rich and varied life, stands the Ron Series. Each issue focuses on a specific LRH profession: *Auditor, Humanitarian, Philosopher, Artist, Poet, Music Maker, Photographer* and many more including his published articles on *Freedom* and his personal *Letters & Journals.* Here is the life of a man who lived at least twenty lives in the space of one.

FOR FURTHER INFORMATION VISIT
www.lronhubbard.org

GUIDE TO THE MATERIALS

YOU'RE ON AN ADVENTURE!
HERE'S THE MAP.

- All books
- All lectures
- All reference books

All of it laid out in chronological sequence with descriptions of what each contains.

Your journey to a full understanding of Dianetics and Scientology is the greatest adventure of all. But you need a map that shows you where you are and where you are going.

That map is the Materials Guide Chart. It shows all Ron's books and lectures with a full description of their content and subject matter so you can find exactly what *you* are looking for and precisely what *you* need.

Since each book and lecture is laid out in chronological sequence, you can see *how* the subjects of Dianetics and Scientology were developed. And what that means is by simply studying this chart you are in for cognition after cognition!

New editions of all books include extensive glossaries, containing definitions for every technical term. And as a result of a monumental restoration program, the entire library of Ron's lectures are being made available on compact disc, with complete transcripts, glossaries, lecture graphs, diagrams and issues he refers to in the lectures. As a result, you get *all* the data, and can learn with ease, gaining a full *conceptual* understanding.

And what that adds up to is a new Golden Age of Knowledge every Dianeticist and Scientologist has dreamed of.

**To obtain your FREE Materials Guide Chart and Catalog,
or to order L. Ron Hubbard's books and lectures, contact:**

WESTERN HEMISPHERE:
**Bridge
Publications, Inc.**
4751 Fountain Avenue
Los Angeles, CA 90029 USA
www.bridgepub.com
Phone: 1-800-722-1733
Fax: 1-323-953-3328

EASTERN HEMISPHERE:
**New Era Publications
International ApS**
Store Kongensgade 53
1264 Copenhagen K, Denmark
www.newerapublications.com
Phone: (45) 33 73 66 66
Fax: (45) 33 73 66 33

Books and lectures are also available direct from Churches of Scientology.
*See **Addresses**.*

ADDRESSES

Scientology is the fastest-growing religion in the world today. Churches and Missions exist in cities throughout the world, and new ones are continually forming.

To obtain more information or to locate the Church nearest you, visit the Scientology website:

www.scientology.org
e-mail: info@scientology.org

or

Phone: 1-800-334-LIFE
(for US and Canada)

You can also write to any one of the Continental Organizations, listed on the following page, who can direct you to one of the thousands of Churches and Missions world over.

L. Ron Hubbard's books and lectures may be obtained from any of these addresses or direct from the publishers on the previous page.

CONTINENTAL CHURCH ORGANIZATIONS:

UNITED STATES
CHURCH OF SCIENTOLOGY
CONTINENTAL LIAISON OFFICE
WESTERN UNITED STATES
1308 L. Ron Hubbard Way
Los Angeles, California 90027 USA
info@wus.scientology.org

CHURCH OF SCIENTOLOGY
CONTINENTAL LIAISON OFFICE
EASTERN UNITED STATES
349 W. 48th Street
New York, New York 10036 USA
info@eus.scientology.org

CANADA
CHURCH OF SCIENTOLOGY
CONTINENTAL LIAISON OFFICE
CANADA
696 Yonge Street, 2nd Floor
Toronto, Ontario
Canada M4Y 2A7
info@scientology.ca

LATIN AMERICA
CHURCH OF SCIENTOLOGY
CONTINENTAL LIAISON OFFICE
LATIN AMERICA
Federacion Mexicana de Dianetica
Calle Puebla #31
Colonia Roma, Mexico D.F.
C.P. 06700, Mexico
info@scientology.org.mx

UNITED KINGDOM
CHURCH OF SCIENTOLOGY
CONTINENTAL LIAISON OFFICE
UNITED KINGDOM
Saint Hill Manor
East Grinstead, West Sussex
England, RH19 4JY
info@scientology.org.uk

AFRICA
CHURCH OF SCIENTOLOGY
CONTINENTAL LIAISON OFFICE AFRICA
5 Cynthia Street
Kensington
Johannesburg 2094, South Africa
info@scientology.org.za

AUSTRALIA, NEW ZEALAND & OCEANIA
CHURCH OF SCIENTOLOGY
CONTINENTAL LIAISON OFFICE ANZO
16 Dorahy Street
Dundas, New South Wales 2117
Australia
info@scientology.org.au

Church of Scientology
Liaison Office of Taiwan
1st, No. 231, Cisian 2nd Road
Kaoshiung City
Taiwan, ROC
info@scientology.org.tw

EUROPE
CHURCH OF SCIENTOLOGY
CONTINENTAL LIAISON OFFICE EUROPE
Store Kongensgade 55
1264 Copenhagen K, Denmark
info@scientology.org.dk

Church of Scientology
Liaison Office of Commonwealth
of Independent States
Management Center of Dianetics
and Scientology Dissemination
Pervomajskaya Street, House 1A
Korpus Grazhdanskoy Oboroni
Losino-Petrovsky Town
141150 Moscow, Russia
info@scientology.ru

Church of Scientology
Liaison Office of Central Europe
1082 Leonardo da Vinci u. 8-14
Budapest, Hungary
info@scientology.hu

Church of Scientology
Liaison Office of Iberia
C/Miguel Menendez Boneta, 18
28460 - Los Molinos
Madrid, Spain
info@spain.scientology.org

Church of Scientology
Liaison Office of Italy
Via Cadorna, 61
20090 Vimodrone
Milan, Italy
info@scientology.it

BECOME A MEMBER
OF THE INTERNATIONAL
ASSOCIATION OF SCIENTOLOGISTS

The International Association of Scientologists is the membership organization of all Scientologists united in the most vital crusade on Earth.

A free Six-Month Introductory Membership is extended to anyone who has not held a membership with the Association before.

As a member, you are eligible for discounts on Scientology materials offered only to IAS Members. You also receive the Association magazine, *IMPACT*, issued six times a year, full of Scientology news from around the world.

The purpose of the IAS is:

"To unite, advance, support and protect Scientology and Scientologists in all parts of the world so as to achieve the Aims of Scientology as originated by L. Ron Hubbard."

Join the strongest force for positive change on the planet today, opening the lives of millions to the greater truth embodied in Scientology.

JOIN THE INTERNATIONAL ASSOCIATION OF SCIENTOLOGISTS.
To apply for membership,
write to the International
Association of Scientologists
c/o Saint Hill Manor, East Grinstead
West Sussex, England, RH19 4JY

www.iasmembership.org

EDITOR'S GLOSSARY
OF WORDS, TERMS AND PHRASES

Words often have several meanings. The definitions used here only give the meaning that the word has as it is used in this book. Dianetics and Scientology terms appear in bold type. Beside each definition you will find the page on which it first appears, so you can refer back to the text if you wish.

This glossary is not meant to take the place of standard language or Dianetics and Scientology dictionaries, which should be referred to for any words, terms or phrases that do not appear below.

—The Editors

′ (prime): a symbol written above and to the right of a name, letter, figure, etc., and used to distinguish it from another of the same kind. For example, Joe and Joe′ are the same name (and person) but the prime symbol represents Joe (prime) in different circumstances, conditions or actions. Page 134.

abandoned: utterly lacking in moral restraint; shameless. Page 45.

aberrated: affected by *aberration*. Aberrated conduct would be wrong conduct, or conduct not supported by reason. Aberration is any deviation or departure from rationality. Page 36.

aberration: any deviation or departure from rationality. *Aberration* is described in Chapter Seven, Communication. Page 30.

abhorred: regarded with horror or disgust, detested. Page 3.

ability: the quality of being able to do something; power or capacity to act. Page 21.

absoluteness: the state or condition of being free from restriction or condition; perfect or complete. The suffix *-ness* is used when forming nouns expressing a state, quality or condition. Page 48.

absolute zero: a theoretical temperature that is thought to be the lowest-possible temperature, the point at which all molecular activity ceases. Page 47.

abstractacity: the quality or condition of being unknown or uncertain or being difficult to understand. Page 3.

accent: stress or emphasis; focus of attention. Page 57.

acceptance level: the acceptance level of a preclear is the condition in which a person or object must be in order that the preclear be able to accept it freely. Page 190.

Acceptance Level Processes: an *Acceptance Level Process* is a process which discovers the lowest level of acceptance of the individual and discovers there the prevailing hunger (what the person desires) and feeds that hunger by means of mock-ups until it is satiated. Acceptance Level Processing works because the individual has been inhibited from having something long enough that he craves it. Page 190.

addled: made confused; caused to be unclear in mind or intent. Page 121.

Adler: Alfred Adler (1870-1937), Austrian psychiatrist and psychologist who theorized that people were primarily motivated to overcome inherent feelings of inferiority. Page 121.

adverbial clause(s): a group of words (acting like an adverb) modifying another word or words, telling how, when, where or to what extent the action of the sentence is performed. For example, in "She will find the letter when she returns," the adverbial clause "when she returns" tells when she will find the letter. Because of their nature, adverbial clauses can be used to greatly expand and lengthen a basic sentence. Page 63.

afield: to a distance; away from a given point. Page 11.

agent: a means by which something is done or caused; a force or substance that causes a change. Page 26.

Alexander: Alexander the Great (356-323 B.C.), military general and king of Macedonia (an ancient kingdom in what is now northern Greece and neighboring countries) who executed people (including his own) if they appeared to be a threat to him. Page 4.

Allied: of or relating to the *Allies* (Great Britain, France and Russia, later joined by the United States, Italy, Japan, etc.) in World War I (1914-1918), the nations allied by treaty against Germany, Austria-Hungary, Turkey and Bulgaria. Page 93.

all manner of: many different kinds of; all sorts of. Page 154.

all very nice: fine or acceptable as far as it goes (implying that it may be unsatisfactory in other ways). Used when something seems good by itself but has problems or situations connected with it. Page 111.

ally: a person who has aided in the survival of the preclear under engramic or highly emotional circumstances and whom the preclear reactively regards as important to his further survival. The individual will go into the personality of an ally just to keep him around. Page 212.

along (the lines): in accordance or conformity with, as in *"it works exactly along the lines it is designed."* Page 17.

AMA: an abbreviation for *American Medical Association*. Page 157.

anchored down: fixed firmly as if held in place with an *anchor,* a heavy device for keeping a ship or other floating object in place. *Down* means into or toward a secure position. Page 170.

anchor points: assigned or agreed-upon points of boundary which are conceived to be motionless by the individual. Page 191.

answer up to: give a (suitable) reply to a question asked. Page 79.

any more than: using a second item of (graphic) comparison to show that the first item being denied must be as stated, as in *"he is not his body any more than he is his house or his car."* Page 35.

arbitrary: based on judgment or useful selection rather than on the fixed nature of something. Page 45.

archangel Smearel: a humorous made-up name for an archangel (an angel of high rank). *Arch* means chief or principal. Page 156.

A-R-C Scale: the Tone Scale, a scale of emotional tones which shows the levels of human behavior. These tones, ranged from the highest to the lowest, are, in part, Enthusiasm, Boredom, Antagonism, Anger, Covert Hostility, Fear, Grief and Apathy. Even lower tones exist which are minus tones, such as -8.0, Hiding. The Tone Scale is described in *Science of Survival* as well as in *Scientology 8-80*. Page 178.

arduous: severe or demanding. Page 44.

ascendance: the action of rising (to a higher state, level or position). Page 98.

ascertain: find out definitely; learn with certainty or assurance; determine. Page 112.

As-ised: erased, made to disappear. *As-is* is a Scientology term meaning causing something to vanish or cease to exist by viewing it exactly as it is. Page 88.

assumption: something taken for granted or accepted as true without proof. Also something accepted as true as a basis for further investigation, research, application, etc. Page 14.

as the case may be: according to the circumstances. Used when referring to two or more possible alternatives. Page 189.

as to: with respect or reference to; with regard to; concerning. Page 150.

astral walking: in spiritualism, an astral body is the belief in a sort of spirit body or a "double" of the physical body. Astral walking is the belief by spiritualists that this astral body could be separated from and journey outside the physical body and when it did so was composed of a spirit *and* mind *and* body. This is in contrast to Scientology where the awareness of awareness unit can *fully* detach, by itself, from both mind and body (exteriorization). Page 42.

at hand: nearby or close. Hence, under discussion or being dealt with in present time. Page 107.

at home: willing to receive visitors. Page 39.

at the hands of: performed by (someone) or through the action or operation of (someone). Page 46.

at the same time: used in introducing a reservation, explanation or contrast with the meaning while saying this; nevertheless; however. Page 65.

atomic fission: the splitting of the central part of an atom (nucleus) which is accompanied by a significant release of energy. The pieces of the nucleus then strike other nuclei (centers of atoms) and cause them to fission (split), thus creating a chain reaction, the principle of the atomic bomb. Page 14.

atomic pile: a nuclear reactor, an assembly of materials and equipment used to initiate, sustain and control atomic fission for the purpose of generating useful energy. The term *pile* came from the fact that the first reactor ever built consisted of special blocks of material stacked into a large "pile" which controlled the nuclear reaction and prevented explosion. Page 14.

attain (to): to arrive at or succeed in reaching or obtaining something. Page 14.

at work: in action or operation, especially directed to a definite end or result. Page 38.

auditing: the application of Dianetics and Scientology techniques and exercises. Page 70.

auditor: one who listens and computes, a practitioner of Dianetics and Scientology. Page 6.

automaticity: a mechanism of the mind set up by an individual to carry out an action automatically for which he then abandons responsibility. It now operates "on automatic," outside his control and awareness. To create a game and have randomity, an individual mocks-up players in the game and then "forgets" he created them. Failing to control the communication of the other players, a scarcity of acknowledgment occurs. Believing he has to have mass to compensate for this lack of communication, the individual sets up automaticities. Page 213.

automatic machinery: the mechanisms or devices the analytical mind sets up to do things automatically, such as carry out commands, perform certain actions, etc. Page 189.

Babylon: the capital of *Babylonia,* an ancient empire of southwest Asia (located in what is now southern Iraq) which flourished ca. 2100-689 B.C. The most important city in western Asia during this time period, Babylon was wealthy through commerce, and famous for its magnificent temples and palaces. However, by 538 B.C. it had been destroyed, rebuilt and finally captured by the neighboring Persians, becoming a region of that empire. Page 4.

back of this: serving as a foundation for or basis of something. Page 96.

balked: 1. thwarted or stopped as if by obstacles. Page 62.
2. stopped short (at); refused to go past. Page 116.

ball, wind up in a: end up in a confusion or tangled mess. Page 123.

banality: something common or ordinary. Page 210.

bank: 1. the mental image picture collection which forms the storage system of the mind, an analogy to memory storage in a computer. Page 27.
2. same as *reactive mind.* For a description of the reactive mind, see Chapter Two, The Fundamentals of Life. Page 107.

bear pit: a large hole dug in the ground, often covered with sticks and leaves, to capture or kill bears. When the intent is to kill, sharp stakes are planted in the pit piercing the bear when it falls in. Page 92.

become: having taken on the characteristics or qualities of; moved from one state of existence to another, as in *"when Man, become a machine, runs wild."* Page 14.

behold: hold in view; look at or observe. Page 25.

beingness: condition or state of being; existence. Page 14.

Bennington: the Battle of Bennington, a battle fought on August 16, 1777, during the American Revolutionary War (1775-1783), near the town of Bennington in southwest Vermont. The battle was a significant victory for the Americans. Page 111.

bent: 1. changed (dishonestly) or corrupted, likened to altering something from an originally straight or even condition. Page 7.
2. strongly inclined; determined to take a course of action, usually with the word *on* or *upon*. Page 44.

besting: winning over, defeating or getting the better of. Page 36.

Better Business Bureau: an organization established in 1912 by businesses supposedly to protect the public from false advertising and unethical selling practices. It consists of some 200 independent organizations. Better Business Bureau reports have consistently been used to attempt to discredit new ideas and innovations. Page 5.

biological: having to do with the use and application of the principles or methods of *biology,* the study of living things, purely from a physical and chemical standpoint. Page 93.

blackboard(s): a sheet of dark, smooth, hard material used in schools, lecture rooms, etc., for writing or drawing on with chalk. Page 122.

blind alley: literally, a *blind alley* is a narrow passageway or lane, especially one running between or behind buildings, which is closed at one end. Hence, a course of action that fails to effect its purpose or from which there is no resultant benefit or apparently leads nowhere. Page 79.

blowing (the session): slang for departing suddenly; leaving hurriedly. Page 196.

blow into view: appear or turn up, especially unexpectedly, likened to something suddenly moved along or carried in by the wind or a gust of air. Page 211.

blown: caused something to dissipate and disappear; discharged. Page 171.

bogged: became mired down, sunk in, as if in a bog (wet, spongy ground). Page 150.

Book Auditor: an auditor without any professional training who audits based on information he has read in Dianetics and Scientology books. Page 77.

botany: the science or study of plants, their life, structure, growth, classification, etc. Page 145.

brave: to meet or face courageously. Page 230.

break: slang used in the wise of *breaking a case,* meaning that one breaks the hold of the preclear on something non-survival. Never breaking the preclear or his spirit, but breaking what is breaking the preclear. Page 182.

breed of feline: coined variation of *breed of cat,* meaning kind or type of person. A *feline* means of a cat or the cat family (domestic cats, lions, tigers, etc.). Page 6.

bric-a-brac: small, miscellaneous objects which may be pretty or of interest but which have little artistic or monetary value. By extension, miscellaneous, nonessential things or objects of little worth. Page 44.

brief: of limited extent. Page 147.

bring (someone) up: elevate, raise or cause to move in the direction of a higher position or grade. Page 179.

bunk, doing a: making an escape; departing hurriedly. In Dianetics and Scientology it refers to the awareness of awareness unit compulsively going outside the body (running away). Page 221.

buster: something which breaks something up, blows something open or apart, as in *"planet buster."* Page 90.

but: no more than; only, as in *"a prima donna who can but croak."* Page 5.

buttered: smeared or spread out or distributed over a surface or space, likened to the action of spreading butter over something. Page 241.

button: literally, a rounded switch which when pushed operates a machine, light, etc. Figuratively, anything resembling such a button for its ease of use in quickly producing a single effect. Page 38.

bypasses: roads diverging from and reentering a main road, especially ones constructed as alternative routes to relieve congestion or traffic in a town. Page 87.

byproduct(s): something produced in addition to or as a result of the principal thing being referenced. Page 25.

by their fear you shall know them: a reference to a line from the Bible, "by their fruits [results] ye [you] shall know them" meaning one knows someone or others by the results or outcome of their actions. Hence, in this sense, if one observes that certain individuals are in fear, he will know more about them and the consequences of their actions. Page 44.

byword: a word, statement or phrase expressing the guiding principle or rule of action of an individual, group or time period. Page 242.

call back: re-create (in the mind). Page 29.

calling: one's job, profession or trade. Page 16.

canned: prerecorded in a standardized form for general and repetitive use, thought of as patterned and unoriginal. For example, many weekly radio and television shows are recorded in advance for later broadcast, utilizing prerecorded laughter, clapping and other predictable, repetitive elements. Page 137.

capital: the general body of capitalists, especially with regard to their political interests. *Capitalists* are people who have wealth, especially extensive wealth, invested in business enterprises and are thought of as being primarily motivated by self-interest and profit. Page 5.

cards (card-file system): cards with patterns of holes punched in them, used to store information in early computers of the 1950s. The information was stored in the cards by making holes or notches that represented letters and numbers. The filed card(s) could be retrieved and fed into a machine which was able to read the pattern and thus work with the stored information. Page 27.

carrier wave: waves are the form in which things such as sound, light and radio signals travel. A *carrier wave* is a special type of wave used in radio transmission that carries another communication or signal on top of it so that it can be received correctly and heard on a radio. Hence, by extension, any wave that carries something else along with it from a source. Page 211.

case(s): 1. a general term for a person being or about to be audited, as in *"A recent series of cases...has now concluded successfully."* Page 39.
2. the entire accumulation of the facsimiles, energy masses, machinery, stimulus-response mechanisms, etc., of the individual, as in *"'Self-clearing' has not been found possible where the individual was badly mired in his own case."* Page 46.

cataloged: systematically arranged and listed. Page 13.

causation: the power, influence or source by which something comes into existence, an action takes place or by which an effect is created. Page 6.

causative: characteristic of or having the nature of being cause as opposed to effect; originated or produced by one's own efforts; able to cause things, effective. Page 13.

Cause: *Cause* is simply the source-point of emanation of the communication. Page 60.

cause: *cause* is a potential source of flow. Page 42.

cause-point: the source of emanation; the basic point of emanation. Page 26.

cell(s): a small group dedicated to the study and development of communism, especially, the smallest organizational unit of the Communist Party often located within and made up of employees of a particular business, industry, school, etc. Page 93.

Central Organization: the main Scientology organization responsible for its geographical zone or area and which delivers training and processing. See *Addresses* for current locations. Page 39.

Chaldea: a region of ancient *Babylonia,* an ancient empire of southwest Asia (located in what is now southern Iraq). Chaldean leaders developed a vast civilization in Babylonia (625 B.C.) called the New Babylonian Empire which gained control of a large part of the present-day Middle East until destroyed by neighboring Persia about 100 years later. Page 4.

Chaldean priest: a reference to the priests of *Chaldea,* an ancient region that formed part of the empire of *Babylonia* (located in what is now southern Iraq). Renowned as fortunetellers for predicting movements of the Sun, Moon and stars, the Chaldean priests used their knowledge to control their kings, who came to rule over all of the Babylonian Empire (625 B.C.) until destroyed by neighboring Persia about 100 years later. Page 4.

change off: move from one method or procedure or the like to another one. Page 80.

changingness: a state or condition of *change,* that is, an alteration or modification of characteristic, quality, form, etc. Any change involves time. For there to be time, there must be change. Page 29.

charlatan: one who pretends to have expert knowledge or skill; a fake. Page 4.

Chart of Human Evaluation: the Hubbard Chart of Human Evaluation, contained in the book *Science of Survival,* which gives a complete description of the Tone Scale. It includes the components and characteristics of the human mind, each one plotted on the Tone Scale, providing a complete prediction of an individual's behavior and an index of their survival potential from lowest to highest. *Science of Survival* is written around the Hubbard Chart of Human Evaluation with a chapter devoted to and describing each section of the chart. Page 178.

cheery word, a: a remark or comment showing or suggesting optimism, good spirits, etc. Page 38.

chronic somatics: suboptimum physical conditions or pains which resist change and remain over a long period of time or recur frequently. *Somatic* here means a physical feeling. Page 232.

circuit: a division of the mind that behaves as though it has a life of its own and dictates to the preclear. Page 26.

Clear: the name of a state achieved through processing or an individual who has achieved this state. A *Clear* is simply an awareness of awareness unit which knows it is an awareness of awareness unit, can create energy at will and can handle and control, erase or re-create an analytical mind or a reactive mind. See *Dianetics: The Modern Science of Mental Health.* Page 6.

cleared: brought to the state of Clear. A *Clear* is simply an awareness of awareness unit which knows it is an awareness of awareness unit, can create energy at will and can handle and control, erase or re-create an analytical mind or a reactive mind. See *Dianetics: The Modern Science of Mental Health.* Page 6.

cliché object, the minister's son: a *cliché* is something that has lost its originality through overuse and constant repetition. In this case, the often-told story of the minister's son who turns out to be committing sins or doing evil. Page 45.

climb (up): to move or ascend upward with effort. Page 172.

clinical: purely scientific. Also based on actual observation of individuals rather than theory. Page 128.

clinical psychology: *clinical,* in this sense, means involving or based on direct observation of a patient. *Clinical psychology* refers to the supposed study, diagnosis and treatment of mental and behavior disorders. Frequently, clinical psychologists work in a medical setting with psychiatrists and other physicians and employ both psychotherapy as well as psychological tests. The practice of psychoanalysis was at one time strictly limited to psychiatrists (medical doctors working in the field of "mental illness"). Page 76.

close: done in a careful and thorough way. Page 40.

close (theory): strictly logical. Page 196.

closing with: drawing near; gradually getting nearer to something; approaching. Page 39.

cocked: (of a gun) having the firing mechanism in a position ready to shoot. Page 93.

codes: a system of symbols, letters or words given certain meanings, used for transmitting messages requiring secrecy. Page 3.

codified: arranged into an organized system or orderly collection. Page 40.

coffin into which (one) nails himself: a variation of *the final nail in the coffin* meaning an event which causes the failure of something that was already failing. Page 63.

cog: a *cog* is literally part of a cogwheel, a wheel that has teeth (called cogs) of hardwood or metal made to insert between the teeth of another wheel so that they mesh. When one cogwheel is rotated, the other wheel is turned as well, thus transferring the motion to drive machinery. The term *cog* can be used to describe an individual carrying out minor, automatic actions as part of a larger, uncaring "machine." Page 13.

colonial America: pertaining to the thirteen British colonies that won their independence from Great Britain and became the United States of America. Also pertaining to the time period they existed as colonies from 1607 to 1775. Page 87.

come to pieces: to break up, dissolve, fall apart. Page 209.

commodities: useful or valuable things, likened to raw material or a primary agricultural product that is needed and sought after. Page 4.

common coin: a thing that is customary or current due to being commonly discussed, mentioned or accepted. Page 110.

common denominator: something common to or characteristic of a number of people, things, situations, etc.; shared characteristic. Page 70.

communication lag: the length of time intervening between the posing of the question, or origination of a statement, and the exact moment that question or original statement is answered. Communication lag is fully described in Chapter Ten, Communication Lag. Page 78.

Communist Party: a group which forwards the political theory or system in which all property and wealth is owned by all the members of a classless society and the Party, with absolute power, runs the economic and political systems of the state. Extensive restrictions are enforced on personal liberties and freedom, and individual rights are overruled by the collective needs of the masses. Page 5.

compliances: actions or directions agreed to, obeyed or taken because they are required or expected. Page 13.

concentrated: increased in strength, intensity or power, as if by being focused or gathered together. Page 207.

conception: beginning, origination. Page 12.

concerned, as (so) far as (something) is: used to give facts or an opinion about a particular aspect of (something). Page 11.

confreres: fellow members of a profession; colleagues. Page 126.

connotates: has an additional sense or senses associated with or suggested by a word. Page 92.

consciencelessly: in a manner without conscience (the internal sense of what is right and wrong in one's motives or conduct, impelling one toward right action). Page 17.

consideration(s): an idea or opinion or thought. Page 60.

constitute: make (a person) something; appoint to a function; designate. Page 196.

constricted: held in; limited; slowed or stopped. Page 95.

contagious: for the care of patients whose diseases are contagious (able to spread to others by direct or indirect contact), as in "contagious wards." Page 66.

contemplated: looked at, viewed with continued attention; studied thoughtfully. Page 37.

contemplating: having in mind as an intention or possibility; thinking about something as a possible course of action. Page 14.

conundrum: a puzzle or problem that is usually intricate and difficult to solve. Page 204.

conviction: a belief that excludes doubt; a strong belief. Page 16.

convulsions: extreme disruptions or disturbances; periods of violent turmoil. Page 40.

couched: expressed or manifested in a veiled or nonobvious manner. Page 66.

credence: acceptance based on the degree to which something is believable or thought of as real or valid. Page 4.

cubic: of or pertaining to a cube, a solid figure of six equal square sides. A cubic inch refers to the amount of space or volume inside a cube with all sides one inch in height and width. Page 230.

cubist: having to do with cubism, a French art movement of the early twentieth century, in which images are separated into abstract arrangements of cubes and other geometric forms. In literature, to reflect this abstract arrangement, writers use unusual and unexpected associations and disassociations in imagery, different points of view, etc. Page 109.

currency: that which is current as a means of exchange, such as a coin, paper currency, etc. Hence, the language or communication used in intellectual exchange or expression. Page 110.

cycle-of-action: the sequence that an action goes through, wherein the action is started, is continued for as long as is required and then is completed as planned; start, change and stop. Page 106.

dabbler: one who engages in an activity superficially or without serious intent and who lacks professional skill. Page 6.

daresay: to be as bold as to say, because one is prepared to state it is a fact or true. Page 92.

Dark Age of Reason: a period of severe decline within a civilization which is without knowledge or culture; a period characterized by ignorance and a lack of intellectual and spiritual activity. Page 4.

day and age, in this: at the present time; at the moment of speaking or writing. Page 157.

debars: prevents from an action; sets a barrier or prohibition against. Page 94.

decisional: able to decide, choose, conclude or determine. Page 28.

deeper significances: the profound, mysterious or hidden meanings or influences of something, as contrasted with the direct simplicity of what actually is. Page 38.

delineated: represented or expressed. Page 61.

delineation: description or precise outlining (of something). Page 25.

demon circuits: in Dianetics, a "demon" is a parasitic circuit. It has an action in the mind which approximates another entity than self and was considered in Dianetics to be derived entirely from words in engrams. Their phenomena are described in *Dianetics: The Modern Science of Mental Health.* Page 95.

determinism: the ability to determine the course of or the decision about. Page 36.

detonative: explosive; capable of exploding or making something else explode. Page 14.

dichotomy: a pair of opposites. Page 91.

digestible: readily or easily absorbed or assimilated. Also, able to be endured. Page 14.

diplomas: certificates issued by an educational institution (school, university, etc.) certifying that the person has satisfactorily completed a course of study. Page 3.

disenfranchised: removed from or deprived of something such as a right, object, pleasure, etc. Page 40.

dismayed: worried, upset or agitated. Page 104.

disseminated: distributed or spread, as information and knowledge. Page 77.

dissertation: an extended usually systematic written or verbal treatment of a subject. Page 26.

distortion: a condition of the body or any part of the body being twisted out of the natural shape. Page 87.

do (someone) wrong: to harm or injure (someone). Page 44.

doggedly: with determination to continue without giving up in spite of difficulties. Page 139.

doing a bunk: making an escape; departing hurriedly. In Dianetics and Scientology it refers to the awareness of awareness unit compulsively going outside the body (running away). Page 221.

drag: a force or action that slows down movement or hinders progress in a direction. Page 94.

drop back to: to fall or pass into some previous (worse) condition or situation. Page 195.

drops into (something): falls or passes into some (unexpected) state or condition. Page 231.

drowned in: completely covered with, as if submerged in a liquid. Page 12.

dustbinned: a chiefly British term meaning ignored or discarded to a place of neglect or oblivion, as being thrown into a trash can (dustbin). Page 4.

dwindling spiral: the worse an individual gets, the more capacity he has to get worse. *Spiral* here refers to a progressive downward movement, marking a relentlessly deteriorating state of affairs, and considered to take the form of a spiral. The term comes from aviation where it is used to describe the phenomenon of a plane descending and spiraling in smaller and smaller circles, as in an accident or feat of expert flying, which if not handled can result in loss of control and a crash. Page 64.

dyed-in-the-wool: wholeheartedly and stubbornly attached to something and totally convinced of its merits (good or praiseworthy characteristics). *Dyed-in-the-wool* is a reference to raw wool that has been dyed before being spun into yarn, serving to more firmly fix the color in the material because the dye permeates the fibers more thoroughly than would be achieved by dyeing the wool after it has been made into yarn. Hence, someone who is totally or thoroughly permeated with some characteristic or thoroughly devoted to something. Page 48.

Dynamic: an urge, a thrust, a motion toward survival; an energetic urge in a certain direction. The dynamics are described in Chapter Eleven, Pan-determinism. Page 61.

Dynamic, First: is the urge toward survival as self. Page 126.

Dynamic, Fourth: is the urge toward survival through all Mankind and as all Mankind. Page 97.

Dynamic, Second: is the urge toward survival through sex or children and embraces both the sexual act and the care and raising of children. Page 115.

Dynamic, Third: the urge toward survival through the group and as the group. Page 61.

dynamics: the forces that characterize something or the laws that relate to them. Page 11.

Eastern: of, relating to or characteristic of the *East,* the southern and eastern part of Asia, including India, China and Japan. Page 116.

East, the: used to refer to the southern and eastern part of Asia, including India, China and Japan. Page 42.

echelon: a level, as in a steplike arrangement or order; one of a series in a field of activity. Page 112.

Effect: *Effect* is the receipt-point of the communication. Page 60.

effect: *effect* is a potential receipt of flow. Page 42.

efficacity: capacity for producing a desired result or effect; effectiveness. Page 203.

egress: a going out or issuing forth. Page 204.

electric shock: the firing of 180 to 460 volts of electricity through the brain from temple to temple or from the front to the back of one side of the head. It causes a severe convulsion (uncontrollable shaking of the body) or seizure (unconsciousness and inability to control movements of the body) of long duration. Page 11.

electrodes: a reference to the cans a person holds in his hands when connected to an E-Meter. Page 28.

electrodes: a reference to the metal discs placed on a person's head through which a heavy electrical current is passed through the brain, as used by psychiatrists in administering electric shock. An *electrode* is a contact through which an electric current enters or leaves a machine, appliance, instrument or device. Page 4.

electronic brain: a computer. Page 21.

electronics: the science dealing with the development and application of devices and systems involving the flow of electrical energy in vacuums, gases and solids. Page 28.

Elementary Straightwire: simply a communication with the past and securing of answers from the past. Elementary Straightwire is described in Chapter Twelve, The Six Basic Processes. Page 177.

elicited: drew out, caused or produced something as a reaction or response. Page 152.

emanates: flows out, as from a source or origin. Page 60.

embedded: firmly or deeply fixed (in the mind or memory). Page 81.

E-Meter: short for *electropsychometer,* a specially designed instrument that can detect the production of energy by the analytical mind. (*Electro* means electric or electricity, *psycho* means soul, and *meter* means measure.) The E-Meter is described in Chapter Two, The Fundamentals of Life. Page 196.

Emotional Scale: the Tone Scale. Page 167.

encroaching: advancing gradually into an area, often lessening its power or authority. Page 5.

Encyclopaedia Britannica: a large comprehensive reference work containing articles on a wide range of subjects. It is the oldest continuously published reference work in English, first printed in 1771. *Britannica* is Latin for British. Page 25.

endeared: regarded with affection; valued highly. Page 3.

endeavor(s): 1. an earnest and industrious effort, especially over a period of time. Page 12.
2. an undertaking or purposeful activity. Page 25.

endowed: (of qualities, abilities or characteristics) provided or given to. Page 21.

ensnare: to catch or entangle (persons) in difficulties; to entrap. A *snare* is a trapping device, often consisting of a noose, used for small animals. Page 4.

ensue: follow as a consequence or result. Page 98.

enters into: becomes or is one of the factors or ingredients that are a part of or relevant to something. Page 171.

entheta: in Scientology, theta is life. *Entheta* is enturbulated theta–theta which has been confused and chaotically mixed with the material universe. Page 170.

entities: ridges that think. They form a very complex pattern. They have geographical areas in the body. These areas are standard, preclear to preclear. These areas answer up like actual minds rather than compartments of a mind. They are actually the basis of "demon circuits" (as covered in *Dianetics: The Modern Science of Mental Health*). Page 95.

enturbulation: the state of being turbulent, agitated or disturbed. Page 170.

equanimity: mental or emotional stability or composure, especially under tension or strain; calmness. Page 15.

equatorial: relating to or present near the *equator*, the imaginary great circle around the Earth that is the same distance from the North and South Poles. The Sun's rays are most direct at the equator and very intense. Page 92.

equilibrium: a state of rest or balance due to the equal action of opposing forces, such as a glass sitting on a table. According to physics theory, the glass is pushing down as much as the table is "pushing up." Page 47.

erasure: the recounting of an engram until it has vanished entirely. See *Dianetics: The Modern Science of Mental Health*. Page 27.

esoteric: intended for or understood by only a limited (small) group who have special knowledge, such as those of a particular profession. Page 4.

esoteric schools: originally the word *esoteric* was coined in the second century A.D. to describe Aristotle's (Greek philosopher 384-322 B.C.) more complex writings. It was believed that these works contained "secrets" only divulged to those who would spread Aristotle's teachings. Hence, *esoteric* came to mean, a philosophical doctrine intended to be revealed only to a select group. *Esoteric schools* are those of philosophy, theology, spiritualism, etc., that search for a higher meaning in life which is said to be knowable only through direct experience and impossible to teach or express in words. For comparison *see* monotony schools. Page 4.

euthanasia: the act of putting to death or allowing a person suffering from an incurable disease or condition to die. Page 68.

evaluation: the act of telling a person what is wrong with him or what to think about his case. Page 76.

event, in any: used to emphasize or show that something is true or will happen in spite of other circumstances. Page 82.

expectance level: a future-type "acceptance level." The acceptance level of a preclear is the condition in which a person or object must be in order that the preclear be able to accept it freely. Page 190.

expectancy: the state or condition where one is waiting for (expecting) an acknowledgment, answer or origination from another. Page 109.

exteriorization: the act of moving outside of the body. *Exteriorization* is described in Chapter Three, The Awareness of Awareness Unit. Page 38.

face of, in the: when confronted with. Page 15.

facet: one of the several parts or sides of something; a particular aspect of a thing. Page 203.

fact (that), in view of the: for the reason (that); since; because. Page 30.

fall away: move away, often into a lessened or diminished state, as in *"Stupidity, ignorance, illness, aberration, incapability are only a fall away from 'understanding.'"* Page 58.

falling off: moving away from; withdrawing from, often into a lessened or diminished state. Page 166.

fantastic: highly unrealistic or impractical. Page 15.

fascist: one who practices *fascism,* a governmental system led by a dictator having complete power, which forcibly suppresses opposition and criticism and regiments all industry, commerce, etc. Page 58.

fates: the supposed forces, principles or powers that predetermine events, the results of which are unavoidable. The word comes from the belief in three Greek and Roman goddesses (the Fates) who were thought to control the course of human events. Page 15.

feline, breed of: coined variation of *breed of cat,* meaning kind or type of person. A *feline* means of a cat or the cat family (domestic cats, lions, tigers, etc.). Page 6.

First Dynamic: is the urge toward survival as self. Page 126.

fishnet: like a net used to catch fish. Used figuratively. Page 140.

fission, atomic: the splitting of the central part of an atom (nucleus) which is accompanied by a significant release of energy. The pieces of the nucleus then strike other nuclei (centers of atoms) and cause them to fission (split), thus creating a chain reaction, the principle of the atomic bomb. Page 14.

fission fascist: a coined term from *fission* and *fascist*, describing government leaders who favor and promote the development and aggressive use of nuclear weapons. Page 58.

fixated: having the attention commanded exclusively or repeatedly (on something). Page 97.

flagrant: shockingly obvious or evident. Page 135.

flatten: flattening a communication lag is described in Chapter Ten, Communication Lag. Page 81.

fleet: a number of warships under one command, usually in a definite area of operation. Also, used to refer to the entire naval force of a country. Page 93.

fleet, grand: a reference to the naval force of Germany prior to World War I (1914-1918). Having built up its number of warships in the years before the start of the war, the German Navy was one of the most powerful in the world. However, in the final months of the war, political unrest among the crews made operation of most of the ships impossible and they were even being sunk by their own personnel. Page 93.

float: remain suspended so as to stay in a certain position or condition. Page 29.

flounder: to move or act clumsily and in confusion. Page 93.

flying the red flag: under communist rule, or supporting communism; from the red flag flown on a ship indicating that it is under communist command. The red flag is a common symbol of communism. Page 93.

formidable: difficult to overcome or deal with; challenging. Page 94.

formula(s): in mathematics, a rule or principle represented in symbols, numbers or letters, often equating one thing to another. Example: $A + 4 = 7$. From this one can figure out that $A = 3$. Page 47.

for that matter: used to add a comment about something just said with the meaning as far as that is concerned; as for that. Page 11.

Fourth Dynamic: is the urge toward survival through all Mankind and as all Mankind. Page 97.

frame of conduct: a set of ideas, concepts, views, etc., by means of which a group or individual evaluates or interprets how to behave or act, especially in regards to morality and ethics. Page 76.

frame of reference: a set of concepts, values, customs, views, etc., by means of which an individual or group perceives or evaluates data, communicates ideas and regulates behavior. Page 23.

freakish: of the nature of a *freak,* extremely unusual or oddly different from what is normal. Page 80.

freethinker: a person who rejects authority and tradition as the basis of knowledge in favor of rational methods of investigation. Page 4.

Freudian analysis: also called psychoanalysis, a system of mental therapy developed by Sigmund Freud (1856-1939) in Austria in 1894 and which depended upon the following practices for its effects: the patient was made to talk about and recall his childhood for years while the practitioner searched for hidden sexual incidents believed by Freud to be the cause of aberration. The practitioner read significances into all statements and evaluated them for the patient (told him what to think) along sex-related lines. Page 68.

from terms of: with respect to, in relation to, or in ways of thought belonging to (a particular category); in comparison with. Page 168.

from the same mold: from the exact same origin and hence were identical. An allusion to forming a series of objects from a mold or form, resulting in a multitude of things that are the same shape, design, form, etc. Page 169.

from the standpoint of: a position from which things (such as objects, principles or the like) are or may be viewed and according to which they are compared and judged. Page 108.

galaxy: a huge system of billions of stars and their planets, gas and dust held together by gravitation and isolated from similar systems by vast regions of space. Page 47.

gamut: a complete range or extent of something. Page 182.

germinated: began to grow, developed; came into existence. Page 12.

get (one) into: cause (someone) to take part in, perform or undertake, as in *"to get him into communication."* Page 209.

getting on with: continuing to do something, especially after an interruption; proceeding with. Page 135.

get very low on: become extremely close to having one's supply of something exhausted. *Low* in this sense means nearing depletion or not adequately supplied. Page 137.

glut on the market: something that is overabundant or is no longer in demand in the market and so has lost its value or use and can no longer be sold. A *glut* is an excessive supply of something. *Market* is the whole area of economic activity where buyers are in contest with sellers and in which the laws of supply and demand operate. Used figuratively. Page 125.

godlings: minor gods, especially those whose influence or authority is entirely local. Page 162.

goes about: begins or carries on work at (something); undertakes. Page 46.

go in for: engage or participate in; attempt or try. Page 221.

going around: being spread from one person to another. Page 147.

good and solid: used ironically to mean MEST. *Good* in this sense means very and is used to intensify the word that follows it. *Solid* means filled with matter throughout; compact in substance. Page 5.

goose egg: zero or nothing, a reference to the egg-shaped numeral 0. Page 47.

go out of: to cease to take part in; perform or undertake. Page 60.

grace, saving: a quality or characteristic that makes up for other generally negative characteristics; redeeming feature. Page 12.

grade: of or pertaining to a degree or rating in a scale classified according to quality, rank, worth, intensity, etc. Page 64.

gradient scale: a scale of lessening or increasing degrees of condition. The difference between one point on a gradient scale and another point could be as different or as wide as the entire range of the scale itself. Or it could be as tiny as to need the most minute discernment for its establishment. Page 91.

grand fleet: a reference to the naval force of Germany prior to World War I (1914-1918). Having built up its number of warships in the years before the start of the war, the German Navy was one of the most powerful in the world. However, in the final months of the war, political unrest among the crews made operation of most of the ships impossible and they were even being sunk by their own personnel. Page 93.

grant beingness: admit the existence of; give life to. *Grant* means to give, hand out, etc. *Beingness* means existingness in a form. Page 78.

graphic: giving a clear and effective picture as if represented in a picture or drawing. Page 60.

grave: any scene or occasion of utter loss, extinction or disappearance; ruin. Page 63.

Great Chinaman of Königsberg: a reference to German philosopher Immanuel Kant (1724-1804), who was born and lived in the city of Königsberg (part of Germany in Kant's time). German philosopher

Friedrich Nietzsche (1844-1900) referred to Kant as the Great Chinaman of Königsberg due to the similarities between Kant's views on virtue and duty and those of the ancient Chinese philosopher Confucius (fifth century B.C.). Page 63.

grind: a continuing action requiring a great deal of effort; laborious work. Page 80.

groggy: sleepy or semiconscious. Page 81.

Group Processing: processing given by a single auditor to a group of individuals gathered in one room. Page 70.

hallmark: literally, a mark put on gold, silver and other fine metal objects that shows the quality of the metal and gives information about when and where the object was made. Hence, any distinguishing or identifying feature or characteristic. Page 82.

hand, at: nearby or close. Hence, under discussion or being dealt with in present time. Page 107.

hands of, out of the: away from the power, influence or direction of. Page 52.

hand, to: near or close by; easily available and ready to be used. Page 70.

hanging to: holding firmly to; clinging tightly to. Page 231.

hang up: to suspend from a hook or rail. Hence, the reference to engrams having a tendency to "hang up" means they become suspended in time. Page 30.

hard: difficult to bear or endure; causing strain, as in *"hard on the eyesight."* Page 112.

hard put, be: have considerable difficulty or trouble. Page 169.

have: acquire or be in possession of. In the process Remedy of Havingness one remedies the preclear's ability to have (or not-have) energy. Page 190.

have or not-have: acquire or be in possession of or not acquire or be in possession of. In the process Remedy of Havingness one remedies the preclear's ability to have or not-have energy. Page 189.

held: (of an opinion, etc.) accepted or believed as true; kept in the mind as a conviction or point of view. Page 126.

held to: adhered to or kept to; remained faithful or attached to, as in *"the description of characters should be held to a 'cubist rendition.'"* Page 109.

high-toned: high on the Tone Scale. Page 88.

hit upon: come upon or encounter; meet with; discover. Page 62.

hobby therapy: a productive or creative activity undertaken or assigned to someone in order to improve their mental or physical condition. A *hobby* is normally an activity engaged in for pleasure during one's own time. Page 41.

hold (into): keep or maintain in a certain condition, state or the like. Page 170.

how's tricks?: a friendly inquiry about a person meaning, How are things? How are you getting on? Page 134.

Hubbard Certified Auditor: a basic auditor training level at which one learned the theory and practice of Scientology. The Hubbard Professional Auditor was the British equivalent. (*Certified* meant insane in Britain so was not used.) Page 198.

Hubbard Dianetic Auditor: the first Professional Auditor training level delivered in Dianetics, as early as 1950 and which certified one as skilled in the technique of Dianetics. Page 198.

Hubbard Professional College: a former training school in Phoenix, Arizona, that offered a training program (series of courses) for auditors. Auditor training is now done in Churches of Scientology around the world. See *Addresses* for current locations. Page 28.

humanities: branches of learning concerned with human thought and relations, as distinguished from the sciences; especially literature, philosophy, history, etc. (Originally, the humanities referred to education that would enable a person to freely think and judge for himself, as opposed to a narrow study of technical skills.) Page 25.

hypothetical abstracts: complicated theories divorced from reality. *Hypothetical* refers to an unproved theory or idea assumed or accepted temporarily to provide a basis for investigation. *Abstracts* are concepts or ideas separate from any material objects or concrete reality. Page 125.

immediately: 1. right away; without any delay; at once. Page 16.
2. directly; in direct connection or relation. Page 40.

imperiled: put at risk of injury or harm. Page 156.

impinged: caused to have an effect, impact or influence; made an impression (upon), as if contact was made between two things, one of which at least was affected by the other. Page 27.

imposed upon: forced upon, as something to be endured, subjected or submitted to. Page 156.

impunity: freedom or exemption from harm, detrimental effects or danger. Page 67.

incidence: rate or range of occurrence or influence of something, especially of something unwanted. Page 70.

indicated: of a course of action, treatment, etc., to be pointed out or suggested as desirable or necessary. Page 82.

indigestible: not readily or easily digested, absorbed or assimilated. Also, not able to be endured. Page 37.

indulging: engaging or taking part in, often with the idea of freely or eagerly doing so. Page 146.

in effect: so far as the result is concerned; in practice; essentially; basically. Page 107.

in every tradition: in the greatest possible degree of a long established and generally accepted practice or method of procedure. Page 28.

infiltrated: moved into or entered gradually and secretly, especially with hostile intent. Page 93.

ingress: a means or place of entering. Page 204.

injunction: the act of directing or ordering somebody to do or not to do something; an earnest warning. Page 82.

inkling: a vague idea or notion; slight understanding. Page 91.

innovations: alterations of what is established or standard by the introduction of new or novel practices or methods. Page 17.

innuendoes: indirect remarks or gestures, usually implying something derogatory or critical. Page 13.

in one's view: the way one thinks of or regards something; one's opinion or attitude. Page 123.

in short: introducing a summary statement of what has been previously stated in a few words; in summary. Page 114.

insidious: intended to entrap; seeming to be harmless yet actually dangerous. Page 41.

intelligible: capable of being understood. Page 153.

intents and purposes, to all: for all practical purposes; practically speaking. Page 153.

intent upon: with full attention concentrated or focused on one thing. Page 80.

interiorized: inside or stuck in something, such as a mass or body. Page 39.

interposed: put forward or introduced by way of interference or intervention. Page 207.

in that: used after a statement to begin to explain in what way it is true; because; it being the case that, as in *"Dianetics is in an interesting position in that it is* itself." Page 77.

in the light of: with the help afforded by knowledge of (some fact, data, etc.). Page 205.

into yesterday: into a time in the past; into such a state or condition that it no longer existed except as a thing of the past. Page 4.

inversion: a reversal of position; a change to the opposite state or condition. Page 165.

invested: installed or put some quality or characteristic into something. Also, spent or devoted money, time, activities, etc., to or in something in the hopes of gaining benefit. Page 66.

irregular verbs: in German (as well as English), a regular verb is one that predictably changes when showing a different use of the verb, such as when showing past tense (in English a regular verb would show past time by adding an -ed or -d to the end). For example, the German word for "play" is regular (in English, present tense is "they play" and past is "they played"). An irregular verb is one that does not change predictably when showing a different use of the verb such as past tense. For example the German word for "think" is irregular (as it is in English: "they think" and "they thought"). Page 110.

javelin: a long, thin piece of wood or metal with a pointed end, used as a weapon; spear. Used figuratively. Page 5.

jaw-cracking: hard to pronounce, as if one's jaw would be displaced from the difficulty of saying a large word. Page 110.

Johnny (John) Jones: a common name representing an ordinary or typical citizen. Page 3.

jump up: suddenly emerge or come to light. Page 212.

Kant, Immanuel: German philosopher (1724-1804), who was born and lived in the city of Königsberg (part of Germany in Kant's time). German philosopher Friedrich Nietzsche (1844-1900) referred to Kant as the Great Chinaman of Königsberg due to the similarities between Kant's views on virtue and duty and those of the ancient Chinese philosopher Confucius (fifth century B.C.). Because of how Kant wrote, his works are considered difficult to understand. Page 63.

Keats: John Keats (1795-1821), English poet who wrote that "Beauty is truth, truth beauty–that is all ye [you] know on Earth and all ye [you] need to know." Page 3.

keyed: activated or brought about or into action, likened to an electrical key, a small manual device for opening, closing or switching electronic contacts. Page 93.

knowingness: the state or quality of knowing. In Scientology it is a specialized term. *Knowingness* is not data. It is a feeling of certainty. It can be best defined by knowing that one knows. True knowingness is a capability to know and to ascertain within oneself, truth. Page 12.

Komroff, Manuel: (1890-1974) American reporter, editor and novelist. Page 96.

labyrinths: any confusingly intricate state of things or events; entanglements. Literally a *labyrinth* is an intricate combination of paths or passages in which it is difficult to find one's way or to reach the exit. Page 63.

lag: a period of time between one event and another event. Page 7.

laid waste: severely damaged or destroyed. Page 14.

Lake Tanganyika: the longest freshwater lake in the world, located in east-central Africa. Page 92.

large, at: as a whole; in general. Page 232.

last-ditch: made or done in a final effort or act. Page 213.

law and order: the stability created by the observance and enforcement of the law within a community. Page 45.

laws of energy: a reference to the predictable and invariable behavior of various forms of energy under specific conditions in the physical universe. For example: the law of the conservation of energy states that energy, itself, cannot be created and destroyed but can only alter its forms. If one burned a piece of coal and collected all the smoke, ash and other particles which radiated from the burning and weighed them, one would have the same weight as before the coal was burned. Another example: the law of inertia states that an object at rest tends to stay at rest and an object in motion tends to stay in motion unless acted upon by an outside force. (*Inertia* is the resistance an object has to a change in its state of motion.) Page 25.

lay in: consisted of; had its grounds or basis in. Page 69.

ledger: an official book of record or account. Page 82.

lengths: a degree or extreme to which a course of action is taken. Page 5.

let us say: used as a way of introducing a possible situation or when giving an example. Page 108.

libido theory: a theory originated by the Austrian founder of psychoanalysis, Sigmund Freud (1856-1939), that the energy or urges motivating human behavior are sexual in origin. *Libido* is Latin for desire or lust. Page 76.

light of, in the: with the help afforded by knowledge of (some fact, data, etc.). Page 205.

light-year(s): the distance light travels in a year, which is approximately 5.88 trillion miles (9.46 trillion kilometers). The term is also informally used to refer to a very long time. Page 229.

limited processes: auditing processes that are limited in terms of the time they can be audited. Page 233.

limping(s): state or condition of moving or proceeding haltingly or unsteadily, likened to someone walking with a labored, irregular movement. Page 7.

linear: of, relating to or resembling a straight line. Page 88.

livingness: the state or quality of living. The suffix *-ness* is used when forming nouns expressing a state, quality or condition. Page 115.

lock: an apparently minor incident which assumes an unreasonable importance due to its containing some similarity to and restimulating an earlier engram or engram chain. Page 27.

lock the door after the horse is stolen: figuratively, to take actions to safeguard or handle something after damage has already been done. Literally, the phrase means that the barn (or stable) door was left open, the horse was stolen or ran away and, then, one locked the barn door; however, the horse was already gone. Page 90.

long run: for a long time. Page 214.

looming: coming into sight especially above the surface (as of the sea or land) in enlarged form. Hence, coming into view in such a manner. Page 96.

Lord knows: a phrase used for emphasis and meaning nobody can say, as something is unknown to the person speaking and probably to others. Page 241.

loss, at a: uncertain or puzzled. Page 28.

lost to: 1. to be so morally bad or wicked as to be no longer affected by or accessible to some good influence; to have no sense of right, shame, etc., as in *"an individual who can contemplate this with equanimity ... is so lost to the race and lost to himself."* Page 15.

2. to no longer belong to or be accessible to, as in *"If these people were lost to us with current Dianetic processes, we would still have gained many percentiles."* Page 38.

low-toned: low on the Tone Scale. Page 37.

machine-motivated: a *machine* is a system or device that performs or assists in the performance of a human task, often repetitive and without the need for full human participation. *Motivated* means moved to action. Hence, *machine-motivated* would be repetitive action or laborious work driven as if by or in the manner of a machine. Page 80.

machinery: a mental computing system or device set up by the individual to perform certain functions for him. Page 26.

magnitude: relative size, amount, scope, importance, extent or influence. Page 13.

Malayan: of the Malay Archipelago (a large group of islands), the largest system of island groups in the world located off the southeast coast of Asia. It includes the Philippines and many other islands. Page 90.

maligning: saying or writing bad or unpleasant things about someone or something. Page 42.

manner, in some: in some way, in some degree. Page 147.

many-evented: having or containing numerous occurrences or happenings, especially those viewed as important, interesting or unusual. Page 122.

Marathon: a coastal plain near Athens, site of a decisive battle in 490 B.C. in which Greek states defeated an invading Persian army. According to tradition a runner was sent from Marathon to Athens with news of the victory. He raced many miles at top speed, delivered the message and fell dead to the ground. Page 111.

marathon: any contest or event requiring prolonged effort or exceptional endurance, such as a footrace covering 26 miles, 385 yards (about 42 kilometers). Hence, any activity that requires prolonged effort or endurance. Page 80.

markedly: noticeably; to a significant extent. Page 42.

mass: 1. a body of matter (with no specified shape or size). Page 22. 2. togetherness, formed by a coming together or an association of particles, parts, objects, things, entities, etc. Page 61.

mathematicity: the quality or condition of dealing with the relationships between numbers, quantities or spaces as expressed in symbols. Used here to imply complication. Page 3.

matter: condensed or solidified energy. Page 22.

measure, in good: to a great or large extent or degree. Page 165.

mechanics: any and all of the objects, motions or spaces which exist; space, energy, matter and time. Page 21.

mechanism(s): the agency or means by which an effect is produced or a purpose is accomplished. Page 12.

medieval torture: crude torture like that used in Europe from about the twelfth century to the end of the sixteenth century such as that used to gain confessions from those accused of "crimes." In the fourteenth century the Roman Catholic Church gave approval to use such torture in cases of heresy (beliefs viewed as not in agreement with the Church). Page 68.

memoirs: an account of one's personal life and experiences. From the French word *mémoire* meaning memory. Page 111.

meter: same as *E-Meter,* short for *electropsychometer,* a specially designed instrument that can detect the production of energy by the analytical mind. (*Electro* means electric or electricity, *psycho* means soul, and *meter* means measure.) The E-Meter is described in Chapter Two, The Fundamentals of Life. Page 28.

Middle Western: of the Middle West, the northern central part of the United States, which has some of the richest farming land in the world. Page 90.

militant: vigorously active and aggressive, especially in support of a cause. Also, using strong and violent action as one would in war. Page 93.

mimicry: mimicry is demonstrated in Chapter Seven, Communication. Page 108.

minister's son, cliché object, the: a *cliché* is something that has lost its originality through overuse and constant repetition. In this case, the often-told story of the minister's son who turns out to be committing sins or doing evil. Page 45.

-8.0: the numerical designation for the level of Hiding on the Emotional Tone Scale. Page 178.

mired: involved in difficulties that are hard to escape from; entangled. Literally, a *mire* is a wet, slimy soil of some depth or deep mud. Page 46.

mirror: to reflect or represent something. Page 67.

mirror maze: a system of paths lined with mirrors, built for amusement and designed to confuse persons trying to find their way out. Page 98.

mirrors of truth, the very: things which give a true representation or description of something or serve as a model of. Page 207.

mis-abilities: *mis-* means incorrect or improper; wrong. *Abilities* are natural talents (physical and mental); special skills or aptitudes. Hence, *mis-abilities* are "natural talents" that are incorrect or wrong, such as psychosis, neurosis or psychosomatic illnesses. Page 69.

mis-emotion: *mis-* abbreviation of miserable, misery. *Mis-emotion* is anything that is unpleasant emotion such as Antagonism, Anger, Fear, Grief, Apathy or a death feeling. Page 183.

mock-up: 1. make or create; make a mock-up of. Page 125.
2. a mock-up is simply something an individual makes or creates. The term is military in origin and referred to the construction of models or objects such as tanks, airplanes, etc., which were made in order to create an illusion of the real thing. Page 169.

"mock-up" processing: processes which have the preclear mock-up (make or create), in his own mind, various forms, objects, distances, spaces, etc. For example, the preclear is asked to mock-up someone and have this "person" give him answers. In making the other "person" talk, the preclear is exercising his Pan-determinism, hence "mock-up" processing restores a preclear's Pan-determinism. Page 171.

mode: a style, manner, way or method of doing something. Page 5.

modus operandi: a Latin term meaning mode of operation; way of doing or accomplishing something; procedure. Page 76.

monopoly: the exclusive possession or control over something. Page 5.

monotony: of or related to a state of utter sameness that provides no challenge, interest or insight; tedious sameness. Page 4.

monotony schools: *monotony* refers to a type of instruction based on teaching unchanging ideas or principles while preventing the introduction of new data, concepts or facts. *Monotony schools* are the traditional universities and schools that force-feed "facts" to students, insisting on rote memory while discouraging reasoning, application and the attainment of higher knowledge. For comparison *see* esoteric schools. Page 4.

moot: without significance, through having been previously decided or settled; of no practical importance; irrelevant. Page 169.

more or less than, nothing: exactly; precisely that and nothing else, as in *"and which is composed of nothing more or less than the usual meters and gauges and electrodes."* Page 28.

motes: numerous tiny specks of dust or other similar material floating in the air (visible in a shaft of sunlight). Page 4.

move off: depart or diverge away from something (such as a method, practice or the like). Page 124.

much less: used to characterize a statement or suggestion as still more extreme than one that has already been stated; and certainly not. Page 17.

murderous: very difficult, disagreeable, trying, etc. Page 223.

muscle-bound: having muscles so bulky and large that movement and swift response is restricted. Page 87.

mystic: a person who claims to attain, or believes in the possibility of attaining, insight into mysteries transcending ordinary human knowledge, as by direct communication with the spiritual or divine. Page 51.

mysticism: the doctrine and belief that it is supposedly possible to achieve knowledge of spiritual truths and God through meditation (concentration of the mind on something in the belief that it aids mental or spiritual development) or through a state of spiritual ecstasy. Page 42.

native: belonging to, or connected with, a person or thing by nature or natural constitution, in contrast to what is acquired or added, especially said of qualities which are essential, permanent and inseparable. Page 126.

natural selection: the process by which forms of life having traits that better enable them to adapt to specific environmental pressures such as predators, changes in climate, competition for food or mates, will tend to survive and reproduce in greater numbers than others of their kind, thus ensuring the perpetuation of those favorable traits in succeeding generations. A *predator* is an animal that hunts, kills and eats other animals to survive, or any other organism that behaves in a similar manner. Page 109.

necessity level: the degree of emergency in present time environment; that amount of commotion necessary to extrovert an individual into action in present time. Page 209.

"necessity level" Other-determined forces: most of humanity is involved in an Other-determined causation or communication. They have an exterior origin of communication which then swings them into communication lines. They see an accident, which serves as an impetus, kicking them into action. These people can't act until they get an Other-determined necessity level. They get down to a point after a while where they only act in terms of emergency. That *is* necessity level. It *is* necessity. It is an other origin of sufficient magnitude to put them on a communication line. Page 209.

nice, all very: fine or acceptable as far as it goes (implying that it may be unsatisfactory in other ways). Used when something seems good by itself but has problems or situations connected with it. Page 111.

noble: having or showing qualities of high moral character, such as courage, generosity or honor. Page 52.

no more and no less than: exactly; precisely that and nothing else. Page 26.

non sequitur: something (such as a statement) which does not logically follow from what came before. Page 108.

north: in or to a more favorable or better position, condition or situation; upward, above, in or at a higher position, level, etc., likened to a map where north is up and south is down. Page 185.

notion: general understanding; conception; idea. Page 88.

not so much: used in a comparison of two things to emphasize that the second of the two items is more suitable or correct, as in *"This matter is not so much composed of action moments as silent moments."* Page 155.

nuclear physicists: scientists who deal with the behavior, structure and component parts of the center of an atom (called the nucleus) and which constitutes almost all the mass of the atom. Page 13.

nymphomania: abnormally excessive and uncontrollable sexual desire in a woman. Page 168.

obtained: existed or was in effect. Page 170.

obtaining: holding good, true or valid. Also, existing in force or effect. Page 67.

occasion: 1. bring about, cause. Page 17.

2. a need arising from or created by circumstances. Page 52.

oddity: something peculiar or unusual. Page 104.

odds and ends: miscellaneous small matters (as of business) to be attended to. Page 154.

off: not (any longer) occupied with, partaking of or engaged in, as in *"being off the Second, Third and Fourth Dynamics."* Page 115.

oil the flow of data from the rostrum to the student bench: smooth the way for the easy, accurate and useful transmission of information from the instructor (conceived of as standing on the *rostrum,* a platform at the front of the classroom) to the students (thought of as seated at a *bench,* a long hard seat for several people as used in earlier schools). Page 76.

on close questioning: when being examined or asked questions in a way involving great care and thoroughness. (*Close* in this sense means done in a careful and thorough way.) Page 40.

One-shot Clear: one phrase or one action given once, or repeated, which would bring into being the Clear as described in Chapter Two of *Dianetics: The Modern Science of Mental Health.* Page 37.

"only one": a person who thinks that he "must be the only one" and that there must not be any other Cause but himself. Page 109.

on that score: concerning the particular thing just mentioned. Page 179.

on the other hand: used to introduce a different idea, especially when opposite or in contrast to something. Page 138.

Opening Procedure by Duplication: a process that gets a preclear to duplicate his same action, over and over again, with two dissimilar objects. Opening Procedure by Duplication is described in Chapter Twelve, The Six Basic Processes. Page 80.

Opening Procedure of 8-C: a process that places into the realm of knowingness, communication with the physical universe. Opening Procedure of 8-C is described in Chapter Twelve, The Six Basic Processes. Page 139.

optics: the branch of science that deals with vision and light, including the behavior of light when transmitted through a lens. Page 107.

outflowing: moving out from one place to another as in a stream. Page 104.

out of order: performing an action incorrectly for the given situation. Page 104.

out of the hands of: away from the power, influence or direction of. Page 52.

paces, put through one's: a reference to the various steps or actions which a person can be put through with the idea of testing or demonstrating their abilities in learning something requiring great skill. Page 209.

parlance: language; the style of speech or writing used in a particular context. Page 88.

participial phrase: a *participle* is a verb used as an adjective, such as "the *opened* book." A *participial phrase* is the participle plus other words that together function as an adjective modifying some other word in the sentence. In "He showed us the book, opened at the first page" *opened at the first page* is the participial phrase modifying *book.* Page 63.

particular: very precise, careful and extremely attentive to details, as in *"We would be getting too particular for our purposes."* Page 114.

passing upon: (of a jury) deciding or adjudicating on or upon; giving a judgment for or against. Page 111.

passport: an official government document that certifies one's identity and citizenship and permits one to travel to other countries. Hence, something that gives one the right or privilege of passage, entry or acceptance. Page 16.

patch up: mend or repair; put together. The use of the word *up* here means to a state of completion; to an end. Page 41.

pat on the back: a word or gesture of encouragement, approval or praise. Page 38.

pays token nod: appears to agree to do something as if nodding one's head in agreement or as an acknowledgment. *Pay* means to give and a *token* in its earliest use was a sign or symbol. Hence something done merely as a symbolic gesture or for the sake of appearance. Page 196.

peculiar: 1. distinctive in nature or character from all others; unique or specific to a person or thing or category, as in *"the awareness of awareness unit has peculiar abilities."* Page 42.

2. belonging distinctively or primarily to one person, group or kind; special or unique (usually followed by *to*), as in *"a 'Third Dynamic' manifestation peculiar to two or more individuals."* Page 61.

3. strange; curious; odd, as in *"an awareness of awareness unit can get (in addition to the Communication Formula) a peculiar idea concerning just exactly how communication should be conducted."* Page 109.

percentiles: percentages. A *percentage* is most strictly a relation to 100 of anything. If 20 out of 100 children enjoy sports, then the percentage is 20. More generally, a proportion or share in relation to a whole. Page 38.

Perfect Duplication: a process that involves a person making perfect duplicates of objects, incidents, etc. When this is accomplished, the original vanishes. (A *perfect duplicate* is a copy made in the same time, in the same place, with the same energies as the original.) Page 23.

perforce: of necessity; by force of circumstances. Page 148.

perfunctory: performed merely as a routine; hasty and superficial. Page 149.

periodicals: magazines, especially those about serious or technical subjects, that come out at regular times, weekly, monthly or quarterly. Page 42.

perusal: the act of reading or examining something. Page 77.

pervasive: dominant; occupying great attention. Page 91.

pet: cherished by, special or favorite (to somebody). Page 198.

phase, out of: not in the same period or stage of something else; not synchronized or coordinated. Page 232.

physics: the science that deals with matter, energy, motion and force, including what these things are, why they behave as they do and the relationship between them, as contrasted to the life sciences such as biology, which studies and observes living organisms such as animals and plants. Page 23.

pick (something) clean: remove every smallest bit or portion from something in order to eliminate anything on or in it. Page 224.

pick (something) up: to notice and take action regarding something. Page 149.

pieces, come to: to break up, dissolve, fall apart. Page 209.

pikes: weapons, formerly used by foot soldiers, consisting of metal spearheads on long wooden poles. Page 172.

Pilate, Pontius: the official of the Roman Empire who interrogated Jesus prior to his crucifixion. While being questioned Jesus told Pilate "… all who are on the side of truth listen to my voice," to which Pilate replied "What is truth?" Although believing Jesus innocent, Pilate under pressure from the crowds condemned him to death. Pilate then proceeded to wash his hands in front of the crowd to symbolically rid himself of any responsibility for the action. Page 4.

pile: a reactor, an apparatus in which a nuclear reaction can be initiated, sustained and controlled for generating useful energy. The term *pile* came from the fact that the first reactor ever built consisted of special blocks of material stacked into a large "pile" which controlled the nuclear reaction and prevented explosion. Page 14.

pilloried: held up to public contempt, ridicule or scorn; from a *pillory,* a device used in the past as a means of public punishment, in the form of a wooden frame with holes into which a person's head and hands were locked. Page 12.

pinched nerves: nerves that have been pressed, stretched or crushed between muscles, bones, etc., causing numbness or pain, and preventing the nerve from working properly. (*Nerves* are bundles of fibers forming part of the system that carries messages about motion, sensation, etc., between the brain and other parts of the body.) Page 220.

placed (someone) on (something): identified and assigned to a particular category such as a level of a scale. Page 241.

Plan C: one of the three plans described in the last chapter of *Dianetics: The Modern Science of Mental Health:* "Plan C includes an effort to discover a higher echelon of universal origin and destination, if the problem is one of origin and destination, and the factors and forces involved to the end of securing a better understanding and useful application of the knowledge so gained, if gained, and if so gained, its dissemination." Page 6.

plastered: covered or affixed to a surface, likened to applied plaster, a thick, liquid paste covering ceilings and walls, that dries to a smooth hard surface. Page 240.

platform: a horizontal surface or structure raised above the level of the surrounding area and upon which things can be placed or persons can stand. Hence, a declaration of principles on which a person, group, science, etc., stands or is based. Page 51.

plight: a bad or unfortunate situation. Page 115.

plus: 1. the positive (as opposed to the negative) of a pair of opposites, thought of as constructive, beneficial, etc., as in *"Freedom is not the 'plus' of the condition where slavery is the 'minus.'"* Page 91.
2. a quantity or an amount of something that is more than is needed, as in *"since there is a scarcity of phrases and a plus in masses."* Page 128.

poliomyelitis: a highly infectious disease, widespread in the 1950s, that usually occurred in children and young adults. It affected the brain and spinal cord, sometimes leading to a loss of voluntary movement and muscular wasting (loss of muscular strength or substance). Page 66.

"pool of life": a reference to the belief by various schools of thought, political philosophies, etc., that all men rather than being separate individuals are the same or are merged together with everyone else, as in a *pool,* a common place where things are kept or stored. Page 169.

postulate: the word *postulate* is used slightly differently to its English definition and means causative thinkingness; to say a thing and have it be true. Page 42.

power of decision: the ability to decide or to determine the course of something. Page 184.

practitioner(s): a person engaged in the practice of a profession. Page 12.

predicated: based or founded on or upon (facts or conditions). Page 23.

prelude: an action or event coming before and introducing another. Page 149.

prenatal bank: the area of the reactive mind concerning conception to birth. Page 210.

pressed: urged or pushed forward. Page 204.

prevailing: most common or influential; most widely occurring or accepted; generally current. A *prevailing mode* would be a mode (style, manner, way or method of doing something) that is widespread in a particular area at a specific time. Page 5.

Preventive Dianetics: that branch of Dianetics that has as its basis the prevention of acquisition of an engram; secondarily, when an engram has been received in spite of all due care and caution, the prevention of restimulation of the engram. Preventive Dianetics is fully described in *Dianetics: The Modern Science of Mental Health,* Book Two, Chapter Ten, "Preventive Dianetics." Page 81.

priest: a person having the authority to perform and administer religious duties and ceremonies and sometimes thought of as a spiritual leader. Page 4.

prima donna: the principal female singer in an opera or concert and often thought of as self-centered and temperamental. Page 5.

primal: being first, original. *Primal impulses* would be some form of communication originated first by someone or something else. Page 137.

′ (prime): a symbol written above and to the right of a name, letter, figure, etc., and used to distinguish it from another of the same kind. For example, Joe and Joe′ are the same name (and person) but the prime symbol represents Joe (prime) in different circumstances, conditions or actions. Page 134.

processed: received *processing,* the application of Dianetics and Scientology techniques and exercises. Also called *auditing.* Page 6.

processes: exact series of directions or sequences of actions that, when applied, help a person find out more about himself and his life and improve his condition. Page 6.

Professional Auditor's Bulletins: a series of bulletins written by L. Ron Hubbard between 10 May 1953 and 15 May 1959. The contents of the bulletins were technical and promotional–carrying the newest technical advances, reprints of the latest processes and technical issues released. Available in the *Technical Bulletins* volumes. Page 179.

projected: extended forward or out. Page 42.

promulgated: made widely known, taught publicly. Page 13.

proposition: something proposed or offered for consideration, acceptance or adoption. Page 88.

province: the range of one's proper duties and functions; sphere or field of activity or authority. Page 25.

proviso(s): a section, as in a document, listing a condition or requirement. Page 79.

psychoanalysis: a system of mental therapy developed by Sigmund Freud (1856-1939) in Austria in 1894 and which depended upon the following practices for its effects: the patient was made to talk about and recall his childhood for years while the practitioner searched for hidden sexual incidents believed by Freud to be the only cause of aberration. The practitioner read significances into all statements and evaluated them for the patient (told him what to think), along sex-related lines. Page 76.

psychoanalyst: a person who practices *psychoanalysis,* a system of mental therapy developed by Sigmund Freud (1856-1939) in Austria in 1894. Page 38.

psychologist: a specialist in modern psychology, the study of the human brain and stimulus-response mechanisms. Its code word was "Man, to be happy, must adjust to his environment." In other words, Man, to be happy, must be a total effect. Modern psychology, developed in 1879 by Marxist Wilhelm Wundt (1832-1920) at Leipzig University in Germany, conceived that Man was an animal without a soul and based all of his work on the principle that there was no psyche (a Greek word meaning soul). Page 6.

psychosomatic: *psycho* refers to mind and *somatic* refers to body; the term *psychosomatic* means the mind making the body ill or illnesses which have been created physically within the body by the mind. A description of the cause and source of psychosomatic ills is contained in the book *Dianetics: The Modern Science of Mental Health*. Page 17.

psychotherapy: 1. from psyche (soul) and therapy (to cure). A means of improving an individual's mental or spiritual condition. Page 16.
2. the use of psychological methods in the supposed treatment of disorders of the mind including physical methods such as drugs, medication and surgery. Page 185.

psychotic break(s): the action of someone suddenly becoming psychotic. Page 81.

pull back: withdraw from; decide not to do or involve oneself with something. Page 116.

pulled (someone) out of: removed from involvement in. Page 154.

purge: the act or process of *purging,* ridding (a nation or political party, for example) of things or people considered undesirable. Page 12.

put forth: to offer or present for consideration; make something known. Page 138.

put through: caused (a person) to go through a plan, course of action, exercise, course of study, etc. Page 204.

put through one's paces: a reference to the various steps or actions which a person can be put through with the idea of testing or demonstrating their abilities in learning something requiring great skill. Page 209.

put up: mock-up (make or create) something. Page 191.

quality: an essential, inherent or distinctive characteristic, property or attribute; personality or character trait. Page 21.

quantitative: having quantity (mass, extent in space or duration in time), capable of being measured. Page 22.

quantity: a material object or objects regarded in the concrete (an actual thing, not just an idea); the measurable, countable, or comparable property or aspect of a thing. Page 21.

quarters: unspecified persons, groups of people, places or areas. Page 4.

questioning, on close: when being examined or asked questions in a way involving great care and thoroughness. (*Close* in this sense means done in a careful and thorough way.) Page 40.

quibbling: arguing over minor matters, making unimportant objections. Page 13.

race: 1. humanity considered as a whole, as in the human race. Page 15. 2. a class or kind of individuals with common characteristics or interests, as if derived from a common source. Page 110.

radiated: sent or spread out as if from a center. Page 23.

radiation: energy that is emanating (flowing or coming out from a source) in the form of either waves or particles. *Nuclear radiation* is the form of energy that comes especially from radioactive materials and which in large amounts is harmful to living things. Page 14.

radioactive: used to describe a substance that sends out harmful energy in the form of streams of very small particles due to the decay (breaking down) of atoms within the substance. This energy is damaging or fatal to the health of people exposed to it. Page 94.

ramifications: effects or results of something. Page 232.

randomity: it is a ratio: the amount of predicted motion in ratio to the amount of unpredicted motion which the individual has. He likes to have about 50 percent predicted motion and about 50 percent unpredicted motion. Page 106.

ran out: exhausted the negative influence of; erased. Page 155.

reactive bank: same as *reactive mind*. For a description of the reactive mind, see Chapter Two, The Fundamentals of Life. Page 42.

reactive memory bank: same as *reactive mind* (defined in Chapter Two, The Fundamentals of Life). A *memory bank* is a storage device of a computer where data was once stored on a group or series of cards called a bank. Figuratively, it is used to describe a storage of memory information in the mind. Memory banks are fully described in *Dianetics: The Evolution of a Science*. Page 27.

ready-made: prepared beforehand and existing in a finished or complete form, ready for use by anyone with no regard or allowance for individual needs. Page 76.

recourse to: the act or instance of turning to something for aid, use or help. Page 45.

red flag, flying the: under communist rule, or supporting communism; from the red flag flown on a ship indicating that it is under communist command. The red flag is a common symbol of communism. Page 93.

regimen: a specific system, program, plan or course of action to attain some result; a systematic plan. Page 98.

regimented: organized in a rigid system under strict discipline and control. Page 93.

registering: recording as of items, actions, perceptions, etc. Page 82.

religionists: people professionally occupied with religion, such as ministers or preachers. Page 3.

Remedy of Havingness: a process that remedies the ability of the preclear to "have" or "not-have" at will. Remedy of Havingness is described in Chapter Twelve, The Six Basic Processes. Page 23.

remote viewpoint(s): a technical term, meaning an awareness of awareness unit who is afraid to look from where he is; he puts a viewpoint over there and looks from that. Page 241.

resistive: tending toward or marked by *resistance,* the opposition offered by one thing, force, etc., to another. Page 39.

restimulate: reactivate; to stimulate again. *Re-* means again and *stimulate* means to bring into action or activity. Page 29.

restimulation: restimulation is fully described in Chapter Two, The Fundamentals of Life. Page 30.

restimulators: those things in the environment which reactivate a facsimile which then acts back against the body or awareness of awareness unit of the person. Page 27.

reverable: worthy of deep (and sometimes fearful) respect and honor, the object of which is thought of as being hard to approach. Page 5.

-ridden: a combining form at the end of a word meaning full of, burdened with, as in *somatic-ridden.* Page 207.

ridges: essentially suspended energy in space existing around a person. It is an apparent no outflow, no inflow. Flows have direction. Ridges have location. Page 207.

right, in its own: by reason of its own quality, character, ability, etc.; in or of itself, as independent of other things. Page 6.

rigor: strictness or inflexibility; severity; harshness. Page 76.

rigorous: careful, thorough and exact; rigidly precise; strict. Page 28.

rocket jockey: one who pilots or operates a rocket; astronaut. A *jockey* is slang for one who operates a specified vehicle, machine, etc. Page 87.

rostrum: a platform or stage such as that used by an instructor in a classroom. Page 76.

Route 1: a special series of processes as contained in *The Creation of Human Ability,* which are run on someone who is exterior and which improve his abilities as an awareness of awareness unit. Page 220.

run: audit or process; apply a process or processes to someone. Page 6.

run(s) into: encounter (something), meet or find by chance. Page 124.

run out: exhaust the negative influence of; erase. Page 210.

runs off: exhausts the negative influence of something. Page 186.

sacrosanct: something considered sacred and not to be violated; of persons and things above or beyond criticism or interference. Page 5.

Saki: pen name of Hector Hugh Munro (1870-1916), British novelist and short-story writer who wrote *The Chronicles of Clovis,* which includes "Tobermory," a story about teaching animals to talk. Page 110.

sanitariums: institutions for the mentally ill. Page 67.

satyrism: excessive or abnormal sexual craving in a male. Page 168.

save: with the exception of; except. Page 25.

saving grace: a quality or characteristic that makes up for other generally negative characteristics; redeeming feature. Page 12.

scheme: an orderly and systematic combination of related parts. Page 22.

school(s): group or succession of persons in some field or practice who are followers of the same teacher or who are united by a general similarity of principles, beliefs and methods. Page 4.

school board(s): a group of people elected or appointed in each county or local school system in the United States to make decisions about education in public schools. Page 76.

science: knowledge; comprehension or understanding of facts or principles, classified and made available in work, life or the search for truth. A science is a connected body of demonstrated truths or observed facts systematically organized and bound together under general laws. It includes trustworthy methods for the discovery of new truth within its domain and denotes the application of scientific methods in fields of study previously considered open only to theories based on subjective, historical or undemonstrable, abstract criteria. The word *science,* when applied to Scientology, is used in this sense – the most fundamental meaning and tradition of the word – and not in the sense of the *physical* or *material* sciences. Page 12.

Scientology: Scientology embraces and treats of human ability. The term Scientology is taken from the Latin word *scio* (knowing, in the fullest meaning of the word) and the Greek word *logos* (study of). Scientology is further defined as "*the study and handling of the spirit in relationship to itself, universes and other life.*" Page 21.

Second Dynamic: is the urge toward survival through sex or children and embraces both the sexual act and the care and raising of children. Page 115.

Secretary of War: a reference to the head of the United States Department of the Army (formerly known as the War Department), established to supervise all military activities and national defense. Page 14.

semantic: of, pertaining to or arising from the different meanings of words or other symbols; of or relating to meaning in language. Page 47.

senior: superior; of greater influence; on a higher level than (something). The use is military in origin and refers to an individual holding a position of higher rank. Page 109.

sense of: a keen perceptive awareness of or sensitivity to the presence or importance of something. Page 45.

serves: meets the needs or requirements of; is useful for a particular purpose. Page 210.

servomechanism: a device or system which serves, services or aids something. Page 21.

session: a period of time given to or set aside for the pursuit of a particular activity. In Dianetics, it refers to a period of time set aside for processing, the application of Dianetics techniques and exercises. Page 78.

set(s) up: establish; create. Page 189.

1790: the year by which German philosopher, Immanuel Kant (1724-1804) had written his key philosophical works. In these works, Kant declared that things lying beyond experience such as human freedom, the soul, immortality or God were unknowable. His stress on the "unknowable" discouraged further investigation of the actual beingness and soul of man. Kant, who had one time despised the masses of people, was also a university professor and heavily influenced by the grammatical style of other

German philosophers. Upon publication, his works and writings were considered very difficult to comprehend and met with great controversy. Despite this, Kant had a greater influence than any other philosopher of modern times. Page 110.

shaman: a priest or priestess who is said to act as an intermediary between natural and supernatural worlds and to use magic to cure ailments, foretell the future and to contact and control spiritual forces. Page 4.

short, in: introducing a summary statement of what has been previously stated in a few words; in summary. Page 114.

side: accompanying as a secondary fact or activity outside of the main one being discussed or referenced. A *"side comment"* would be a remark that is indirect or added as a secondary or accompanying statement. Page 152.

signalizes: is a clear sign of; points out or indicates. Page 82.

signpost(s): literally, a long piece of wood or other material set upright into the ground bearing a sign that gives information or directions, such as the proper road to a place or the like. Hence, any guide, indication, clue, etc. Page 77.

situated on: placed in a context; brought into defined relation to something else, as in *"all this is basically situated on answers."* Page 198.

Six Basic Processes: a series of processes that bring an individual up a gradient scale of *tolerance* for more and more communication. The Six Basic Processes are listed and described in Chapter Twelve, The Six Basic Processes. Page 148.

slats: thin, narrow strips of wood, metal, etc. Page 92.

slim: small in quantity or amount; slight. Page 191.

snarled: caught in a *snare,* a trapping device, often consisting of a noose, used for capturing small animals. Hence, confused or disordered; complicated, as if entangled with a cord or rope. Page 98.

so as to: used to show a result; in order to; as a means to. Page 75.

social machinery: automatic social response, so as to result in a socially acceptable answer. *Machinery* refers to a mental computing system or device set up by the individual to perform certain functions for him. Page 154.

solar system: the Sun together with all the planets and other bodies that revolve around it. *Solar* means of, relating to or proceeding from the Sun. Page 47.

somatic: *somatic* means, actually, "bodily" or "physical." Because the word "pain" is restimulative and because the word pain in the past led to a confusion between physical pain and mental pain, the word *somatic* is used in Dianetics to denote physical pain or discomfort of any kind. It can mean actual pain such as that caused by a cut or a blow. Or it can mean discomfort as from heat or cold. It can mean itching. In short, anything physically uncomfortable. It does not include mental discomfort such as grief. Hard breathing would not be a somatic. *Somatic* means a non-survival physical state of being. Page 91.

some such (time, thing): like the one (or ones) just mentioned; any of the same kind. Page 96.

sonic: the perceptic of sound; hearing. Page 208.

sound: based on good or valid reasoning; competent or valid. Page 93.

south: in or to a less favorable or worse position, condition or situation; downward, below or at a lower position, level, etc., likened to a map where south is down and north is up. Page 179.

spare: save or relieve from experiencing something. Page 82.

specific: something that is a particular remedy for a physical condition. Page 207.

sphere, the: a reference to the whole of planet Earth. Page 90.

spin: cause (someone) to go into a state of mental confusion, likened to spinning or rotating around. Page 233.

spirit: the attitude or intentions with which someone undertakes or regards something. Page 53.

spiritualism: the doctrine or belief that the spirits of the dead can and do communicate with the living, especially through another person known as a medium. Page 42.

spontaneous combustion of mud: a humorous reference to spontaneous generation, the view that certain forms of life can develop directly from nonliving things. The Greeks believed that flies and other small animals arose from the mud at the bottom of streams and ponds; this has been carried forward by most scientists in the theory that spontaneous generation took place when certain chemicals somehow came together in mud to form the first simple living organism billions of years ago. A cell was eventually formed which collided with other cells and through accident formed a more complex organism – eventually leading to the appearance of Man. (*Spontaneous* means having no apparent external cause or influence; occurring or produced by its own energy, force, etc.; self-acting.) Page 13.

spotty: inconsistent or irregular in quality or result. Page 180.

square away: put in proper order for use or action. Page 220.

squarely: directly; straight. Page 91.

stage fright: nervousness felt by a performer or speaker when appearing before an audience. Page 169.

stake: a strong stick or metal bar with a pointed end, sometimes placed at the bottom of a trap (consisting of a large hole) to pierce an animal that has fallen in. Page 92.

state of mind: 1. one's attitude or mental state in reference to a particular situation or condition. Page 114.
2. a condition or a form of existence of the mind. Page 169.

status quo: the existing state of affairs, especially regarding political or social conditions or states. Page 58.

steamroller: a heavy, steam-powered vehicle having a massive roller for crushing or compacting materials or smoothing road surfaces or the like. Page 122.

stimulus-response: a certain stimulus (something that rouses a person or thing to activity or that produces a reaction in the body) automatically giving a certain response. Page 13.

stir-crazy: mentally nervous and disturbed as a result of being confined as in prison. From the word *stir,* an informal word for prison. Page 96.

story: the situation with regard to the subject being discussed; the facts or circumstances involved, as in *"which was not the story of 1950."* Page 195.

Straightwire: same as *Elementary Straightwire,* which is simply a communication with the past and securing of answers from the past. It is called Straightwire because it puts one into better communication with his mind and the world. It is so called because the preclear is being directed, much like a telephone wire, directly to a memory in the past. Communication is opened between the past and the present. The person undergoing processing is in present time and in contact with present time and he is asked questions which restore to him certain memories. Elementary Straightwire is described in Chapter Twelve, The Six Basic Processes. Page 154.

stratum: a horizontal layer or section of material, especially any of several lying one upon another. Hence, anything (such as a level, part, etc.) conceived as resembling such a layer. Page 208.

string beads: literally, the putting of beads on a string. Bead stringing is done for decoration, making jewelry and other such activities, and can range from a single bead on any threadlike material to complex creations having multiple strands or interwoven levels. Page 145.

strong, silent men: men of few words, who conceal and control their feelings but who are thought to be strong and powerful. The *strong, silent man* was a highly popular and romantic character, especially in novels by and for women around the beginning of the twentieth century. Page 135.

stuck flow: a *flow* is a transfer of energy from one point to another (such as from cause to effect). A *stuck flow* is one-way communication. Stuck flows are described in Chapter Eight, The Application of Communication. Page 127.

stumbled: missed one's step in walking or running; tripped and almost fell. Hence, proceeded unsteadily or falteringly; came to a block or obstacle. Page 150.

subjective process: an out-of-sight, in one's own mind process. Page 179.

subordinate: of less or secondary importance. Page 28.

such an extent, to: used to show how great an effect something has; so much that. Page 150.

such a thing as, there is: a phrase used to hint, suggest or emphasize that the thing referred to exists and therefore must be taken into account. Page 165.

suction: the force that, by sucking or drawing away, attracts a substance or object. *Suction* is the process of removing air or liquid from a space such as in a container or from between two surfaces so that something else can be pulled (sucked) into it or so that two surfaces can pull and stick together. Page 94.

summate: add together, sum up. Page 98.

surplice: a loose white piece of clothing with wide sleeves and varying in length, worn by priests. Page 4.

swerve: to turn aside or be turned aside from a straight course. Page 123.

symbolic logic: the use of the concepts and techniques of mathematics to solve situations in logic. *Symbolic logic* uses those parts of logic that can be modeled mathematically and manipulates these in attempting to solve problems of logic. One is manipulating meanings instead of numbers. Page 61.

system: an organized and coordinated method or procedure followed to accomplish a task or attain a goal. In this sense, it means a (complicated, mechanical) via, as in *"you wouldn't have to use a 'system' for finding out what you know."* Page 44.

tablet: a number of sheets of writing paper fastened together at the edge; a pad (of paper). Page 122.

takes one into: leads one, as if toward or into a particular state, condition, situation or the like. Page 222.

takes to: takes up as a practice or habit. Page 112.

telegram: a message sent by telegraph, a method of long-distance communication originally conveying messages as coded electric impulses transmitted through wires. Page 62.

telekinesis: the apparent production of motion in objects by a person without contact or other physical means. Page 110.

telepathy: supposed communication directly from one person's mind to another's without speech, writing or other signs or symbols. Page 44.

terminal(s): in common usage, a terminal is a conductor attached at the point where electricity enters or leaves a circuit. The word is used analogously in Scientology since there is a flow of communication from one person to another. A person who sends or receives a communication is referred to as a terminal. *Terminal* can be used to refer to things other than a person, such as an object. Page 108.

terms: particular requirements or guidelines which specify how something is done, as in *"they violate the terms of this process."* Page 211.

tertiary: third in order. Page 112.

there is such a thing as: a phrase used to hint, suggest or emphasize that the thing referred to exists and therefore must be taken into account. Page 165.

thereto: to that thing just mentioned. Page 36.

thetan: in Scientology, the *awareness of awareness unit* is called a *thetan* – from the Greek symbol *theta* (θ). Page 162.

thetan exterior: awareness of awareness unit exteriorized. Page 219.

Third Dynamic: the urge toward survival through the group and as the group. Page 61.

threshold: any place or point of entrance or beginning. Page 15.

tie into: to connect, associate or fit with something else. Page 170.

time: the relative change of position of particles or objects. Page 22.

time of it: an experience of a specified period, as in *"we would have a difficult time of it."* Page 90.

time payments: a method of paying for something (such as an automobile) where one pays a portion of the overall amount in specified intervals until the entire debt or purchase is paid off. Such payment plans carry with them an extra charge (profit for the person or institution lending the money) that must be paid in addition to the cash price of the item. Page 88.

time track: the consecutive moments of "now" from the earliest moment of life of the organism to present time. Page 29.

token nod, pays: appears to agree to do something as if nodding one's head in agreement or as an acknowledgment. *Pay* means to give and a *token* in its earliest use was a sign or symbol. Hence something done merely as a symbolic gesture or for the sake of appearance. Page 196.

tokens: reminders of something. Page 222.

toll: the extent of loss, damage, suffering, etc., resulting from some action or disaster. Page 70.

tone: one's emotional level. *See* **Tone Scale** below. Page 69.

Tone Scale: a scale of emotional tones which shows the levels of human behavior. These tones, ranged from the highest to the lowest, are, in part, Enthusiasm, Boredom, Antagonism, Anger, Covert Hostility, Fear, Grief and Apathy. Even lower tones exist which are minus tones, such as -8.0, Hiding. The Tone Scale is described in *Science of Survival*. Page 35.

torch: a long stick with burning material at one end, used to give light or set things on fire. Figuratively, something considered to be a source of light, guidance or enlightenment. Page 3.

touchy: requiring expert handling; not to be touched without great precision. Page 80.

tracing back: locating or discovering by searching or researching evidence, often with the idea of following down something or going backward step by step from its latest or most evident existence. Page 26.

track: *time track*, the consecutive moments of now from the earliest moment of life of the organism to present time. Page 112.

tractor-type beams: force beams that pull or drag objects. Page 94.

tradition, in every: in the greatest possible degree of a long established and generally accepted practice or method of procedure. Page 28.

traffic: communication, dealings or contact between. Page 3.

treble: triple; three times as much or as many. Page 70.

tricks?, how's: a friendly inquiry about a person meaning, How are things? How are you getting on? Page 134.

tripped: stumbled or fell as by catching the foot. Hence, failed or hindered. Page 150.

truism: a self-evident, obvious truth. Page 61.

trust, we: it is hoped. Page 104.

turn (it) off: cause to stop operating as if by means of a switch, button or valve; deactivate. Page 214.

turns on: causes to start operating as if by means of a switch, button or valve; activates. Page 214.

2.0: the numerical designation for the level of *antagonism* on the Emotional Tone Scale. From 0.0 (Body Death) to 2.0 is the band of operation of the reactive mind. From 2.0 to 4.0 (Enthusiasm) is the band of operation of the analytical mind. Page 240.

two-way communication: two-way communication is described in Chapter Nine, Two-way Communication. Page 78.

tyranny: a government in which a single ruler has absolute power and uses it unjustly or cruelly. Page 93.

Ugluks: a made-up name for an ancient people. Page 156.

unconscious: performed, employed, etc., without excessive thinking or forced action, as in *"has to be able to practice it with the same unconscious ease as a pilot flies a plane."* Page 77.

UNIVAC(s): abbreviation for *Universal Automatic Computer,* a large, general-purpose commercial computer designed to process data. Completed in 1951, it marked the beginning of the computer era. Page 4.

unlimited processes: auditing processes that are unlimited in terms of the time they can be audited. Page 233.

unlooked-for: not anticipated; unexpected; not hoped for. Page 107.

unpalatable: unpleasant and not easy to accept, as facts or ideas. Page 4.

unpardonable: so wrong or bad it cannot be forgiven or excused. Page 45.

unscrupulous: unrestrained by ideas of right and wrong; unprincipled. Page 12.

unswervably: in a manner that is firm and unchanging in intent or purpose; constant and steady; not veering or turning aside. Page 12.

untoward: unfavorable or unfortunate. Page 240.

up against: faced or confronted by (questions, difficulties, problems, etc.). Page 204.

upwards of: more than; in excess of. Page 23.

vacuum-packed: packed and sealed in a container, as a can or jar, with as much air as possible evacuated before sealing, chiefly to preserve freshness. Page 52.

validates: confirms, demonstrates or supports something as true or existing. Page 80.

vanquish: to defeat or conquer in battle. Hence to overcome or subdue or put an end to. Page 69.

vault: accomplish something, as if by leaping or jumping suddenly. Page 39.

vellum: a fine quality calfskin or lambskin used in binding books. Page 122.

Velocity: one of the Component Parts of Communication, including the Velocity of the impulse or particle. *Velocity* is the rate of speed with which something happens or moves. Page 60.

verbose: using or containing a great and usually an excessive number of words; wordy; talkative. Page 110.

very: exact or precise as opposed to approximate, often used with *this* or *the,* as in *"at this very point"* or *"the very processes which lead up to Clear."* Page 39.

vested interest: those people and groups who have a special interest in having something or wanting something to happen which is to their own personal advantage or for reasons of private gain. Page 4.

via(s): *via* means a relay point in a communication line. For example, to talk *via* a body, to get energy *via* eating alike are communication by-routes (secondary or side routes). Page 3.

vilified: subjected to false and malicious statements; spoken evil of. Page 12.

violence: 1. great force; intensity, as in *"It moved with violence although its message was peace."* Page 4.
2. the exercise of physical force so as to inflict injury on, or cause damage to, persons, property, etc., as in *"None of these ways include violence or revolution."* Page 17.

violent: very strong or intense; able to produce a very marked or powerful effect, as in *"a very violent process."* Page 222.

visio: the perceptic of sight, vision. Page 191.

vitals: those parts or organs of the body essential to life, or upon which life depends. Hence, the parts essential to continued functioning, as of a system. Page 5.

waging: engaging in or carrying on a war, battle or conflict. Page 16.

walks in on: enters a situation, set of circumstances, etc., as in *"An auditor walks in on a preclear who has a scarcity of answers."* Page 124.

Ward 9: a *ward* is a division, floor or room of a hospital for a particular class or group of patients, often designated by number or name, as in Ward 9, Maternity Ward, etc. Page 67.

waste: throw away; give away; render unusable. In the process, the Remedy of Havingness, one wastes things based on the theory that if a person can't have something, one can have him waste it enough and he will be able to have it. Page 191.

Waterloo: site in Belgium of the defeat of Napoleon by an Anglo-Prussian-Dutch army on June 18, 1815, thus ending Napoleon's plans to rule Europe. (*Prussia* was a former state and kingdom in Northern Europe.) Page 111.

wavelength: a wavelength is the distance from the peak to the peak of a wave. The relative distance from peak to peak in any flow of energy. Page 25.

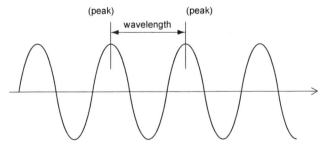

weeds out: removes something undesirable or unwanted, likened to removing *weeds,* unwanted wild plants. Page 109.

weighs against: counterbalances; has equal force or weight on the contrary side. Page 68.

wended: directed, as on or along one's way. Page 63.

wend one's way: go or journey in a certain way or direction. Used figuratively. Page 98.

we trust: it is hoped. Page 104.

whence: from where? from what place, source, cause, etc.? Page 4.

white cross: a cross-shaped marker, first employed in 1953, indicating the site of a fatal highway accident, intended to remind passing motorists of the dangers of the road as well as the lives that have been lost. Page 103.

whole track: the entire track of the individual beyond (earlier than) the present life. Page 103.

wide-open cases: cases which are possessed of full perception except somatic. *Wide-open* does not refer to a high-tone individual, but to one below 2.0 who *should* be easy to work but is often inaccessible and who finds it difficult to regain a somatic and simple to regain perception. Page 40.

wild: beyond reason; not sensible or accurate, as in *"This is not a wild statement."* Page 70.

wild variable: a factor in a situation or problem that behaves in an uncontrolled, strange or unpredictable fashion. *Variable* is most commonly used in mathematics and science where it represents something unknown or unpredictable. A variable is often contrasted with a constant which is known and unchanging. Page 47.

winding up: arriving in a place, situation or condition at the end or as a result. Page 115.

wind up in a ball: end up in a confusion or tangled mess. Page 123.

win friends or influence professors: a humorous reference to the principles in the book *How to Win Friends and Influence People* by American author and lecturer Dale Carnegie (1888-1955). In the book Carnegie purports to advise on how to win friends and influence people and advocates agreeing with *anything* anybody says. *Friends* means people whom one knows; acquaintances, particularly with the idea of entering into close relations with. Page 51.

wire: a telegram, a message sent by telegraph, a method of long-distance communication originally conveying messages as coded electric impulses transmitted through wires. Page 62.

wise, in such a: way of proceeding, manner, etc. Page 107.

witch doctor: in certain societies, a person supposed to have the power of curing disease, getting rid of evil, etc., through the use of magic. Page 38.

witnessing: showing evidence of; testifying to. Page 46.

worked: 1. arranged through questionable or deceitful methods, as in *"who have worked themselves into the position of being able to."* Page 53. 2. performed, acted upon or practiced (a course of action, procedure, etc.), as in *"Some interesting variations can be worked on this. They are not advised."* Page 211.

working: operating; functioning; producing effects, results, etc., as in *"There is a primary rule working here."* Page 65.

work loose: become disengaged or unstuck from some place or position, as if by the action of random motions. Page 81.

writhing: twisting of the body; squirming as if from worry or nervousness. Page 169.

wrong, do (someone): to harm or injure (someone). Page 44.

yesterday, into: into a time in the past; into such a state or condition that it no longer existed except as a thing of the past. Page 4.

zest: animating spirit, lively energy; great enthusiasm. Page 51.

INDEX

A

aberrate
  definition, 107

aberration, 67–68, 114
  common denominator, 70
  control over, 68
  definition, 107
  difference between sanity and, 165
  most aberrative conduct in society, 82
  start, change and stop of, 194
  "strong, silent men" and, 135
  understanding and, 58
  violations in the Communication Formula, 126

ability
  accent on, 57–70
  awareness of awareness unit, 42, 50
  communication and, 103, 204
  control and, 66
  creation of, 194
  demonstrated by, 22
  description, 165
  emphasis on, 41
  freedom and, 87
  inability and, 165
  increasing, 41, 243
  mechanics and, 21

  processing toward, 233
  restoring freedom and, 87
  to be and vary beingness, 126
  to handle energy, 51
  to handle mass, 51
  understanding and, 64
  validate, 242

absolute zero, 47

acceptance level, 190

Acceptance Level Processes, 190

accidents, 103
  seen from different points of view, 110
  shock reaction after, 154

acknowledgment, 134–135, 139, 148, 172, 208–214
  auditing and, 139
  automaticity and, 213
  case results and, 139
  example, 149
  executed command, 184
  lack of, 148
  lag, 147
  mocking-up, 210
  perfunctory, 149
  remedy scarcity of, 171
  running of, 213
  unwillingness in, 115

Acknowledgments, 208
  auditing commands for, 214

Adler, 121

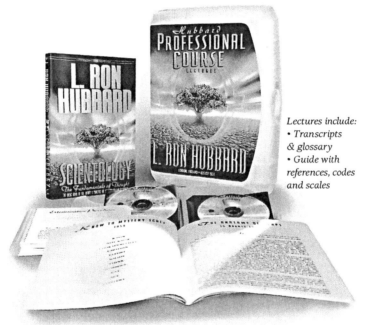